Group Treatment for Hoarding Disorder

✓Treatments *That Work*™

Group Treatment for Hoarding Disorder

Therapist Guide

Jordana Muroff • Patty Underwood • Gail Steketee

OXFORD
UNIVERSITY PRESS

OXFORD
UNIVERSITY PRESS

Oxford University Press is a department of the University of Oxford.
It furthers the University's objective of excellence in research, scholarship,
and education by publishing worldwide.

Oxford New York
Auckland Cape Town Dar es Salaam Hong Kong Karachi
Kuala Lumpur Madrid Melbourne Mexico City Nairobi
New Delhi Shanghai Taipei Toronto

With offices in
Argentina Austria Brazil Chile Czech Republic France Greece
Guatemala Hungary Italy Japan Poland Portugal Singapore
South Korea Switzerland Thailand Turkey Ukraine Vietnam

Published in the United States of America by
Oxford University Press
198 Madison Avenue, New York, NY 10016

Library of Congress Cataloging-in-Publication Data
Muroff, Jordana.
Group treatment for hoarding disorder : therapist guide / Jordana Muroff, Patty Underwood, Gail Steketee.
pages cm.—(Treatments that work)
Includes bibliographical references and index.
ISBN 978–0–19–934096–5
1. Compulsive hoarding. 2. Group psychotherapy. I. Underwood, Patty. II. Steketee, Gail. III. Title.
RC569.5.H63M87 2014
616.89'152—dc23
2013035310

9 8 7 6 5 4 3 2 1
Printed in the United States of America
on acid-free paper

About Treatments *ThatWork*™

Stunning developments in healthcare have taken place over the last several years, but many of our widely accepted interventions and strategies in mental health and behavioral medicine have been brought into question by research evidence as not only lacking benefit but, perhaps, inducing harm. Other strategies have been proven effective using the best current standards of evidence, resulting in broad-based recommendations to make these practices more available to the public.

Several recent developments are behind this revolution. First, we have arrived at a much deeper understanding of pathology, both psychological and physical, which has led to the development of new, more precisely targeted interventions. Second, our research methodologies have improved substantially, such that we have reduced threats to internal and external validity, making the outcomes more directly applicable to clinical situations. Third, governments around the world and health-care systems and policymakers have decided that the quality of care should improve, that it should be evidence based, and that it is in the public's interest to ensure that this happens (Barlow, 2004; Institute of Medicine, 2001).

Of course, the major stumbling block for clinicians everywhere is the accessibility of newly developed evidence-based psychological interventions. Workshops and books can go only so far in acquainting responsible and conscientious practitioners with the latest behavioral health-care practices and their applicability to individual patients. This new series, Treatments *ThatWork*™, is devoted to communicating these exciting new interventions to clinicians on the front lines of practice.

The manuals and workbooks in this series contain step-by-step detailed procedures for assessing and treating specific problems and diagnoses.

But this series also goes beyond the books and manuals by providing ancillary materials that will approximate the supervisory process in assisting practitioners in the implementation of these procedures in their practice.

In our emerging health-care system, the growing consensus is that evidence-based practice offers the most responsible course of action for the mental health professional. All behavioral health-care clinicians deeply desire to provide the best possible care for their patients. In this series, our aim is to close the dissemination and information gap and make that possible.

This group treatment therapist guide and the companion workbook for patients address the puzzling and difficult problem of hoarding and acquiring. Hoarding Disorder, characterized by a profound inability to discard material items that are no longer useful and a compulsive urge to acquire unneeded or excessive possessions, can result in severe disruption of interpersonal relationships, threats to health, and even death in some extreme cases from the dangerous accumulation of "clutter." Estimates suggest this problem afflicts as many as 1 to 2% of the population, who seldom present for treatment until late middle age when, evidently, they have had sufficient opportunity to accumulate overwhelming clutter.

This evidence-based group treatment program, created by Jordana Muroff, Patty Underwood, and Gail Steketee, leads to substantial improvement in most patients. A single experienced clinician can lead the group intervention or a co-therapy model can be used with two clinicians, one of whom is experienced and one of whom may be in training. This group treatment uses a session-by-session approach so group leaders are well-informed about methods to use in any given session. In groups of 6 to 8, participants receive education about hoarding and the CBT model and discuss therapy goals and personal values. They are guided to practice motivational enhancement methods, including identifying barriers to progress, and receive training in organizing and problem-solving. Final sessions focus on reviewing the most effective therapy methods, coping with change, ending treatment, and highlighting strategies for maintaining gains. With the designation of hoarding as its own distinct disorder in the *Fifth Edition of the Diagnostic and Statistical Manual of Mental Disorders* (DSM-5), more people affected by this problem will be recommended treatment. The timely creation of this group program will give many patients hope to reduce clutter, organize their lives, and restore a peaceful order in their homes.

David H. Barlow, Editor-in-Chief
Treatments *ThatWork*™
Boston, Massachusetts

References

American Psychiatric Association (2013). *Diagnostic and Statistical Manual of Mental Disorders* (5th ed.). Washington, D.C.: APA.

Barlow, D. H. (2004). Psychological treatments. *American Psychologist, 59*, 869–878.

Institute of Medicine. (2001). *Crossing the Quality Chasm: A New Health System for the 21st Century*. Washington, D.C.: National Academy Press.

Contents

Appendices

Acknowledgments

We thank the many people with hoarding problems who have contributed to this book as they shared their experiences struggling to overcome their problem. We also thank their family members and friends and the committed professionals from many disciplines who have worked with them in a variety of ways and shared their insights. We wish to thank Drs. Randy Frost, David Tolin, Renae Reinardy, Suzanne Meunier, and Amanda Gibson for their contributions informing the development of this manual. We express our sincere gratitude to Drs. Christiana Bratiotis, Jessica Rasmussen and Cristina Sorrentino Schmalisch, Suzanne Otte, Sarah Dowal, Jennie Davidow as well as numerous other therapists, trainees, research assistants, and home based coaches who have generously shared their reflections over the years, shaping our thinking and the evolution of this manual. Without the input of all of these people, we would not have been able to discover and test effective group treatment approaches for hoarding disorder. We also wish to thank the Oxford University Press Editorial team Andrea Zekus and Sarah Harrington for their support.

Jordana thanks her husband Steve, children Aiden and Scarlett, and other family and friends for their patience and cheer throughout this process.

Patty thanks her amazing children, Jordan and Myles.

Gail thanks her husband Brian McCorkle for his support.

Group Treatment for Hoarding Disorder

Chapter 1 *Introduction*

This chapter contains summary information about hoarding disorder (HD) and about group treatment methods and their efficacy for HD. For more details, please review the first two chapters of Steketee and Frost's 2013 *Treatment for Hoarding Disorder: Therapist Guide & Workbook* (2nd edition), and additional references in the Appendix to this manual.

Background Information

Ordinary people own many more objects than they did even a generation ago. Reasons for saving possessions range from purely utilitarian to intensely emotional, and for most people possessions provide a sense of security, comfort, and pleasure. But almost all of us keep some things we don't need and don't use, and eventually, as these types of items impinge on our living space, we usually get rid of them. But people suffering from hoarding disorder have significant problems doing just that—getting rid of items. For them, possessions rarely seem unwanted or not useful, and trying to get rid of them is an excruciating emotional ordeal, resulting in clutter that prevents them from living normally. This manual is the culmination of years of work on understanding hoarding and developing effective cognitive and behavioral treatment (CBT) methods to address the many components of HD.

First, we'd like to recommend avoiding language that some clients may find stigmatizing. The term "hoarders" describes a person rather than a behavior and can be experienced as pejorative. We suggest using "hoarding behavior," or words like "saving," "collecting," or "cluttering." Try to use the client's own words, or choose neutral ones like "your things" instead of "junk" or "trash," unless the client uses these terms. Agreeing on terminology early in treatment helps establish the shared understanding necessary to treat this problem.

Unlike the individual treatment manual for HD by Steketee and Frost (2013), which uses a modular format, this manual uses a session-by-session approach to address clients' symptoms in a logical order based on our experience conducting more than a dozen CBT groups for hoarding. We recommend that you read the entire manual before starting treatment so you are familiar with the sequence and content of therapy methods. Co-leadership is especially helpful for groups larger than 4 to 6 clients to permit practice exercises in smaller groups monitored by one of the clinicians. Throughout these chapters, we illustrate the use of various forms for assessment and treatment. Blank copies of all forms are available in the accompanying client *Workbook* and on the Treatments *ThatWork*™ website at www.oup.com/us/ttw.

Hoarding Disorder (HD) Diagnosis

The first operational definition of hoarding in 1996 (Frost & Hartl, 1996) was followed by an ongoing surge in research on hoarding by research teams mainly in the United States and Europe. Early research assumed that hoarding was a subtype of obsessive-compulsive disorder (OCD), but subsequent investigations suggested that it was a distinct but related condition (Mataix-Cols et al., 2010; Pertusa et al., 2010). The fifth edition of the *Diagnostic and Statistical Manual of Mental Disorders* (DSM-5; APA, 2013) added HD as a separate diagnosis among the OC spectrum disorders, which also include OCD, body dysmorphic disorder, excoriation (skin picking), and trichotillomania (hair pulling). HD criteria can be found in Chapter 4, Session 1.

"Difficulty discarding" is the hallmark symptom of HD and must be persistent to qualify for an HD diagnosis, ruling out temporary difficulties that might follow recent inheritance of parents' possessions or a move to a new home. Many clients also have significant problems with excessive acquiring. Clutter is a serious consequence of these behavioral problems, and group treatment therefore focuses on changing the behaviors that lead to clutter. Clearing and sorting the clutter will only be effective to the extent that clients learn to discard items and reduce their acquiring. Engaging cleaning services to clear the home might improve the condition of the home temporarily, but this will not resolve the fundamental behavioral problems (and is likely to create additional problems of trust if the cleanout is done involuntarily).

Urges to save and distress at the loss of items are also at the heart of the hoarding problem. People who hoard imbue their possessions with sentimental (emotional), utilitarian (useful), or intrinsic (aesthetic) value, the same reasons that most people save objects. But in the case of hoarding, these are applied to many more possessions and are experienced more intensely. The treatment described in this manual helps clients understand the nature of their attachments and beliefs about possessions.

Clutter typically occupies the active living areas of the home and compromises the person's ability to use these spaces (e.g., eating at the table, sitting in chairs). When clutter is confined to only non-living areas like the attic, basement, or other storage areas, this does not qualify for a diagnosis of HD. In its severe form, HD can make the home unsafe with regard to fire or structural danger, pest infestation, squalid conditions, and/or health problems (e.g., Norberg & Snowdon, 2013; Tolin, Frost, Steketee, Gray & Fitch, 2008a), and quality of life may be seriously impaired (Saxena et al., 2011). Assessment of these problems helps ensure that the most dangerous conditions are tackled first in treatment.

Note that a diagnosis of HD requires ruling out other disorders that might be causing hoarding, as these are unlikely to respond to the group CBT described here. For instance, contamination fears that lead clients to drop objects and refuse to pick them up again, or repetitive checking that leads clients to avoid getting rid of papers should be treated with CBT methods designed for OCD.

Current or past acquiring is a common cause of clutter (Frost & Mueller, 2013). Compulsive buying may occur via retail shopping, the Internet, and neighborhood tag or garage sales. Free things often come from giveaway items (promotions) and items left for trash pickup or in dumpsters; stealing occurs in about 10% of HD cases (Frost, Steketee & Tolin, 2011b). Acquiring is often associated with positive feelings, even euphoria, that encourage the behavior and make it difficult to stop. Accordingly, excessive acquisition and avoidance behaviors must be carefully assessed and require the direct intervention described in this guide.

Many people who hoard do not consider their behavior unreasonable (Tolin, Fitch, Frost & Steketee, 2010a), and have limited awareness of their problem, making treatment more challenging. Also, in response to previous efforts by others to resolve the hoarding problem, some clients may have developed strong defensive reactions that resemble poor insight (Frost, Tolin & Maltby, 2010). In any case, even voluntary help-seekers can become ambivalent when faced with difficult decisions about removing clutter. These problems are addressed in Chapter 6, Session 3.

Differential Diagnosis and Comorbidity

Up to 20% of clients also have OCD symptoms that may require separate treatment beyond this group CBT (GCBT). Many HD clients also suffer from major depressive disorder (MDD) (Frost et al., 2011b), although a recent study did not indicate that baseline depression predicted individual treatment outcomes (Muroff, Steketee, Frost & Tolin, under review). Attention problems (but not hyperactivity) are also common in clients with HD (Frost et al., 2011b; Tolin & Villavicencio, 2011) and may require strategies to manage attention during sorting and discarding tasks. Social phobia and generalized anxiety disorder (GAD) occur in up to a third of HD cases, and may make it difficult for clients to get the social support they need, especially elderly clients who experience social isolation (Kim et al., 2001). Perfectionism is common and may be associated with worse outcomes from individual treatment (Muroff et al., under review). Group CBT as described in this manual includes cognitive and behavioral strategies to reduce perfectionistic standards and rigid rules for saving and discarding, while also improving decision-making.

Prevalence, Course, and Family Patterns

Epidemiological studies indicate that hoarding occurs in 2% to 6% of the population, making it one of the most frequent mental disorders (e.g., Bulli et al., 2013; Iervolino et al., 2009; Samuels et al., 2008). HD begins early, usually in the teenage years and rarely after age 25, although it does not become seriously problematic until around age 40 (Grisham, Frost, Steketee, Kim & Hood, 2006; Tolin, Meunier, Frost & Steketee, 2010b). In some cases trauma can precipitate hoarding, but this is usually seen with later onsets (Grisham et al., 2006), and HD is associated with an increased frequency of adverse life events but not post-traumatic stress disorder (Frost et al., 2011b). Both men and women suffer from hoarding, although women appear to be more likely to seek treatment (Steketee & Frost, 2013). People with HD are less likely to be married (Samuels et al., 2002; Kim et al., 2001), and may have difficulty with motivation to change their hoarding if they are living alone. Often, people who hoard have a family history of hoarding, which appears to have a genetic component (Hirschtritt & Mathews, 2013; Samuels et al., 2002), and may have family members who hoard and condone their hoarding behavior; this will require thoughtful attention during GCBT.

Development and Benefits of Individual CBT for Hoarding

CBT for HD based on a cognitive behavioral model of this problem has shown good benefit. From our work with single cases and pilot studies (e.g., Hartl & Frost, 1999; Steketee, Frost, Wincze, Greene & Douglass, 2000), we have learned that experienced and novice clinicians (Turner, Steketee & Nauth, 2010) can accomplish good outcomes. In-home sessions approximately monthly seem important in many cases, although not necessarily all, as some clients may benefit from "coaches" who are available to assist them at home.

Steketee and Frost's (2013) individual CBT manual for HD provides more detail on treatment outcomes. In brief, an open trial with 10 women using 26 sessions of CBT and monthly home visits over six to nine months (Tolin, Frost & Steketee, 2007a) produced significant reductions ranging from 25% to 37% in overall hoarding severity, difficulty discarding, and acquiring, and 31% improved on an observational measure of clutter. A subsequent waitlist-controlled study showed that CBT outperformed a waitlist control condition and the 37 clients who completed treatment showed a 27%–39% reduction on various measures of hoarding symptoms. Clinicians rated 71% of clients "much" or "very much improved," and 81% of clients rated themselves in these categories. When 31 patients were followed 3 to 12 months after CBT, nearly all maintained their gains, and the percent rated "much" or "very much improved" by clinicians and clients were fairly stable at 62% and 79% (Muroff et al., under review).

Development and Efficacy of Group CBT for Hoarding

Group treatment offers a potentially cost-effective and accessible alternative to individual CBT, while also reducing the stigma and social isolation that can be a problem for some clients. In turn, working alongside others in groups seems to improve clients' motivation. Below, we provide a brief summary of clinician-led group treatments for hoarding that have been reported in the psychological literature.

In our first test of group treatment for HD (Steketee, Frost, Wincze, Green & Douglass, 2000), we found modest benefits for six clients who participated in a group treatment, plus one who was treated individually. Group CBT (GCBT) consisted of 15 two-hour sessions (the first 10 sessions were weekly, and the remaining five convened every other week), plus home-based sessions. Five of the seven clients reduced their acquisition and improved on the measures of problematic beliefs, decision-making, and organizing. Clutter was slower to reduce, and participants showed a modest overall reduction of 16% in overall hoarding behavior. Improvement seemed greatest in acquisition, confidence in reducing hoarding, and recognition of erroneous thinking about hoarding. Four clients (including three group participants) who received 14 additional sessions showed an overall 28% reduction in symptoms at the one-year follow-up assessment. Taking medication was not associated with more improvement.

Muroff and colleagues (2009) completed a larger study of GCBT with 32 participants who were mainly white middle-aged women (average age of 53, range 38–65). Social work and psychology clinicians co-led four groups of 5 to 8 people each. Groups met for 16 two-hour weekly sessions, and one group continued for 20 weeks. Each participant also received two 90-minute home visits. Mean scores on the Saving Inventory–Revised (SI-R; Frost, Steketee & Grisham, 2004, see Appendix 3) showed a 14% reduction, and improvement was also evident on the pictorial Clutter Image Rating scale (CIR; Frost, Steketee, Tolin & Renaud, 2008, see Appendix 4), clinical ratings of illness severity, and on depression.

The group that followed a more formal protocol and had telephone-based assessments appeared to show somewhat more improvement (22%). GCBT also appeared to reduce social isolation and the stigma felt by participants with hoarding. Therapists and patients alike thought that additional home visits would have been beneficial.

Another study of GCBT, by Gilliam and colleagues (2011), omitted home-based sessions in order to test a group therapy that could be more easily disseminated in community mental health settings. Of the 45 clients who started the study, only 30 (67%) completed it. Participants were similar to other studies in being mainly middle-aged white single women with a college education; most had another psychiatric problem and were taking medications for mental health reasons. Five treatment groups had 4 to 12 members each, with an average of 9 people per group. Groups led by advanced trainees met for 90 minutes for 16 sessions (3 groups) or 20 sessions (2 groups). Among those who completed treatment, 31% showed clinically significant improvement on HD symptoms and benefits on anxiety, depression, and quality of life. The attrition rate of 33% was high for this study, and it is hard to know whether the lack of home visits may have contributed.

In a recent study, Muroff and colleagues (2012) tested GCBT for hoarding compared to benefit derived from reading *Buried in Treasures*, a popular self-help book that uses similar CBT methods (Tolin, Frost & Steketee, 2007b). The researchers also explored the effects of additional home visits with non-clinician "coaches." The 38 participants were assigned randomly to GCBT with extra home assistance by coaches (11 people), GCBT with minimal home assistance (14 people), or reading the book individually (13 people). Everyone received 20 weekly sessions plus four 90-minute home visits from one of the therapists. Those in the coaching condition had four additional home visits from a student trained to help clients with de-cluttering, applying CBT skills at home, and improving attention and motivation (Davidow & Muroff, 2011). Those in the bibliotherapy condition were asked to read *Buried in Treasures* and only had calls to complete their assessments. Only one person dropped out (from the GCBT coaching condition).

The group with additional home visits showed a 30% reduction in hoarding, and 36% were considered clinically significant improved. GCBT members without extra home visits improved by about 23%, similar to our earlier 2009 study, and 21% were clinically improved. In contrast, bibliotherapy participants had only a 9% reduction in hoarding symptoms. Both group treatment methods were significantly better than bibliotherapy, and clutter was reduced slightly more with extra coaching visits. It is also noteworthy that these groups produced benefits similar to people in individual CBT, who achieved 27% overall improvement (Steketee et al., 2010).

Overall, these studies support the benefit of group CBT for hoarding disorder.

Risks and Benefits of GCBT for Hoarding

We believe the risks associated with group treatment for hoarding are small and easily outweighed by the potential benefits. As for any group treatment, participants are asked to respect each other's need for confidentiality, but it is not possible to guarantee this right to privacy. The privacy risks for GCBT for hoarding do not seem to be any greater than those for group therapy for other problems. In fact, we suspect that people who hoard may be more than usually attuned to the need for control over belongings and perhaps also private information. Group treatment for HD could trigger clients' traumatic memories and unresolved grief reactions that provoke strong emotions and require clinical time outside of the group to help clients process their feelings. However, given the relatively low rate of post-traumatic stress disorder encountered among those with HD, this problem does not appear to rise to the level of serious risk for GCBT.

Another risk could arise when a client's home is in a squalid or structurally dangerous condition that requires mandated reporting if children or elders (including the client) are living in the home. Such clients should be referred to appropriate regulatory authorities. Accordingly, if the baseline office assessment indicates that such conditions might be present, clinicians should warn clients prior to a home visit that they are obligated to report conditions that may impair the health or safety of children or older adults to the relevant authorities. With over 90 hoarding task forces in communities across the United States and recent efforts to inform the public about hoarding disorder, we have found that investigative authorities will often allow appropriate time for those in violation of the law to correct the dangerous problem. In such cases, individual treatment may be warranted if the group intervention may not be of sufficient duration to resolve the risk. Extreme hoarding cases with substantial squalid conditions may require aid from a sanitation crew to remove waste that could cause health problems.

Other potential risks related to GCBT for hoarding disorder include potential dual roles for the clinician and coaches who work with clients in their homes with regard to removing discarded clutter. Those assisting in the home may want to help clients remove bags of trash or take unwanted items to donation centers; such activities require that they not accept items (gifts) from clients in order not to compromise their independent role as facilitator of progress in treatment. As always, cultural competence is needed in delivering GCBT, as reasons for saving some items may be idiosyncratic to certain cultures and religious beliefs.

The benefits of treatment are apparent in the above description of positive outcomes following GCBT in research studies. Many, if not most, people experience a significant reduction in their clutter, difficulty discarding, and excessive acquiring, and have gained important skills to continue their work independently or with the help of a coach. These comprehensive group treatment methods typically have positive side effects of reducing stigma; improving self-esteem, mood, and functioning; along with apparent improvements in hoarding behaviors and clutter. However, many clients may be improved but not recovered at the end of the intervention, and some may require further assistance to benefit adequately. Referral for additional group or individual treatment may be needed for the HD itself, or for other problems that appear to be impeding progress.

Alternative Interventions

As noted, individual CBT has been shown to be highly effective for HD and is available in manual form (Steketee & Frost, 2007; 2013). Few of the current alternative treatments are evidence-based. Standard exposure and response prevention (ERP) for OCD symptoms does not appear to be very effective for HD (Abramowitz, Franklin, Schwartz & Furr, 2003). Medications for HD specifically have not been identified or tested in controlled trials (see below). Although as noted earlier, reading a book about CBT for hoarding does not produce much improvement, structured support groups using the *Buried in Treasures* book and facilitated by non-clinicians have shown promise in recent studies (Frost, Pekarava-Kochergina & Maxner, 2011a; Frost, Ruby & Shuer, 2012). Some clients who have experienced forced cleanouts by authorities or relatives react with anger and hurt and do not appear to benefit from such efforts in understanding their problem, improving their skills, reducing their emotional attachment, or changing their behavior. Their continuing struggles with hoarding suggest that involuntary cleanouts are not effective alternatives to treatment. Such cleanouts should only be used if required for health and safety and should involve HD participants as much as possible in decision-making about possessions.

Role of Medications

A number of studies (although not all) have reported limited benefit from selective serotonin reuptake inhibitors (SSRIs) in retrospective studies. For example, Black et al. (1998) found that hoarding symptoms were a strong predictor of non-response to medication, and Mataix-Cols et al. (1999) found that severer hoarding predicted worse outcomes. Winsberg and colleagues (1999) also reported poor response to medication by those with hoarding. However, in a prospective study, Saxena, Brody, Maidment, and Baxter (2007) reported that the SSRI paroxetine produced similar benefits for both hoarding and non-hoarding OCD patients, although improvement was modest in both groups. In a small uncontrolled trial, Saxena et al. (2011) reported good outcomes with venlafaxine. Furthermore, these investigators (Saxena et al., 2002) reported benefits from a combination of hoarding-specific CBT plus SSRI medication in an intensive six-week intervention program. As in other trials, OCD clients without hoarding improved more than those with hoarding problems, but the latter group showed significant reductions in Yale Brown Obsessive Compulsive Scale (YBOCS) scores (average of 10 points) following the intervention. Thus, medication combined with CBT tailored to hoarding led to clear improvement, and SSRIs could help clients tolerate the CBT more easily. Unfortunately, few prospective treatment studies have included or studied the impact of medications with or without CBT, and we therefore have too little information to provide recommendations.

Chapter 2 *Group Formation and Assessment*

Outline of the Intervention Program

The group CBT treatment program for hoarding described in this guide utilizes the protocol outlined in Chapter 1, delivered in a time-limited 20-week closed group (new members are not permitted to enter once the group has begun). We recommend including at least two home visits to complete a before-and-after assessment of progress on hoarding symptoms. We also recommend one or more visits (usually 1–2 hours) to the home or to common acquiring locations by the clinician or "coach" for treatment purposes (see Home Visit section below), and understand that clinician visits may not be feasible in some settings. The 20-week duration of group treatment was derived from earlier research described in Chapter 1. Ideally, the group treatment sessions are two hours in length. However, when agency billing constraints have limited the time, we have conducted 90-minute group sessions with good outcomes.

Each group session covers the topics in this box.

Session Number	Session Topics
1	Introduction and Education
2	Model Building
3	Motivation
4	Goals and Treatment Planning
5	Reducing Acquisition
6	More on Acquisition
7	Exposure Practice for Non-Acquisition
8	Decisions about Saving and Discarding

9	More on Decisions about Saving and Discarding
10	Skills Training for Organizing
11	Organizing Paper
12	Cognitive Strategies
13	Cognitive Therapy Skills for Letting Go
14	Coaching and Letting Go
15	Non-Acquisition Practice
16	Barriers to Progress
17	Maintaining Systems and Gains
18	Review of Treatment Methods
19	Assessment and Review of Progress
20	Graduation and Next Steps

Session Structure

Each group treatment session follows a basic format that begins with a "check-in" or "go-round" in which each client reports very briefly (1 min.) on hoarding-related events that have occurred since the intervening session. While group members briefly review their progress with their home commitment assignments, the group leaders complete the compliance ratings on the Clinician's Group Progress Notes (see Appendix 15 for a blank form and Appendix 16 for an example). Co-leaders distribute Group Sessions forms (see Appendix 12 for a blank form and Appendix 11 for an example) to each member, state the agenda for the current session (noted on the form), and ask whether group members have additional agenda items. Experiences with the week's home commitment assignments are discussed first, followed by the session content. New home commitments for the week are developed during the discussion or devised at the end of the session to fit the topics covered. Group participants bring their client *Workbook* (see discussion below) to each session to follow along with relevant information, exercises, and forms pertinent to the topic. We also recommend requiring or providing 1-inch 3-ring binders for each group member to organize their handouts. At the end of each group session, group members make notes and record their home commitment assignments on the Group

Session Forms and put these into the binder. These forms help members remember treatment methods and remind them of their home commitment assignment.

Co-Leadership

We have utilized a co-leadership model in our hoarding groups and find this especially helpful. The benefits include increased opportunities to model desired behaviors, enhanced ability to manage the group process, easier problem-solving, potential for professional development, and may offer a cost-effective training model. Some of the challenges include the added cost and time-commitment incurred by two leaders, problematic style differences, power differentials, and conflicts between co-leaders. Recommended guidelines for successful co-leadership relationships include clarifying in advance the nature of the co-leaders' relationship (e.g., senior and junior clinicians; mentor and student) and their roles within the group. This typically includes discussing the co-leaders' styles, defining the division of group tasks, conducting intake assessments jointly or separately, meeting regularly to review group sessions and client progress, and receiving group supervision or consultation together when possible (Hepworth, Rooney, Rooney & Strom-Gottfried, 2013; Shulman, 2011).Throughout this Guide, we will refer to the clinicians leading the group in the plural as "leaders," but understand that your group may have a single leader. The benefits of a single-leader group include lower cost; less time required for coordinating, planning, processing, and supervision of the group; and no co-leadership challenges. The disadvantages of leading the group independently are decreased collaboration and support, more challenges in responding to group conflicts and group members' needs, and possibly inability to model effective communication to group members.

Group Formation

We recommend that the group have no more than eight members (although we have conducted groups of nine successfully). Group composition is a critical part of the group planning process. Typically, members will be adults (age 18 or older) who have a clinical level of hoarding according to the DSM-5 criteria (see Chapter 4, Session 1). We prefer that clients have access to an individual therapist who can address coexisting mental health problems so these do not interfere with focusing on hoarding in the group. Note that group treatment may not be advisable for clients who have psychiatric conditions that require immediate clinical care (e.g., suicidality, psychosis, substance abuse), severe interpersonal problems, are homeless, and/or live in a home with serious squalid conditions that will require public health intervention to restore an appropriate sanitary environment. Bieling, McCabe, and Antony (2006) suggest that clinicians ask themselves the following three questions to help determine which clients may be suitable for group treatment:

- What kind of relationships will this person wish to form with other group members?
- What interpersonal behaviors of this person will support group cohesion and process?
- What interpersonal behaviors have the potential to undermine group cohesion and process?

Diversity is also an important aspect of constituting the group. While all group members will have a hoarding problem in common, they may differ with regard to economic status, race, ethnicity, age, physical ability, and sexual orientation. When making decisions about the racial and gender composition of the group, be thoughtful about the balance of group membership (Shulman, 2011). For example, an "extreme" composition wherein one group member is substantially younger or older, or is the only member of a race/ethnic group or gender may lead to their discomfort, isolation, and disconnection. This may ultimately affect the mutual aid system and success of the group. A demonstration group illustrating some of these issues is described at the end of Chapter 3.

Office Assessment

The intake process will typically follow your agency's protocol for referral and evaluation procedures. Much of the initial assessment takes place with the client individually in the group leader's office, and includes interviews about hoarding symptoms, comorbid health and mental health problems, previous treatment, and other aspects of the client's life. It is recommended that assessments of potential members be completed within a month of the initiation of group or that the intake be updated to confirm appropriate fit. Several questionnaire measures of symptoms can be completed by clients in your office, and some should be done during the home visit. We strongly recommend that you complete a home visit at the outset of treatment before the group begins to accurately assess the hoarding environment, the severity of clutter, and the need to address any dangerous conditions. Collaboration with outside providers is also recommended, including individual and/or group therapists, in-home supporters, or others who may be helping the client de-clutter. During the intake process, discuss and identify helpful persons whom the group leaders will contact (e.g., other providers, family, friends, housing managers). As per the Health Insurance Portability and Accountability Act (HIPAA) Privacy Rules, you must request releases to speak with anyone about your client. For more information about HIPAA, please go to the U.S. Health and Human Services website: http://www.hhs.gov/ocr/privacy/hipaa/understanding/index.html.

Assessing Hoarding Symptoms

A variety of measures are available to assess hoarding and related symptoms. The Hoarding Interview provides a template for collecting detailed information about clients' hoarding symptoms, degree of impairment, and general life situation. We suggest incorporating Hoarding Interview questions into the initial intake session(s), as this may help in developing the conceptual model for each client's hoarding symptoms as described in Session 2.

In addition to this interview, we recommend using the following standard measures of hoarding symptoms. These can be found in the Appendix 1–8, with a scoring key and information about typical scores for each measure. These instruments can be given as self-report measures, but you may prefer to administer some directly with the client in their home, depending on the nature and severity of their hoarding and on their capacity to complete the forms accurately by themselves.

- Hoarding Rating Scale (HRS; Tolin, Frost & Steketee, 2010b; Tolin, Frost, Steketee, Gray & Fitch, 2008a) is a very brief five-item scale that assesses the major features of HD (clutter, difficulty discarding, acquisition, distress, interference). The HRS takes 5 to 10 minutes and can be administered as an interview during intake, and as a self-report questionnaire to track progress during treatment. The HRS can be found in the client *Workbook* and Appendix 2.

- Saving Inventory–Revised (SI-R; Frost, Steketee & Grisham, 2004) is a 23-item scale with three subscales: (1) Acquiring, to determine the extent of buying and acquisition of free things; (2) Clutter, to report the amount of clutter and associated problems; and (3) Difficulty Discarding, to measure discomfort about getting rid of items. This scale can be found in the client *Workbook* and Appendix 3.

- Clutter Image Rating (CIR; Frost, Steketee, Tolin & Renaud, 2008) is a pictorial measure that includes nine pictures, ranging from 1 = "no clutter," to 9 = "severe clutter" for three rooms: kitchen, living room, and bedroom. A rating of 4 or higher represents clinically significant clutter characteristic of HD. Clients simply select the number of the picture that most closely matches the level of clutter in their own room. This instrument is very easy to use for the initial assessment of clutter and also helps gauge progress during treatment. The CIR works best when printed in full color. We have included black and white samples in the Appendix 4 and in the client *Workbook*. You can download color versions from the Treatments *ThatWork*™ website at www.oup.com/us/ttw. Both clients and clinicians can complete this measure for each room in the home.

- Saving Cognitions Inventory (SCI; Steketee, Frost & Kyrios, 2003) is a 24-item self-report questionnaire that assesses beliefs and attitudes clients experience when trying to discard items. Four subscales focus on emotional attachment to objects, beliefs about objects as memory aids, responsibility for not wasting possessions, and the need for control over possessions. This questionnaire can be found in the client *Workbook* and Appendix 5.

- Activities of Daily Living for Hoarding (ADL-H; Frost, Hristova, Steketee & Tolin, 2013) inquires about how much the clutter interferes with clients' ability to complete ordinary activities like bathing, dressing, and preparing meals (15 items). Items are rated from 1 (none) to 5 (severe). This scale can be found in the client *Workbook* and Appendix 6.

- Safety Questions help identify common hoarding situations that compromise the safety of people's homes. These include questions about fire hazards, blocked exits, whether emergency personnel can get through the house with equipment, and so forth. Items are rated from 1 (none) to 5 (severe). Evaluation of client safety is critical early in treatment (especially if there are children or elders living in the home) and helps identify priority areas for treatment. A score of 2 or above on any item warrants attention to that item early in treatment. You can complete these questions during a visit to the client's home. Safety Questions can be found in the client *Workbook* and Appendix 7.

Squalor is a concern in some hoarding cases and is best assessed by clinicians during a home visit. The Home Environment Index (HEI; Rasmussen et al., under review) includes 15 questions that provide a useful index of the extent of a squalor problem in the home, including the presence of moldy or rotten food, dirty surfaces, odor in the home, etc. Each question is rated from 0 = "no problem" to 3 = "severe problem." A score of 2 or above on any item warrants attention to that item early in treatment. The HEI can be found in the client *Workbook* and Appendix 8.

If both you and your client complete the HRS, CIR, and ADL-H, you can determine whether there are substantial discrepancies in your scores. If your client rates himself or herself significantly lower than you do on any of these measures, there may be problems with insight that will require your attention using motivational strategies described in Session 3. All of these measures are included in the Appendix 1–8, and the self-report measures are in the client *Workbook* as well.

Identifying Other Psychiatric Problems

As noted in Chapter 1, several psychiatric problems are often comorbid with hoarding disorder, and you should be aware of their presence to determine whether they affect the hoarding problem or the treatment. These conditions include major depression, social phobia, obsessive-compulsive disorder, and attention-deficit hyperactivity disorder (ADHD). Depression and attention deficit tend to be the most frequent and problematic of these conditions during the treatment process. Session 16 provides recommendations for managing these other psychiatric, as well as health and safety, conditions if you encounter them.

In-Home Assessment

A home visit is important to confirm impressions gained during the office interview. During the home visit, you can determine the amount and type of clutter and whether the home environment poses an immediate health or safety threat. You can also meet with family members if this is appropriate (see below). If at all possible, schedule the home appointment prior to the first group treatment session. Assume your client is worried and embarrassed about the visit and will find your walking through the home and taking photographs intrusive. Many hoarding clients have had no visitors for years, and in some cases, relatives or local officials have removed their belongings against their will. To allay their fears, describe the goals of the home assessment and the procedures you will follow during the visit. Indicate that you will not touch any items and that any photos taken are part of the client's confidential record and will not be shown to anyone else, including members of the group. Language similar to the following may be helpful:

> *The home visit is very important for us to understand your thoughts and experiences about the things you own. So far, I've asked you a lot of questions about the hoarding problem during this office visit. When we are at your home, I'll be asking how you feel and think about your things as you actually look at them, and also what you typically do at home and how the clutter affects this. The home visit helps me understand how you think and feel about your home and*

your things. We can take pictures of your home to use during treatment to decide on next steps and to track your progress. Of course, I will keep the pictures strictly confidential and not show them to anyone else, including other members of the group. If you decide to show the pictures to anyone, that will be entirely your decision. Do you have any questions about the process or about anything else so far?

On entering the home for the first time, be careful not to react with shock or dismay, regardless of the level of clutter or state of the home. This avoids confirming your client's worst fears that you will judge them harshly. As in all treatment sessions, begin the home visit by checking-in and establishing the agenda. The major agenda items for this session are (1) completing assessments of daily activities; (2) identifying the type and amount of clutter; and (3) beginning to plan the intervention with clients. You and your client can then complete the assessments, including the Hoarding Rating Scale, Activities of Daily Living for Hoarding, Safety Questions, and the Clutter Image Rating during the walk-through. If you observe squalid conditions, you may wish to complete the HEI after the walk-through. Compare notes with your client on these measures. If you observe a mismatch in your scores, you may decide to explore the discrepancy with the client at that time or make a note to speak with them at a later date. You may also decide that speaking with the individual therapist is the most appropriate approach. These measures will help establish treatment goals to improve clients' functioning.

We recommend photographing all rooms (digital photos from the client's phone are fine) to capture an accurate visual record of clutter contents and provide a baseline assessment of the severity of clutter for reference during therapy to evaluate progress and decide on next steps. Photos help point out visible progress later in treatment when clients may be discouraged during what can be a lengthy treatment process with ups and downs. If clients live too far from the clinic, or if a home visit is not possible, they can take the photographs themselves with a little training. Plan to take 2 to 4 photographs per room to capture the full extent of the hoarding and to help decide which items clients should bring to group sessions for practice during treatment. Try to devise a consistent method that will be easy to follow at the next picture-taking occasion in order to match the first pictures.

Deciding Where to Begin

At some point during the home assessment, or when reviewing pictures of the home, help clients decide where to begin the sorting, organizing, and removing of clutter. This requires a discussion about whether to proceed room-by-room or to use some other system such as one based on types of item (e.g., gathering up all papers or all books from all the rooms, and then sorting these). We usually begin with the easiest space or the one that will have the most immediate benefit for clients. For example, some clients may prefer to begin with a hallway because it impedes access to parts of the home they'd like to use. Others might begin in the kitchen because it is the least cluttered and/or offers the most benefit in terms of resuming important activities like cooking or eating. Other considerations, like reducing family members' criticism or complying with building codes, may also contribute to this decision.

We recommend framing this decision of where to begin as an initial step in the 20-week intervention. It does not signify that the client is ready to de-clutter or has the necessary skills. Explain to clients that they will be learning the required skills for sorting and discarding and will have opportunities during the group to practice those skills. If time allows, help clients assemble a box or bag of typical saved items to take to group sessions to learn and practice new skills. This box should contain a mixture of clutter items, such as junk mail, newspapers, magazines, small objects, receipts, notes, ticket stubs, clothing, books, etc. Select these items mainly from the room where treatment will begin.

Special Issues During the Home Visit

Severe hoarding problems may complicate home visiting procedures. Although it is difficult to know how severe the problem is, you may be able to gauge this based on your client's CIR ratings (6 and above are very severe) and clutter scores on other measures. However, even with moderate scores in the 4 to 5 range on these scales, you may encounter unhealthy and even dangerous problems in the home. If your client has children or elders living at home, have a frank discussion about the level of risk to them and your professional responsibilities for reporting dangerous conditions if they exist. Such a discussion should occur *before* the home visit and should cover information about the reporting process and how you can help them with it. It is important that your client understand that the health and safety of their loved ones may necessitate more drastic action than they may have anticipated. See the Readings and Resources for a list of resources related to mandated reporting laws and procedures.

If the assessment (photos, HEI scores) suggests very serious sanitary or structural problems in the home, you will also need to have a brief discussion before the home visit of steps you may take to protect your own health and safety. These could include wearing gloves, protective clothing, and/or a breathing mask, or avoiding unsafe areas of the home. Please keep in mind the importance of being consistent about wearing gloves or using other protective material in group members' homes, as they may mention such details during group sessions. Take these protective items with you just in case, and use them if you feel it necessary.

The clinicians' personal tolerance for the odor, dust, animal dander, etc., will vary. The use of protective gear is a clinically sensitive issue; and if not handled carefully, it could damage the therapeutic relationship. Here are some statements that may help:

> *I have allergies and need to wear a mask.*
>
> *Our agency requires us to wear protective gear.*
>
> *I need to use the mask and gloves; how do you feel about this?*

In most cases, protective gear is not required; each clinician will make their decision based on the photos of the client's home prior to the visit, their home-based assessment, and/or reports from other in-home providers. In addition, be prepared to have no place to sit down and little room to move around during the home visit. It may be helpful to bring a clipboard for writing notes. Finally, be prepared for some clients to offer food or drinks. You may choose to decline the offer; one way to handle this is to put a bottle of water into your bag.

Should you find serious sanitary or structural problems, we recommend contacting a local area hoarding task force (if available) for help in coordinating the safety assessments and interventions. The hoarding task forces are made up of experts from various fields and public agencies (e.g., public health, fire, police, housing, mental health) who can provide a collaborative approach in helping the person with a severe hoarding problem and serious home safety concerns. Visit the International OCD Foundation website at www.ocfoundation.org for a complete listing of hoarding task forces across the country. Another excellent resource is *The Hoarding Handbook: A Guide for Human Service Professionals* (Bratiotis, Sorrentino, Schmalisch & Steketee, 2011).

If you are conducting home visits during the course of the group, it is probable that group members will discuss their experiences with these visits during group sessions. Be sure to maintain confidentiality about each group member's home visits. Group members must decide how much detail they would like to share about the condition of their home, the types of items in their home, and the family, friends or other supporters who may have participated in home visits.

Use of This Guide

As noted in Chapter 1, this manual is organized as a session-by-session guide. While we recommend proceeding in the order presented, it is not prescriptive, and group leaders should use their clinical judgment in responding to the specific needs of each group. We recommend reading all the chapters of this book to become familiar with the main components of the treatment and the goals and objectives covered in each session.

Use of the Client *Workbook*

The accompanying client *Workbook* contains brief information and instructions to clients that follow the format of this manual. Also included are blank versions of all forms used during treatment and for homework assignments. These include assessment instruments, and various forms for recording behaviors, thoughts, and beliefs as they occur naturally; and case formulation, treatment goals, organizing plans, behavioral experiments, cognitive techniques, and a list of interventions learned during treatment. The client *Workbook* reinforces what is learned during sessions and is therefore a critical part of therapy. We recommend that all group members purchase a client *Workbook* and a binder for their personal use prior to the group. Leaders can have copies available for purchase and/or include the price of the *Workbook* and binder in the cost of treatment. At each session, advise clients what parts to read and which forms to complete before the next session. Because materials are easily lost in the clutter at home, in Session 1, ask clients to put the book and binder in a special place where it is always available for recording notes. Examples are just inside the front door, in the room where they most often sit or lie, or on top of the refrigerator or other surface that they keep relatively uncluttered. Ask them to bring the client *Workbook* and binder to every session.

Chapter 3 *Group Process*

Introduction to Group Process

The group intervention for hoarding described in this book blends the scientist-practitioner approach of CBT and the process-oriented approach of group work (Bieling, McCabe & Antoni, 2006). While much has been written about group process and about CBT treatment for hoarding, little is written specifically about group processes in CBT groups for hoarding. "Group process" refers to the interactions between group members and group leaders; that is, the here-and-now experiences within the group (Brown, 2003). Several therapeutic factors have been identified as useful in planning group treatment for hoarding. These include instilling hope, fostering universality of group members' experience, imparting information, socializing members to communicate clearly, and encouraging group cohesion, mutual aid, and appropriate imitative behavior among group members (Schwartz, 1961; Shulman, 2011; Yalom, 2005). This chapter will review relevant therapeutic factors, and leaders' roles in nurturing helpful group processes and managing therapy-interfering behaviors that can undermine the group process. Attending to the processes of your 20-week hoarding group fosters a group climate that is safe and engaging for all participants.

Phases of Group Development

The 20-week hoarding group has a beginning, middle, and ending phase of treatment (Berman-Rossi, 1993; Garland, Kolodny & Jones, 1965; Gitterman & Shulman, 2005). The therapeutic aspects of group processes evolve during these phases, with group leaders addressing specific tasks throughout as shown in Table 3.1. For example, during the beginning phase, the leaders highlight the commonality or universality of group members' experiences. In the middle phase, the group leaders push group members to work actively on their problems and address conflict between members. In the ending phase, the leaders help group members become more independent and separate from the group, while simultaneously emphasizing the group's shared experience of loss and/or sadness. These phases of the group shape the leaders' responses to interactions among group members as they encourage mutual aid and cultivate other therapeutic factors. These three main phases are described in more detail in Table 3.1.

Beginning Phase

The beginning phase of your hoarding group is the time to orient the clients to the group content and process. Assume that they will be asking themselves questions such as, "Why am I here? Who are these people? Can I trust them? Who is this leader?" and "How is this going to help me?" During this period, the leader is engaged in contracting with group members—clarifying the purpose of the group, defining the role of the leaders, asking for feedback, identifying commonalities among group members, helping group members talk about difficult topics, and addressing issues of authority (Gitterman & Shulman, 2005). At the first group session, begin establishing the cultural norms of your group by encouraging certain behaviors and limiting others. Make the rules of the group explicit by collaboratively setting guidelines such as arriving on time, refraining from side conversations, and agreeing not to share or trade items. Look for connections among the members and identify them to the group to help foster feelings of universality, cohesion, and hope. During the beginning phase, help group members limit excessive disclosure of personal information (especially if it is painful) until a sense of safety within the group has been achieved.

Middle Phase

The middle phase of the group is also known as the "work phase." Ideally, the group has developed a deeper level of cohesion and engages

Table 3.1 Group Session Topics, Phases, and Processes

Session	Group Session Topic	Phases	Process Skills[1]	Processes
1	Introduction and Education	Beginning	Contracting Encouraging specificity Reaching for feedback Identifying connections Pointing out phase (beginning)	Instilling hope Universality Imparting information
2	Model Building			
3	Motivation			
4	Goals and Planning Treatment			
5	Reducing Acquisition	Middle/ Work	Reflecting on dynamics Pushing for work Helping members elaborate Pointing to connections between experiences Reaching for feelings Encouraging support and feedback Addressing conflict Point out phase (Middle)	Altruism Socializing Imitative behavior Interpersonal learning Group cohesion Mutual aid
6	More on Acquisition			
7	Exposure Practice for Non-Acquisition			
8	Decisions about Saving and Discarding			
9	More on Decisions about Saving and Discarding			
10	Skills Training for Organizing			
11	Organizing Paper			
12	Cognitive Strategies			
13	Cognitive Therapy Skills for Letting Go			
14	Coaching and Letting Go			
15	Non-Acquisition Practice			
16	Barriers to Progress	Ending	Point out phase (Ending) Sharing feelings about ending Getting and giving feedback (positive and negative) Celebrating Reminiscing	
17	Maintaining Systems and Gains			
18	Review of Treatment Methods			
19	Assessment and Review of Progress			
20	Graduation and Next Steps			

[1](Berman-Rossi, 1993; Shulman, 2011)

in mutual aid that encourages the intimacy and feelings of safety needed to push each other to work and share more intimate details of their private thoughts and behaviors. At this point, the leader helps group members by reflecting aloud on group dynamics, encouraging elaboration of feelings and thoughts (rather than containing them in the beginning phase), reaching for feelings, and encouraging support and feedback. In this phase, you will also undoubtedly experience conflict in your group. It is helpful to view this conflict as an important expression of difference among members, just as important as the experience of commonality. Steinberg (2010) suggests seven key ways for using conflict to encourage the development of mutual aid:

1. Recognize that conflict can be helpful.
2. Expect conflict to happen and help the group accept it.
3. Treat conflict as a result of difference, not fault.
4. Don't take over when conflict occurs.
5. Engage everyone in the group.
6. Be sure every member feels supported by the leader(s).
7. Help the group keep sight of its common ground.

Ending/Transition Phase

Endings and transitions can be difficult for group members. Accordingly, during the final phase of the group, expect that members may come late, miss a session, or behave in unusual ways in group as a reaction to the impending end of the group. The group leader's task is to help the members understand their feelings and behaviors and make that transition. Schwartz (1961) outlined the stages of the group ending process: denial, indirect and direct expressions of anger, mourning, "trying it on," and "farewell party" syndrome (avoiding discussion of negative aspects). Shulman (2011) suggests some strategies that can help group members through the termination process:

- Discuss termination from the start.

- Point out the stages of grief as the group is going through them (denial, anger, mourning, trying it on, farewell party syndrome).
- Share personal feelings about the group ending.
- Encourage sharing of feelings about the group ending.
- Help group members be specific with their feedback about the group and their work together.
- Encourage negative feedback.

Keeping these phases and process skills in mind will help you respond appropriately to the issues that arise for individual members and for the group as a whole throughout the hoarding group experience.

Therapeutic Factors and Mutual Aid

Various therapeutic factors and mutual aid efforts will play important roles as group members and leaders interact with each other. While the 20-week hoarding group is content-driven, these processes are a critical part of the hoarding group's success. The leaders impart content that helps group members understand and resolve their hoarding problem, and also fosters therapeutic processes and mutual aid efforts, guiding the group towards increased connection and cohesion. The integration of content and process enhances group members' ability to reach their treatment goals (e.g., increase their knowledge about hoarding, develop skills to decrease hoarding behaviors, improve their social support, and decrease their social isolation). Group leaders tune in to, foster, and encourage these therapeutic factors and mutual aid. The group leaders' tasks are to: (1) recognize the common connections between group members, (2) encourage support of members' struggles to understand and change their hoarding behaviors, and (3) develop cohesion and safety so members become comfortable sharing the shame, loneliness, and fear that often accompany hoarding disorder. Here we focus on four therapeutic factors: universality, instilling hope, cohesion, and socializing.

Fostering Universality

Universality occurs when the group members meet others with the same disorder and recognize that they are not alone in struggling with their hoarding problem. Many people who hoard have been isolated in their homes, too ashamed to invite family or friends over or reach out for help. Coming together with others who share a common problem can reduce the stigma, isolation, and shame they feel (Bieling et al., 2006). Sadly, people with hoarding disorder can provoke criticism and rejection from family and friends, similar to those who suffer serious mental illness, and unfortunately, such negative perceptions can become internalized (Tolin, Frost, Steketee & Fitch, 2008b). The sense of universality (being "in the same boat") can generate hope that the group member will be able to make positive changes that lead to an uncluttered home and ultimately a more fulfilling life.

The following examples (see box) demonstrate how the group leader can encourage feelings of universality.

Group member	Group leader response
One member reports being very embarrassed by the people looking at her car at the gas station.	"Has anyone else felt that way?"
Group member reports that the symptoms of depression make it difficult to work on de-cluttering their home.	Notice that several members are nodding their heads and point out that others in the group seem to understand.
Two members state that they have memory problems that make it scary to put items away, for fear of not finding them.	Point out that both members share this concern.

Developing Cohesion

Universality may lead to self-disclosure, which can encourage a sense of safety and group cohesion (Sorrentino Schmalisch et al., 2010). Group cohesion is important to group success and individual goal attainment

(Gazda, Ginter & Horne, 2001). This connectedness refers to the alliance of group members to one another and to the group as a whole, as well as their commitment to the group CBT hoarding treatment program. Cohesion starts during the beginning phase and develops throughout all phases of the group. From the very first session, members commit to confidentiality, attendance policies, and other guidelines generated together, all of which foster a sense of safety and trust between the members. Cohesion also develops as the group members learn about each other's similar beliefs about possessions—for example, beliefs about everyday items (e.g., plastic bags, newspapers) having high value, that it seems wrong to waste items that might be usable (e.g., corks, toilet paper rolls), or that objects have feelings or human traits. Cohesion becomes evident as members join with each other in celebrating their developing understanding and skills.

Socialization Strategies

Socializing techniques applied in group treatment provide opportunities to increase member connectedness and mutual aid (Yalom, 2005). Many group members are isolated and lack opportunities for social interaction, which may be a result of, as well as contribute to, their hoarding problem. These emotional and physical barriers created by hoarding can isolate clients from family, friends, acquaintances, and others with whom they might interact (e.g., shopkeepers, repair people). In some cases, the hoarding symptoms may also provide a protective barrier for those with trauma histories or social anxiety. Through group treatment, members may work to reduce their shame that distances them from others, and interact with peers on an equal footing. Group leaders strive to create safe social environments where members can learn and practice social skills. Additionally, the group offers the opportunity for members to shift their focus from relating to their possessions to relating to other people.

Socializing during and outside of the group sessions may also provide opportunities for members to strengthen their cohesion and mutual aid. Socializing is also encouraged during sessions through activities whereby members break into pairs to practice skills and techniques. We also recommend supporting group member contact outside of group sessions, as long as this is in the service of working on members' hoarding problems. Allowing group members to linger after the sessions can encourage positive interactions and create an opportunity to practice socializing outside of the structured time. When negative interactions occur inside or outside the group session, these need to be processed during the group, as working through conflicts offers an opportunity for cohesion. As group members become more connected to each other, they may experience increased motivation to attend group and arrive on time, and a heightened sense of hope.

Instilling Hope

Instilling hope is another critical component of the hoarding group treatment process. Each group member will already have some hope, as indicated by their willingness to attend the group. The group modality provides the unique opportunity for the members to observe improvement in each other (Yalom, 2005). During the first few sessions, the group leader asks each member to identify their personal goals; this process enhances their motivation to continue and fosters the hope of improving the state of their homes and their lives. Furthermore, as group members gain more understanding of their hoarding behavior and problematic thinking styles, and as they practice skills to address them, they are also likely to feel more empowered, with a corresponding increase in hope.

Encouraging Mutual Aid

"Mutual aid" was first described by Schwartz (1961) as "an alliance of individuals who need each other, in varying degrees, to work on certain common problems" (p. 18). Mutual aid occurs when members offer support, empathy, and understanding to one another (Sorrentino Schmalisch et al., 2010). In delivering group CBT for hoarding, you will need to carefully evaluate the balance between covering manualized content and fostering group process. It is important to protect time for interactions between group members, paying careful attention to the potential for encouraging mutual aid and leaving some time for spontaneous communication and connection (Steinberg, 2010). The questions below may help in this effort (Brown, 2003, p. 234):

1. What is the group doing to promote safety?
2. How is the group establishing norms, and what norms are in place and/or emerging?
3. What is the group's reaction to authority?
4. What is threatening to the group?
5. How does the group manage conflict, anxiety, arousal, and other uncomfortable states?
6. What is the group's reaction to anticipated intimacy?
7. What significant and important feelings are expressed or ignored?
8. What personal feelings and reactions am I [the leader] experiencing?
9. Does the group seem stuck?

To model and encourage mutual aid among hoarding group members, bring individual problems reported by clients back to the group and encourage supportive, empathic sharing of ideas, strategies, and tools to address the problem. Examples of statements that encourage mutual aid include the following:

- "Liz, thank you for letting us know that the bookstore has now started a consignment shop. Some of you might find that helpful for getting rid of some items."
- "Joseph, thank you for passing the tissue to Jennifer. That was really nice."
- "Let's try to help Charlie problem-solve what to do with that old lawn mower. Does anyone have any ideas?"

Such mutual aid efforts afford therapeutic benefits to both the receiver and the giver of information and advice, as the receiver feels emotionally supported while the giver feels gratified to have been helpful. Group members may gain new insights and perspectives from the experiences and advice of others who are struggling with a similar problem. As noted above, mutual aid often occurs during practice exercises (e.g., Socratic questioning, establishing coaching rules, developing hierarchies), which can include the entire group or subsets (usually dyads or triads).

Managing the Roles of Group Co-leadership

Co-leaders are an integral part of the group, and their relationship influences mutual aid and the development of the therapeutic factors. As mentioned in Chapter 2, when planning your group, explicit conversations between the co-leaders about their roles and power differentials is strongly recommended (Nosko, 2002; Shulman, 2011). Many models for the roles of the group leaders exist; for example trainer–trainee; two comparably experienced clinicians; or one leader with greater expertise with group work, hoarding, and/or CBT models. Co-leaders may alternate presenting session content and/or designate specific content based on one individual's expertise. One co-leader may assume more responsibility for managing the content, while the other may have primary responsibility for overseeing group processes. Establish roles and responsibilities prior to each group session, and define them for the group members. For example: "Today, I am going to present the content, and my co-leader is going to be tuning into the group dynamics;" or "Our plan is for the two of us to alternate presenting the content and tuning in to the group process." Regardless of the specific roles, it is most important to lead the group as a well-coordinated team.

Treatment-Interfering Behaviors

Therapy-interfering behaviors are behaviors that negatively affect individual clients' treatment progress and influence the development of the group, therapeutic factors, and mutual aid. Therapy-interfering behaviors includes not completing homework, missing sessions, acting aggressively toward other members or toward the group leader, criticizing the treatment model, denying the problem, providing inaccurate information, refusing home visits or not participating in group, and switching the focus of the conversation (e.g., group member discusses other problems or interests during check-in or proposes goals unrelated to the hoarding problem) (Pollard, 2012). When these behaviors are not isolated events but repeated, ongoing patterns of behavior, they require the leader's attention. Do not rush to fix problems; instead, be patient and allow time for the group to respond. Sometimes the group members will point out these behaviors in others (see Case Example 1 below). If this occurs, it is important to encourage and support the group members' diverse perspectives during the confrontation. That is, support those who point out the therapy-interfering behaviors and those who are being confronted. If group members do not address a member's verbal aggression that threatens the sense of safety in the group, then the leaders should raise this with the group directly and discuss it with the individual separately afterward.

In Case Example 2, the group member's therapy-interfering behavior is denying the efficacy of the group hoarding treatment. In this case, it is important for the group leader to re-contract with this group member (e.g., confirm the client's commitment to the group treatment and willingness to follow group rules) to avoid the undermining of motivation of other group members. This meeting would take place in an individual session.

Case Example 1

A group member was mandated by her town public health department to attend the hoarding group due to concerns about her safety in her significantly cluttered home. A widowed woman with grown children and several grandchildren, she refused home visits and talked about her activities and goals related to her church rather than her home. The group leaders encouraged her to adjust her goals to address the hoarding problem. However, it was another group member's comments that helped her engage more actively in the hoarding treatment. The member asked, "Why aren't you making your goals related to hoarding? This is a hoarding group. I don't understand why you are talking about your need to prepare pies for the church as your goal."

Case Example 2

Sam was a self-referred client who reported significant clutter in his home. He completed the intake evaluation and the initial home visit. Throughout the beginning phase of the group, he often became verbally aggressive towards other group members and to one of the group leaders. He stated during the group that the material didn't resonate with him and that he would stay in the group to find out if there was anything he could learn, but he didn't think he would learn anything he didn't already know. The verbal combativeness and frequent criticizing of the treatment model were undermining the group's cohesion, and several group members' hopes for improvement were diminishing. The group leader(s) requested a meeting with Sam outside the group session in order to directly address his behavior. Sam apologized to the group and the leaders, and members reviewed group rules together.

Motivational interviewing (MI; Miller & Rollnick, 2013) and dialectical behavioral therapy (DBT; Linehan, 1993) share similar assumptions about human behavior and interventions for treatment-interfering behaviors, referring to these respectively as "treatment adherence" behaviors and "therapy-interfering behaviors." DBT attends particularly to both patient and therapist behaviors, pointing to the collaborative nature and shared responsibility for treatment effectiveness. Van Dyke and Pollard (2005) focus on the functional outcomes of clients' behavior patterns that interfere with effective participation in treatment; they suggest that these clients will benefit from an intensive readiness program to address their willingness to engage in therapy to change their behaviors.

The group treatment program for hoarding described here does not require a readiness group to prepare members for the group; but, as suggested in Chapter 2, we recommend that group members have an individual therapist who works with clients on co-occurring mental health disorders. We also recommend that leaders define and discuss treatment-interfering behaviors when they emerge.

Demonstration Group

Next, we introduce eight group members: Sally, Charlie, Liz, Joseph, Maria, Jennifer, Grace, and Carl. They will appear throughout this guide to help us illustrate group processes and therapy methods during group treatment sessions. Their backgrounds and histories reflect the heterogeneous characteristics of a typical hoarding group. Among the five women, one is Latina and two are African American women. Among the three men, one is gay with a long-term partner, one is divorced, and the third is married. The women in the group are either single or widowed. Two people are in the group because they were mandated or pressured into attending—one by the housing court and the other by a partner. All members of the group have hoarding disorder, and many have other comorbid mental health problems. Thus, they represent a typical group that leaders might encounter in clinic settings. Each member is described, and Table 3.2 summarizes their characteristics.

Table 3.2 The Demonstration Group

Name	Age	Marital Status, Living Situation	Co-occurring Disorders	Current Providers	Comments
Sally	65	Single, has life lease of single-family home	MDD,back problems	Individual therapist	Consignment shopping
Charlie	60	Married, owns single-family home	None	None	Wife insisted on treatment
Liz	70	Single, public housing	GAD, fibromyalgia, chemical sensitivity, rule out OCPD	Elder services, case management, housing staff	Eviction notice received
Joseph	59	Divorced, apartment	ADD, MDD	Individual therapist	Trade magazines
Maria	62	Widowed, owns duplex	MDD	Individual therapist	Husband's clothing
Jennifer	45	Single, condominium	OCPD, perfectionism	Individual therapist, DBT group	Accessories
Grace	50	Single, trailer	MDD, specific phobia	Individual therapist	Animal supplies (food, toys, brushes)
Carl	55	Partnered, condominium	Social anxiety	Individual therapist	Trains, music equipment

ADD = attention deficit disorder; DBT = dialectical behavior therapy; GAD = generalized anxiety disorder; MDD = major depressive disorder; OCPD = obsessive-compulsive personality disorder

Sally is a 65-year-old, single, African American woman who was referred to group by her individual therapist. Sally has a moderate hoarding problem (her CIR was scored 5) and suffers from major depression. She is on disability for a back problem. Sally recalls that the hoarding became "really unmanageable" after the death of her fiancé 10 years ago. She still lives in her late fiancé's house. She enjoys shopping at consignment shops, in which she finds great deals on clothing and accessories, but she has no more room to store her clothing and finds it difficult to discard the clothing. She has not had a visitor in 15 years.

Charlie is a 60-year-old married White man who has a family history of hoarding—his father "collected" lots of tools. His wife is threatening to leave if he doesn't clean up their single-family house. Like many mandated clients, he is at the pre-contemplation stage of motivation in that he is aware he has a problem but is not sure he needs treatment. His home is filled with electronics equipment that has some intrinsic value. His CIR score is an 8 in some rooms.

Liz is a 70-year-old single White woman who reports having anxiety, fibromyalgia, and chemical sensitivity. Her CIR score is 7 in most rooms. Referred by the public housing office, she is mandated to attend the group as part of the efforts to prevent eviction. She collects and saves paper, clothing, and containers and picks up many free items. She states that recycling is critically important. She reports memory problems and difficulties with organizing.

Joseph is a 59-year-old divorced White man, the father of four children (2 are over 18, one is in middle school and one in high school). He has major depression and attention-deficit disorder. His kids do not visit him at home due to the clutter. Joseph's business went bankrupt a few years ago just prior to his divorce. His apartment is moderately cluttered, with CIR scores ranging from 4 to 6. Joseph cannot part with his trade magazines, papers, and other items related to his business, fearing that if he gets rid of them, he will be letting go of an important part of his identity. Joseph also has many boxes of his children's artwork from when they were very young. He struggles with attention and focus, and reports he is easily distracted by visual cues or ideas that come to mind.

Maria is a 62-year-old Hispanic widow whose apartment is cluttered with art supplies, clothing, and all of her husband's items. Maria's children urged her to seek treatment so that they could bring their children over for holidays and Sunday dinners. Currently, Maria's home scores in the 5 to 7 range on the CIR. Maria has depression and struggles to find the physical energy to work on de-cluttering her home. She reports memory problems and states that she often feels anxious.

Jennifer is a 45-year-old single White woman who was referred by the local hospital following a stay for suicidality and emotion disregulation. She has also been diagnosed with obsessive-compulsive personality disorder. The home she inherited from her parents is cluttered and disorganized, with a CIR score of 6 in most rooms. She has special difficulty letting go of accessories, cards, and clothing. She also struggles with attention focusing, organization, and anxiety. She cannot seem to find the "perfect" place for her items and has trouble discarding clothing because it's the "perfect" shade or style.

Grace is a 50-year-old single African American woman who rents a trailer that is significantly cluttered throughout (CIR scores range from 5 to 6). She reports a previous diagnosis of depression and a phobia of mice. She has a dog and two cats. She has an excessive number of newspapers, mail, receipts, coupons, and pet items such as food, toys, brushes, etc. She likes to make sure her pets sleep comfortably, so she keeps a clear space for them to sleep, but she is unable to sleep in her own bed due to the clutter. Instead she sleeps on part of the couch in the front room.

Carl is a 55-year-old White gay man who has social anxiety and a trauma history. He works as a sound specialist for local bands and live shows. He lives in a condo with CIR scores of 4 to 5, and is mostly alone, although his long-distance boyfriend visits approximately three times a year. The condo association sent him letters because his clutter has exceeded his storage area (this room has a CIR score of 9). When he was a boy, his parents moved while he was staying with his aunt and threw out his favorite train sets during the move. He has accumulated many tools, trains, models, paints, and musical equipment.

Chapter 4 *Session 1: Introduction and Education*

Materials Needed

- Ink board or flip chart pad
- Poster board for rules
- Name tags or placards and marker
- Workbooks
- Binders
- Binder information sheet insert "Where to Put My Binder" (Appendix 9)
- Session Schedule (Appendix 10)
- Group Session Form (Appendix 12)
- Confidentiality contract (Appendix 13)
- DSM-5 criteria for hoarding disorder (Appendix 14)
- Blank Hoarding Rating Scale (HRS; *Workbook* Chapter 2, p. 12; Appendix 2)
- Clinician Group Progress Notes (Appendix 15)

Session Agenda

- Welcome and introduction
- Discussion of format and development of group rules

- Review of definition of hoarding disorder
- Discussion of home commitments
- Complete brief assessment

Preparations for Group

In preparation for the initial group session, gather the recommended materials. Set up your poster board or white board and write the session number and agenda on the board. As group members arrive, invite them to write their name on a name tag (or small placard). By Session 1, all group members need a client *Workbook* and a binder for their personal use. As discussed in Chapter 2, group leaders can have copies available for purchase and/or include the price of the *Workbook* and binder in the cost of treatment. Distribute copies of the information sheet, and ask group members to place it in the inside pocket of the binder.

Objective 1: Welcome and Introduction

The initial greeting may include a statement of congratulations for group members' courage in taking a big step toward addressing their hoarding by joining the group. Acknowledge the difficulties involved in attending a 20-week group. Emphasize the importance of attending all 20 sessions, as there is a lot of material to cover in a short period of time. Starting with yourselves as group leaders, ask each group member to introduce themselves and make a brief statement about why they are participating in the group and what they hope to gain from the group.

Objective 2: Describe Group Purpose, Structure, and Format

Indicate that the purpose of the group will be to learn skills that have been shown to be effective in treating hoarding symptoms. The group is designed to educate its members about hoarding, develop skills to address hoarding problems, address barriers and learn how to work with setbacks. Note that treating hoarding is a process, and individuals are very likely to experience improvement at the end of the group but will probably not be "cured," because treatment will be an ongoing process and recovery will require further practice beyond the group. Note that recommendations for ongoing support will be made during the final sessions.

Briefly describe the skills and topics that will be covered in the group, including assessment of hoarding symptoms and severity; understanding the nature of hoarding; developing a personalized model of hoarding; setting goals; increasing motivation; reducing acquiring; improving decision-making, problem-solving, and organizing skills; practicing sorting and discarding; addressing unhelpful thoughts using cognitive strategies; managing barriers to progress; accessing support (e.g., through coaches); maintaining gains and preventing lapses; and ending the group.

Describe the basic structure of the group as 20 weekly sessions that meet for two hours (or less if this is not possible). Note that each session will start promptly on time and will begin with a check-in of about 15 minutes in which leaders ask each member for their mood rating (0 = "very positive" to 10 = "extremely negative"), special issues that occurred during the week, and an example of a success with or barrier to completing their home commitments. Indicate that the bulk of each session will be taken up with the specific agenda and topics for that session. Group members can think of this as the educational and practice time for learning about themselves and their hoarding problem and for practicing specific strategies to resolve each aspect of their symptoms. Let members know that sessions will end with a brief "check-out" and establishing each group member's home commitment during the week between sessions. Other topics to cover may include attendance expectations, cancellation policies, parking arrangements, and payment.

Ask group members to use their binders to organize all materials for the group sessions and to store their client *Workbook* (Steketee & Frost, 2013) inside a folder within a binder. Explain that this binder is meant to help them keep track of all their materials for the group and at home. Additional forms that are helpful at the start of the group include a binder information sheet, a session schedule, and a Group Session Form that records information from each session. The binder information sheet is stored in the front of the binder and includes the group leader's contact information and a blank line for clients to note where they will keep their binder at home. The session schedule outlines the session numbers, dates, and topics. At the beginning of each session, distribute the Group Session Form (Appendix 12) and set the agenda for that session. See Objective 8 below for additional information about the Group Session Form.

Objective 3: Establish Group Guidelines

A brainstorming session of group guidelines is helpful to set group norms collaboratively. Begin this discussion by addressing confidentiality and its limits (e.g., mandatory reporting rules). Ask the group to discuss and reach a consensus about how the members will talk about the group outside the group. This agreement typically specifies that members may talk about themselves or about general topics explored in group, but cannot reveal information about other group members. We recommend using a confidentiality contract (see Appendix 13); some shared group agreements and guidelines are listed below. After these guidelines are developed within the group, we suggest posting them in the room where the group meets and providing each group member with a copy for their binders.

Example of Shared Group Agreements/Guidelines

1. Group will start and end on time.
2. Confidentiality as discussed in contract.
3. Members and group facilitators may not touch or throw away anything without the owner's explicit permission.
4. Members make all the decisions about their possessions.
5. Items cannot be traded with others without prior group discussion.
6. Work on non-acquiring first.
7. Group "airtime" will be shared among members.

8. Members' viewpoints and feelings will be respected.
9. Attend each group, call if you cannot.
10. Take care of oneself.
11. Parking lot rule*—members may be asked to hold a comment (e.g., note it on the board) for later discussion.
12. Items that are put in the trash cannot be retrieved.
13. Be respectful and non-judgmental.

*When a group member comments on something that is tangential to the group discussion but important to the individual, co-leaders will use the "parking lot" method, whereby the clinician notes the comment in a box that appears in one of the corners of the ink board, helps recognize the member's concern, and gets to this important item when the time is appropriate.

Objective 4: Define Hoarding Disorder

Discussing the formal DSM-5 definition of hoarding disorder with the group is important, as many have not learned the specific aspects of this disorder. Group members may have diverse reactions to this definition. Given that the group was formed to address HD symptoms, this also initiates a discussion of "Who are we as a group?" and their preferences for terminology such as "hoarding disorder" and "clutter." Hoarding disorder (APA, 2013) is defined below, and the case vignette that follows illustrates these issues. A copy of the DSM-5 criteria for hoarding also is included in the Appendix 14. You may copy it and hand it out to the group for discussion. Group members may read through it as a group and discuss reactions and questions.

Hoarding Disorder 300.3 (F42)

A. Persistent difficulty discarding or parting with possessions, regardless of their actual value.

B. This difficulty is due to a perceived need to save the items and distress associated with discarding them.

C. The difficulty discarding possessions results in the accumulation of possessions that congest and clutter active living areas and substantially compromises their intended use. If living areas are uncluttered, it is only because of the interventions of third parties (e.g., family members, cleaners, authorities).

D. The hoarding causes clinically significant distress or impairment in social, occupational, or other important areas of functioning (including maintaining a safe environment for self and others).

E. The hoarding is not attributable to another medical condition (e.g., brain injury, cerebrovascular disease, Prader-Willi syndrome).

F. The hoarding symptoms are not better accounted for by the symptoms of another DSM-5 disorder (e.g., obsessions in obsessive-compulsive disorder, decreased energy in major depressive disorder, delusions in schizophrenia or another psychotic disorder, cognitive deficits in major neurocognitive disorder, restricted interests in autism spectrum disorder).

Specify if:

With excessive acquisition: If difficulty discarding possessions is accompanied by excessive acquisition of items that are not needed or for which there is no available space.

Specify if:

Good or fair insight: The individual recognizes that hoarding-related beliefs and behaviors (pertaining to difficulty discarding items, clutter, or excessive acquisition) are problematic.

Poor insight: The individual is mostly convinced that hoarding-related beliefs and behaviors (pertaining to difficulty discarding items, clutter, or excessive acquisition) are not problematic despite evidence to the contrary.

Absent insight (i.e. delusional beliefs about hoarding)*: The individual is completely convinced that hoarding-related beliefs and behaviors (pertaining to difficulty discarding items, clutter, or excessive acquisition) are not problematic despite evidence to the contrary.*

Reprinted with permission from the Diagnostic and Statistical Manual of Mental Disorders, Fifth Edition, (Copyright 2013). American Psychiatric Association. All Rights Reserved.

Case Vignette

The following dialogue illustrates varying reactions to the DSM-5 definition of HD and the naming of the group.

GRACE: So it's helpful to hear the definition that you (group leader) just reviewed with us, but it also makes me uncomfortable.

CLINICIAN: Do others have reactions to the definition?

SALLY: It's just so embarrassing and hearing the definition and being in the group makes it seem so real.

LIZ: Everyone knows about it and has been calling me a hoarder and I didn't understand that it was a mental health problem. It makes me feel better that it is a disorder. There is a name for it and a treatment for it.

CLINICIAN: Have others been called a "hoarder?"

CARL: I don't really care about the name of it or the definition. It's just so humiliating when I am at the gas station and someone sees my car and yells out "Hoarder!"

CLINICIAN: You all raise important thoughts and experiences. And it sounds like there are some common emotional responses of embarrassment, humiliation, and shame, as well as discomfort.

SALLY: It feels good to be with others who have the same problem as I do. I feel less alone.

CLINICIAN: It takes courage for you all to come in today.

CHARLIE: I don't like the word "hoarding." My wife has been accusing me of this for years now, and we just fight about it all the time. She doesn't understand and she has to comment on everything I bring into the house. I don't even want to be here, not that I don't like you folks. You seem like nice people, but I don't see it as such a big problem.

CLINICIAN: Charlie, it sounds like this issue is complicating your marriage. Can we "parking lot" how hoarding affects our relationships for the moment, and return to our discussion about the word hoarding?

CHARLIE: Ok.

CLINICIAN: Thanks, Charlie. You had mentioned that you don't like the word "hoarding."

MARIA: Perhaps we could come up with our own word.

CLINICIAN: Good idea, any suggestions?

JENNIFER: How about instead of hoarding we say "clutter?"

CHARLIE: I like "collection" better.

CLINICIAN: Joseph, it looks like you have something to share.

JOSEPH: It is what it is. What is it going to change if we use another word?

MARIA: Maybe it's because of the media, but the word just sounds negative and like something is wrong with me.

CLINICIAN: Can we come up with a term that we all agree on?

LIZ: What if we just use the word "clutter?"

CHARLIE: That's fine with me.

Notice that the leader is pointing out the commonality between the members (e.g., shame and humiliation). The leader is also asserting more authority during this first group (e.g., utilizing the "parking lot" rule), to keep the discussion focused and foster a sense of safety in group.

Objective 5: Assessing Hoarding and Related Problems

Most of the assessment will have been completed during the intake process and the home visit before group Session 1. Depending on the length of time between the assessment and first group session, group leaders may consider re-administering the brief 5-item Hoarding Rating Scale (HRS) as a self-report measure (see Appendix 2 and client *Workbook*, p. 12). Group members can complete the HRS individually and discuss their reactions to it.

Objective 6: Discussion of Home Commitments

We recommend using the term "home commitment" to refer to the work clients will undertake between sessions, as some clients become defensive in reaction to the term "homework," especially when the request is initiated by an authority figure like the group therapist. You may fare better by initiating a group discussion about how to select and structure work between sessions and what to call this. You might emphasize the importance of completing weekly home commitments as follows:

> *Leader: During our sessions, each one of you can be thinking about what tasks make sense for you to do before the next session. We like to call this your "home commitment," but if you prefer, we can use another term. The home commitment is very important because we are only meeting once a week, and you won't be able to make much progress on the hoarding problems without a good bit of effort between sessions. Once we agree on your home commitment, I'll ask you to write this down on your Group Session Form in your binder so you can check it to be sure of what you planned to do that week. This is a sort of contract with all of us, and everyone here will be expected to do their work or explain what happened at the next session. I know this is not going to be easy for everyone, so I want to make sure you agree on this plan. Are you sure you want to do this?*

This final question is intended to help address the common problem of early enthusiasm for treatment followed by waning of motivation and effort. If need be, clients can be reminded of this early agreement later in treatment.

Home commitment assignments for the initial session can be self-education tasks and self-recordings to encourage self-observational skills that will be useful throughout treatment. We have recommended specific home commitments at the end of each session, but you may wish to design your own that follow logically from your discussions during group sessions. In most cases, the assignment will be the same for most or all group members, but individualized commitments are also needed to fit idiosyncratic symptoms or contexts. In general, be thinking in the back of your mind during each session whether some aspect of the topic being discussed might lend itself to a home commitment for one or more members. Be sure clients write their assignment on their Group Session Form so there is no confusion about the task. When clients fail to do the home commitment, do it improperly, or experience unexpected events, you can use these problems as opportunities to learn more and to refine the practice assignments. It is essential during the course of the 20-week group that when group members bring in items, time is specifically protected to review this aspect of the home commitment.

Objective 7: Home Commitment

Ask group members to complete the following tasks prior to the next session:

- Read Chapter 1 of this workbook to learn more about hoarding behavior.
- Assemble the binder and put it in the agreed-upon location.

As noted above, direct the clients to write their home commitment on the Group Session Form (Appendix 12) at the end of each session. Agenda items that are not covered during the present session may be carried over to the Group Session Form for the following session.

Use your Clinician Group Progress Notes (see Appendices 15 and 16) to record clients' home commitments and compliance and your reflections on the group process. This serves as your own record of your notes for each group session and is not distributed to the group members.

Chapter 5 *Session 2: Model-Building*

(Corresponds to Chapter 3 of the Workbook)

Materials Needed

- "What Is Hoarding" reading (*Workbook* Chapter 1, p. 1)
- General Conceptual Hoarding Model (*Workbook* Chapter 3, p. 33, Appendix 17)
- Brief Thought Record (*Workbook* Chapter 3, p. 37, Appendix 18)

Session Agenda

- Work with client to develop their model of hoarding
- Guide clients to complete a Brief Thought Record

CBT Model of Hoarding

As described in Chapter 1, hoarding behavior is complex, deriving from a combination of personal and family vulnerabilities, information-processing problems, beliefs about possessions, positive and negative emotional responses, and learned behaviors. The assessment process has helped identify the features of your client's hoarding problem. Now it is time to draw this information together into a conceptual model that helps clients understand how and why the hoarding symptoms occur.

During this session, each group member will work collaboratively with the leaders and other group members to begin to develop a personal model to understand how their hoarding problem developed and why it continues. Developing a model collaboratively helps clients adopt an external perspective, learning to observe and critically examine their thoughts and emotions to better understand them. Thus, model-building enables clients to take the first step toward distancing themselves from their problem and adopting a more rational rather than purely emotional stance. Model-building also establishes the clients' roles as detectives and collaborators, working with you the group leaders and other group members to understand and resolve the hoarding problems.

This structured activity also provides an opportunity for group members to share their experiences and discover similarities between their own experiences and others'. This experience often fosters a sense of universality and relief that clients are not alone, helping to reduce stigma, isolation, and shame, as well as instill hope. A home commitment is assigned between sessions to collect additional information that helps group members complete the model. Model-building is an ongoing process throughout treatment. As new information emerges from practice experiences, encourage clients to revise their model. Once developed, the conceptual model can be used throughout treatment to determine goals and methods for achieving them.

The overall model of hoarding is depicted in Figure 5.1. This model is based on our research and clinical experience with hoarding disorder. It should be considered a work in progress, although several studies have supported various features of this model (see Frost & Steketee, 2013). The model presumes that problems with acquiring, saving, and clutter result from (1) personal vulnerabilities that include past experiences and training, negative general mood, core beliefs, and information processing problems. These vulnerabilities contribute to (2) beliefs about possessions, which, in turn, result in (3) positive and negative emotional responses that trigger (4) hoarding behaviors——acquiring, difficulty discarding, saving, and disorganized clutter. These behaviors are reinforced positively through the pleasure gained from acquiring and saving, and they are also reinforced negatively through the avoidance of unpleasant emotions of grief, anxiety, and/or guilt. The model includes information about how these features are connected, reinforced, and maintained; for example, drawing arrows leading from the various components to resulting emotions and behaviors. This model is intended to illustrate many variants of hoarding elements seen across clients and

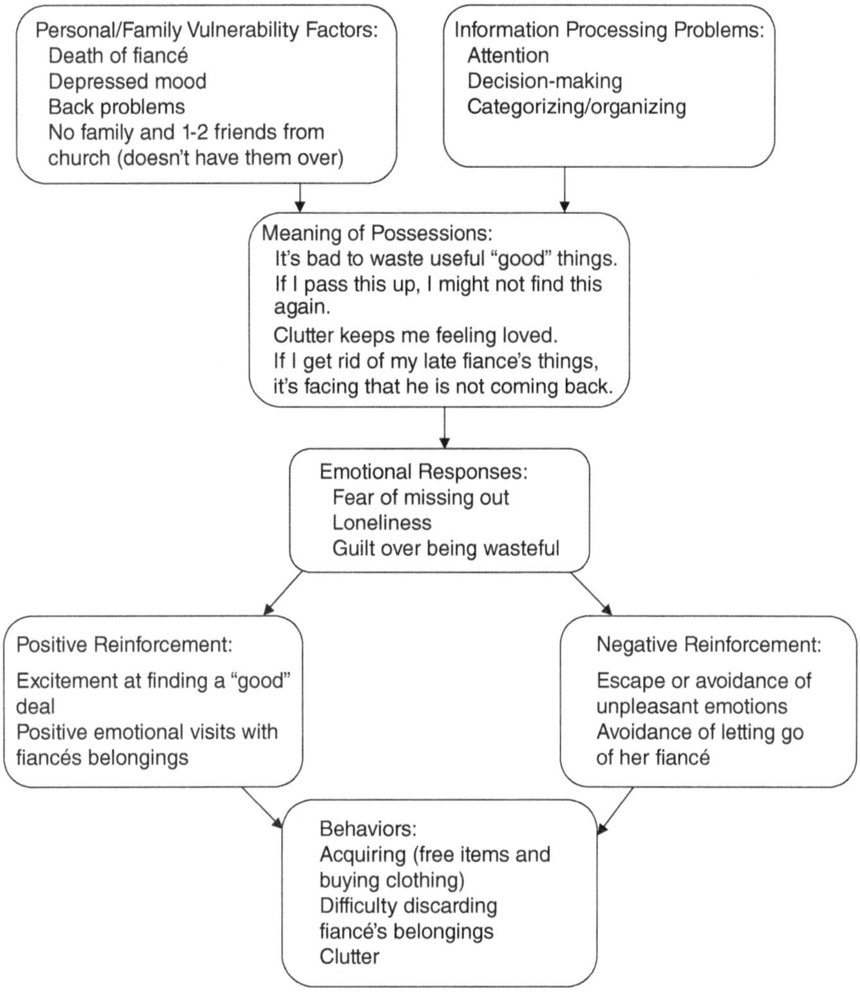

Figure 5.1

A Graphic Representation of the Model as Developed So Far with Sally

help clients understand their behavior in the context of their life experience. The model leads directly to intervention strategies that target the specific problems identified in the models.

Objective 1: Check-in

- Distribute and review Group Session Form and review the session agenda.

- Each group member notes whether they assembled their binder and stored it in the location that they identified in Session 1.
- Clients briefly discuss initial reactions to the "What Is Hoarding?" reading from the client *Workbook* (Chapter 1, p. 1).

Objective 2: Building the General Conceptual Hoarding Model

Extend the check-in conversation about *Workbook* Chapter 1, which introduced group members to the common factors that contribute to and maintain hoarding behaviors. Ask clients to turn to Figure 3.1 in their client *Workbook* (Chapter 3, p. 33) while you draw the model on the board. Remind clients that each element of the model is also described briefly in Chapter 3 of their *Workbook*. Table 5.1 lists the most common factors to look for during the model-building process.

In order to demonstrate the elements of the model in a timely way, it is helpful to focus on one client while guiding the others to complete their own models. Guide group members to begin recording the elements of their model by asking a series of questions and commenting about what you have already learned during group sessions (for example, Sally mentioning her acquiring of clothing). Use open-ended curiosity questions like "That's interesting; where do you think that thought comes from?" and "How do you think these two components are connected?" Then specify the consequences of the elements and their role in reinforcing the behaviors. Review the example in Figure 5.1 to familiarize yourself with the process. Inform the group members that the first "working model" is usually revised a few times before it accurately captures the complete picture.

Let the group members know that developing their model also helps identify goals and points for intervention, such as reducing anxiety about losing valuable information, re-evaluating beliefs about responsibility for possessions, and reducing behavior patterns that result in acquisition (e.g., shopping, visiting dumpsters).

The following example of a beginning dialogue demonstrates how the therapist directs and guides the group in working on the general conceptual hoarding model. Conversations between clients sometimes need to be contained, and it is important to prepare group participants ahead

Table 5.1 Elements Useful in Developing the Conceptual Model

Basic Elements	Components	Examples
Personal and family vulnerabilities	Family history of hoarding	Hereditary traits, biological underpinnings
	Comorbid problems	Depressed mood, social anxiety, obsessive-compulsive symptoms, attention problems
	Parental values and behavior	Acquiring, difficulty discarding, clutter in the home, decision making, beliefs and values about waste, sentimentality
	Physical constraints	Health, time, household space
	Adverse life events	Loss of caregiver, moving, deprivation, assault
Information-processing problems	Attention	Difficulty sustaining attention on a difficult task
	Categorization	Problems grouping and organizing objects into categories
	Memory	Poor verbal or visual memory leading to reliance on visual cues
	Perception	Strong visual attraction to objects, failure to notice clutter
	Associative or complex thinking	Generates many thoughts about or uses for objects, creative ideas, focus on nonessential details, inability to separate important from unimportant details
	Decision-making problems	Considering too many facets of a problem, ambivalence; may be related to fear of making mistakes
Meaning of possessions (What gives them value?)	Beauty	Finding beauty and aesthetic appeal in unusual objects
	Memory	Belief/fear that memories will be lost without objects or that objects contain or preserve memories
	Utility/opportunity/uniqueness	Seeing the usefulness of virtually anything; seeing opportunities presented by objects that others don't
	Sentimental	Attaching emotional significance to objects; anthropomorphism
	Comfort/safety	Perceiving objects (and related behaviors like shopping) as providing emotional comfort; objects as sources of safety (safety signals)

(continued)

Table 5.1 (Continued)

Basic Elements	Components	Examples
	Identity/validation of self-worth	Belief that objects are part of the person or represent who the person can become; objects as representation of self-worth
	Control	Concern that others will control one's possessions or behavior
	Mistakes	Perfectionistic concern about making mistakes or about the condition or use of possessions
	Responsibility/waste	Strong beliefs about not wasting possessions, about polluting the environment, or about using possessions responsibly
	Socializing	Buying or collecting items provides social contact not available in other ways
Emotional reactions	Positive	Excitement, joy, pleasure, comfort, satisfaction
	Negative	Anxiety, guilt, grief, sadness, anger
Learning processes	Positive reinforcement	Saving and acquiring produce positive emotions
	Negative reinforcement	Saving permits escape or avoidance of negative emotions
	Effects of hoarding behaviors	Prevents the opportunity to test current beliefs and develop alternate beliefs
Outcomes	Hoarding behaviors	Acquiring, saving, clutter

of time by making some statement to this effect: "In order to move through the model today, we may include less interaction among all of you than will be typical of most of our group sessions."

Case Vignette

CLINICIAN: Today we are going to work together to better understand how your problems with hoarding have developed and what keeps them going. Let's take a look at the model in front of all of us. I need one volunteer to go through the model.

[*Sally raises her hand*]

CLINICIAN: Great, Sally, thanks. [*The clinician writes out parts of the model on the white board so the entire group can participate and observe Sally's model.*] So, Sally, you have mentioned that the clutter really keeps you from connecting with others, and you still have an acquiring problem, especially clothing from consignment shops. Does that sound right?

SALLY: Yeah, I need to get things under control. I have so much stuff. I get so overwhelmed so I don't do anything.

CLINICIAN: So, as you note you are having difficulty getting rid of stuff and you are still acquiring a lot of items. These have resulted in a substantial clutter [*clinician points to the bottom of the model*]. So, active acquiring and saving are the problematic behaviors. Sally next to acquiring, please note "clothing." For the rest of you, what are some of the types of items that you still bring into the home?

CHARLIE: I still collect printers, routers..... anything, you know, electronic that I can sell. [*Chuckling*] There are a lot of "collectors" in my family. My dad.....

CLINICIAN: [*interrupting*] Great. Okay, so Charlie, next to acquiring you can add "electronics." We will come back to your dad in a moment. Moving on to difficulty discarding or saving, Sally, what are the types of items that you have the most difficult time letting go of?

SALLY: [*sigh*] Anything that was my fiancé's. So things like his books, paper, clothes..... all of it.

CLINICIAN: Okay, please note "fiancé's belongings" next to "difficulty discarding." What do others of you have difficulty parting with?

JENNIFER: Everything..... 'cause I can't make a decision. Funny enough——I have all these boxes, racks, and shelving units. But I can't set them up. I just can't focus.

CLINICIAN: We will get into some of the other processes in a moment. Jennifer, please note the word "boxes" next to the bubble called "difficulty discarding." As you can see, the word "clutter" is also included in the bubble. Sally, it sounds like your clothing and other possessions, in addition to your fiancé's stuff, have resulted in a great deal of clutter. And that has become more than you can manage. Does that sound right?

SALLY: Yes.

LIZ: I have been holding onto all of my mother's stuff, too, since she died decades ago. What am I supposed to do, just throw it out? I have the same things Jennifer has. I have boxes and shelving units, and I just don't get to it.

GRACE: I can't throw away my receipts and financial papers. I'm always afraid I may need to show them to the IRS.

CLINICIAN: Yes, there are many things that contribute to the clutter. Let's take a look at the top left bubble, "Personal and Family Vulnerability Factors," so we can begin to understand major factors that contribute to the hoarding.

Vulnerability Factors

Table 5.1 offers a variety of other vulnerability factors to explore, including early experiences, core beliefs, personality traits, mood, and comorbidity. The group discussion continues as follows:

Case Vignette

CLINICIAN: Sally, earlier you noted that when you feel depressed you have a harder time making decisions. Would you say that your depression makes it difficult for you to manage your stuff?

SALLY: Well, yeah it's an endless cycle because my stuff being so overwhelming makes me feel even more hopeless and upset, and then I don't do anything. I just stay in bed all day.

CLINICIAN: I hear you. Please add "depression" under core vulnerabilities. How about others of you?

JOSEPH: I am down a lot and it really makes things hard. But I am also really struggling with focus. Whenever I try to clean up, I get caught up with other things.

CLINICIAN: Ok, so please add depression and inattention under core vulnerabilities.

JENNIFER: I am not so much depressed but I get super anxious. I just really want everything to be perfect. I just can't tolerate it any other way. So I guess I will add "perfectionism." And yet one would never know that if they walked into my house.

CLINICIAN: Does your clutter remind you of anyone else in your family? Do any of you have family members with similar behaviors?

CHARLIE: Like I said, my dad had lots of "collections." Tools were his thing. And my mom sure liked her jelly jars. My wife says that my clutter is 100 times worse than my parents' ever was.

CLINICIAN: So Charlie, please write "mom collected jelly jars" and "dad collected tools." For those of you with a family history of hoarding, please note that in the bubble.

LIZ: I remember that my father always wanted to save everything. We had to reuse everything. And now the idea of being wasteful, well, it's just wrong. Don't you all agree? We all should recycle.

CLINICIAN: Recycling is an important topic to return to. For now, Liz, please add "father reusing and recycling."

Carl: My parents didn't collect things. They threw my stuff out. One summer we moved and my parents threw out my trains. I was angry and upset.

Maria: Carl, that is terrible that they did that to you.

Clinician: That sounds very hard. Do you think that made you vulnerable to the clutter you have now?

Carl: I think so. . . . I have a lot of trains, tracks, and other stuff in my home. Some aren't even opened. I have them "just in case" others get lost. Some are collectors' items.

Clinician: Okay, Carl. Please write "parents threw out trains" in the "Vulnerability Factors" box.

Information-Processing Components

Table 5.1 lists common information-processing problems related to hoarding. Comment that many people with hoarding problems have one or more of these symptoms. Then ask whether they have difficulties in any of these areas, such as attention problems as children and learning difficulties in school. If other problems emerge later during treatment (for example, in working on organizing possessions), revise the model at that time. The following dialogue illustrates the method of questioning.

Case Vignette

Clinician: As you read in the "What Is Hoarding?" reading in your *Workbook*, most people with a lot of clutter have difficulty processing information. For example, they have difficulty with attention, memory, categorization, and decision-making.

Sally: My decision-making isn't great, but when I am depressed it's impossible to make decisions. Plus, I really want to create a nice way to keep my accessories. I have tried to organize them, but I just get overwhelmed. I used to put all my earrings together, then necklaces, but there are sets of matching ones, and I have also lost some.

JOSEPH: I have all these magazines and papers from when I was working before I lost my job. They are so much a part of who I am. I just can't decide what to do with them. But my therapist suggested that I use an egg timer to keep me focused.

CLINICIAN: It sounds like decision-making, attention, and organizational problems are getting in the way for several of you. Do these problems have anything to do with your clutter?

JENNIFER: I mean I have all the organizational stuff, I just can't focus.

SALLY: I can't get organized. My accessories are all over my room.

JOSEPH: It seems mean to judge my kids' artwork. I can't decide which pictures and crafts to keep.

CLINICIAN: It's not uncommon for people with clutter to get distracted and not focus long enough to complete a task. Certain kinds of items may be more challenging than others to make decisions about. Sally, you also raised problems with categorizing your accessories. So in the "Information Processing" box, please note decision-making, organizational and attention problems related to specific items such as your accessories, Sally, and Joseph, your kids' artwork.

MARIA: I am afraid to put anything away. I know I won't be able to find them if I put them out of my sight. I just don't have the energy these days to search for stuff. I need them out so I can find and remember what I need.

CLINICIAN: I am glad you brought up this concern with putting items out of sight, as it often gets in the way of progress. We will definitely talk more about memory later.

LIZ:	I also have a problem with my memory.
CLINICIAN:	Many people with hoarding doubt their memory and think they need to keep their items in sight. Please write "memory" in the box under information processing, for those of you who experience this concern.

Meaning of Possessions: Thoughts and Beliefs

Emphasize that the information-processing problems and vulnerabilities help define what possessions mean and the role they play in their lives. These meanings are outlined below. As noted in Chapter 1, the meaning we attach to possessions (our beliefs or appraisals) drives hoarding behavior. Various types of attachments are shown in Table 5.1. Ask clients to review the Meaning of Possessions from the *Workbook* (Chapter 3, p. 32) to select those they recognize in themselves, such as emotional comfort in possessions, loss and mistakes, value of possessions, identity, responsibility, memory, control, and perfectionism.

Case Vignette

CLINICIAN:	Sally, you were saying earlier that you acquire a lot of clothing from consignment shops.
SALLY:	Yes, I love going to them. It's so hard for me to drive by and not stop in. It's amazing what people give away. I got this gorgeous red purse some years ago. I mean it was Coach and barely used. It was only $10. That would have been $150 retail.
CLINICIAN:	Sounds like it felt like quite an opportunity and that the bag caught your eye.
MARIA:	I don't really have money to buy stuff. I have a red purse that my husband gave me and can't part with. He gave

it to me for my fortieth birthday and even picked it out himself. It's not from Coach but it reminds me of him.

Jennifer: I can't get rid of gifts other people give me either. It seems rude.

Liz: Sally, I think it's really great that you go to consignment shops. There is no reason to buy new stuff. Plus, you are helping the environment by not adding to the landfill.

Joseph: It's really important to me to recycle all my newspapers after I am done with them.

Clinician: I am hearing that your possessions have a lot of meaning. Looking at the meanings listed here in your workbook, which seem to apply the most?

Liz: It's responsibility for me [*others nod*].

Clinician: So the thought is that "It's my responsibility to recycle."

Liz: Well, yeah. I mean if I throw away plastic bottles and then they go into the ocean, fish are dying. All these plastics——they are just so bad for the environment.

Maria: I can't imagine throwing anything away. I see beauty in everything. Even an old McDonald's cup could have a pretty picture of a Christmas wreath. I could use it when I make my Christmas cards next year.

Joseph: I keep papers. I don't want to miss any information—so I guess mine is related to "loss of information."

Clinician: We could phrase this as "might need to know." Is that a pretty common reason for you to save things?

Joseph: Uh huh.

Clinician: And Maria, that cup had value to you. The thought is "it's useful," for example in making cards. Please note that under Thoughts and Beliefs.

Later on in treatment, clients are likely to discover additional beliefs about acquiring and saving that emerge from using cognitive interventions such as the Downward Arrow method (Session 12) or Behavioral Experiments (Session 9) to test for beliefs and attachments during acquiring and/or sorting and discarding.

Emotional Responses

Comment to clients that most of their thoughts about possessions are followed by immediate emotional reactions that make discarding difficult. Help group members identify their emotional responses while reporting their thoughts (e.g., "What were you feeling when thinking about that?" or "What does it feel like when you think about that experience?" "What sensations did you feel in your body when you had that thought?"). Typically, these emotions are negative—anxiety, fear, sadness, grief, guilt, anger. Explain that these feelings occur when they contemplate or attempt discarding or not acquiring.

Clients often identify positive feelings like pleasure, excitement, joy, comfort, or satisfaction when describing possessions, sometimes even when they are considering getting rid of them. For example, this happens in finding lost objects and in passing items along to someone who might use them. Remind clients that these positive feelings, even if fleeting, help reinforce saving and acquiring behavior. Ask about recent acquiring, sorting, and de-cluttering experiences that are fresh in their minds to determine the emotions and connect them to the triggering thoughts and subsequent behaviors. Apply the usual sequence of thoughts–emotions–behaviors. For example, thoughts about losing items, about vulnerability, and about safety may generate fear and anxiety. Sadness may stem from clients' beliefs about their identity being defined by possessions. Anger could result from perceived threats to free choice and personal control. The following conversation illustrates this type of questioning.

Case Vignette

CLINICIAN: Several reasons for saving have already come up — needing to know information, concerns about being wasteful, object being useful, or being an opportunity. Let's examine the emotions that result from these types of thoughts. Joseph, if you think to yourself, "I need to know what's in this newspaper," but then you threw it out anyway, how would you feel?

JOSEPH: It would make me nervous. What if I miss out on some important information that I should know about?

CLINICIAN: You would feel anxious, on edge.

JOSEPH: Yes. Why would I want to throw out information that could be useful? So I wouldn't like that.

CLINICIAN: So the thought that you might miss important information that you need leads to feelings of anxiety about not knowing something important. In the model, let's connect the thought about missing important information to the emotion of anxiety. What about the idea of wasting something? What emotion does that provoke?

LIZ: I'd be mad if you made me waste it. I would also feel guilty. I'd feel guilty that someone else didn't get a chance to use it. A lot of people have nothing at all. I can't afford to just buy a new one.

SALLY: And I worry about letting a good deal go by.

CLINICIAN: Okay, Liz, please write "guilt about being wasteful" in the box titled Emotional Response. And Sally, please note your "fears about missing opportunities." [*The clinician asks about other negative emotions tied to beliefs before moving on to positive ones.*] How about positive emotional reactions? Sally, do you experience any positive emotions when going through your stuff?

Sally: I was really thrilled to find that Coach bag. How lucky was that! [*grinning*]

Maria: Yes! The other day I was sorting through my stuff and looking for the art supplies I got for my grandkids. Not only did I find the supplies, but I also came upon two boxes that had these ball gowns I hadn't seen in like 25 years. Oh, it took me back.

Clinician: When you say it "took me back," what emotion came up for you?

Maria: Well, I was very excited to see the gowns. It's going to sound nuts I know, but I danced with them and then I started to cry. [*sniffles*]

Jennifer: [*picks up the box of tissues, takes one for herself and hands one to Maria*] That is really hard. Those dresses bring you such joy but the memories are also so painful.

Joseph: I—I save all my kids' art projects from over the years. Sometimes I find them when I'm looking for something else, and it makes me really happy to see them. But it also makes me sad and angry because my ex won't let the kids come to my home. I can't get rid of any of the projects because it's all I have to remind me of when they were younger and I could see them every day.

Clinician: Okay, I hear a number of beliefs and emotions here. Joseph, your first belief that getting rid of your newspapers will cause you to miss some important information and that causes the emotion of anxiety. Liz, you mentioned that thinking that you are wasting something causes guilt for you. Sally, your belief was around the bag being such an opportunity that brought you happiness. Maria and Joseph, your beliefs about holding onto the dress and projects to maintain happy memories cause joy as well as sadness and anger. Let's add those negative and positive emotions to the model. Now, let's go on to see what actually happens when you've had these thoughts and feelings.

Once the meanings and emotional responses are clear, work with the group members to figure out how these features result in clutter. Table 5.1 describes several avenues to hoarding symptoms. Explain to group members that positive reinforcement of saving or acquiring comes from the short-term benefits of acquiring or saving—the excitement, joy, or other positive emotions make it more likely that they will continue to collect and keep things (e.g., Joseph holding on to his children's art projects; Sally getting the Coach bag at the consignment shop). As described, this is most evident when clients feel pleasure at finding a treasured item that has been buried in the pile for a long time, or getting a "good deal."

Caution clients that often the joy is short-lived. Avoidance behaviors are negatively reinforced by removing the distress associated with discarding. For instance, if Joseph puts the newspapers in his garage rather than recycling them, he can avoid the distress associated with the idea of missing out on important information or opportunities. Emphasize that each of these actions (acquiring, putting something in sight) or avoidance behaviors (avoiding discarding, not putting an item away, etc.) contributes to the clutter. Note that at the same time, the actions also help clients feel better by reducing their negative emotions (less anxiety, less guilt). Stress to group members that negative reinforcement is a powerful mechanism for maintaining clutter.

Case Vignette

CLINICIAN: Let's continue and consider the behaviors you do after you have these thoughts about one of your items. You picked up the Coach bag out of the box, thought about the deal you got on it, felt anxious about getting rid of it, and then what happened?

SALLY: Oh, I was so excited to see it. I put it on my shoulder and admired it in the mirror. I love the red color. [*laughs*] Then I thought, "there is no way I am getting rid of this." And I got mad thinking that I might have to. I put it back in the box.

CLINICIAN: Okay, so you were feeling excited to see it but then quickly felt anxious and angry about the possibility of getting rid of it. [*The group nods.*] Have you used it recently?

SALLY: Well, no, I forgot I had it. It was tucked in this box with a bunch of other bags.

CHARLIE: Do you have a lot of bags?

SALLY: I don't know, maybe 30 bags.... But, why should I get rid of a good bag?

JENNIFER: I guess we are here because we all have too much stuff. All I know is that when I think of getting rid of stuff I get overwhelmed and cry, so of course nothing leaves my house.

SALLY: It's too much for me to think about getting rid of the bag.

CLINICIAN: So in your mind you think, "this is a good bag, why get rid of it?" There is so much anxiety about the idea of even letting it go, and you put it back in the box.

SALLY: It would be such a waste to get rid of it. Plus, it's such a beautiful color.

CLINICIAN: How did you feel after you put it back in the box?

SALLY: Well, relieved. It's mine. Though I guess, I felt ashamed too that I haven't used it and have so many bags that I never use.

CLINICIAN: That brief period of relief is an important reinforcer of the whole process. So to recap—you see an object in your home, you have a thought about it, for example about it being valuable and unique, and this triggers an emotional reaction like excitement but also anxiety and anger. Your response is to keep the item, putting it back in the box of bags. This provides immediate relief and helps you avoid the unpleasant emotions of anxiety and anger that you may experience if you got rid of the item. At the same time, it doesn't actually help you take steps toward reaching your goals and reducing the clutter in your home.

SALLY: Yes, I am aware of that. But I don't want to just throw out stuff that is good.

CLINICIAN: I understand. At the moment, we are focusing on learning what your process is like for you, and then we can figure out what to do about it. You have described some important vulnerability factors and processing issues; we have also looked at how your thoughts produce specific emotions that cause your behavior related to your clutter. This model [*showing her the model*] is based on what you have shared.

Special Considerations for Models of Acquiring

Point out to group members that acquiring behaviors are usually based on elements similar to those that drive saving and clutter, but usually there are more positive feelings and fewer negative ones. Describe that acquiring problems can occur in several ways:

- Collecting free items or accepting items from others
- Picking up things others have thrown away
- Compulsive buying in stores, yard sales, flea markets
- Buying multiple items "just in case" something happens to the original
- Stealing
- Ordering subscriptions, mail order items, home shopping networks, etc.

Objective 3: Brief Thought Record

Ask client to notice and report what they are thinking while they are sorting. Use the Brief Thought Record to record triggering events, and to identify thoughts and beliefs, and the emotions and behaviors these provoke. Figure 5.2 depicts a completed record, and blank forms are provided in the corresponding client *Workbook* (Chapter 3, p. 37) and Appendix 18.

Case Vignette

MARIA: I can't bear to let go of any of my husband's things. It's like he is still here when I look at his clothes or magazines.

CLINICIAN: Maria, how about we complete a thought record to investigate the thoughts and feelings that are triggered when looking at your husband's things?

MARIA: Well, okay.

Initials: Maria

Date: 5/16/13

Trigger situation	Thought about Meaning of Possessions	Emotions	Actions/Behaviors
See husband's clothing	I really miss him.	Sad	Hold a piece of his clothing and cry.
See husband's clothing	I can't let go of his clothing because it's like letting go of him all over again	Sad\Irritable	Cry and clench fists
See husband's clothing	I will forget him if I throw out his clothing	Sad	Cry and keep clothing
See husband's clothing	I won't let them make me throw it out	Angry	Yell at family members

Figure 5.2

Example of Completed Brief Thought Record

CLINICIAN: [*stands at the white board and draws a Thought Record, pointing to the first column*]: So let's start with the trigger, seeing your husband's clothing. Right?

MARIA: Yes, and everything else that was his or reminds me of him!

CLINICIAN: Okay, good. What is the very first thought that pops into your head when you see his clothing?

MARIA: I miss him, even now, 10 years later.

LIZ: Oh, Maria, that's sad.

SALLY: I know how you feel.

CLINICIAN: It is sad. Yes, you are all ahead of me! Can we keep going?

MARIA: Yes.

CLINICIAN: Okay, so the thought is [*writing it down on the board*]: "I miss him." What is the feeling following that thought?

MARIA: Sadness.

SALLY: [*nodding head*]

CHARLIE: [*losing attention, appears disengaged*]

CLINICIAN: Okay, let's keep going. Let's focus up here, everyone, because you're next! What did you "do?" What is your action that follows that the thought and feeling?

MARIA: I keep all of his things. I can't even get to the point where I consider letting it go. I know that just because his things are all here, doesn't mean *he* is here. But letting it go feels like I would be letting him go.

JOSEPH: You have his memories though, they will never go away.

CLINICIAN: Thanks for sharing this, Maria. Does anyone have questions about how we do the Thought Record?

GROUP MEMBERS: [*shaking heads no*]

CLINICIAN: Okay, who's next? Charlie?

Between-Sessions Practice

Emphasize to clients that it is very important to the treatment that they gain awareness of their thoughts, emotions, and behaviors related to saving and acquiring. Note that this will require practice between sessions. As noted in Session 1, the Home Commitment is a critical element of the treatment. Ask clients to review the exercise covered during session and to practice using the blank Brief Thought Records in their *Workbook* (p. 37) between sessions. Mention that if new information is learned through their use of the Brief Thought Records, then they should add it to their personal general conceptual hoarding models. You can state this as follows.

CLINICIAN: I would like you to review the thought records that we did during group today and continue practicing this exercise during the week. Would you each be willing to observe yourself at home while trying to sort a little pile of your things, making a decision about a possession, or when you are about to acquire? Using the form in your *Workbook* called a "Brief Thought Record," please write down your thoughts at times when you have a strong emotional reaction. When you start feeling quite anxious or unhappy or guilty or angry, that would be a time to stop what you are doing and ask yourself what you were thinking. You would also do this when you have strong positive feelings of pleasure or enjoyment. This gives us a way to see if there are other thoughts or beliefs besides the ones we have here in your models that contribute to clutter. What do you think? Please focus on those thoughts that produce a strong reaction and fill out 2 to 3 Brief Thought Records for a few situations. These Brief Thought Records may also help determine if there is anything to add to the model.

Objective 4: Home Commitment

- Monitor thoughts and feelings using the Brief Thought Record form (*Workbook*, Chapter 3, p. 37) while sorting at home or when acquiring.

- Review the model (Figure 3.1 in the *Workbook,* Chapter 3, p. 33) at home to identify additional components that contribute to saving or acquiring.

Objective 5: Complete Clinician Forms

- Clinician directs the clients to write their home commitment on the Group Session Form (see Appendix 12) and completes the Clinician's Group Progress Notes (see Appendix 15).

Chapter 6 *Session 3: Motivation*

Materials Needed

- Brief Thought Record (*Workbook* Chapter 3, p. 37, Appendix 18)
- General Conceptual Model of Hoarding (*Workbook* Chapter 3, p. 33, Appendix 17)
- Clutter Visualization Form (*Workbook* Chapter 4, p. 44, Appendix 19)
- Unclutter Visualization Form (*Workbook* Chapter 4, p. 45, Appendix 20)
- Motivational Enhancement Strategies (Appendix 22)
- Signals of Ambivalence and Strategies (Appendix 21)
- Advantages and Disadvantages of Change Worksheet (Appendix 23)

Session Agenda

- Rate motivation for and confidence in change
- Complete visualization and practice exercises
- Examine ambivalence
- Use motivational strategies to address problems with home commitment
- Deal with undermining among group members

Understanding Motivational Challenges

Two major impediments to successful intervention for hoarding disorder (HD) are the lack of insight into the severity of the problem and limited motivation to resolve it. During this session, we recommend ways to recognize and resolve motivational problems, using strategies based on motivational methods developed by Miller and Rollnick (2013). We urge you to read their work, view the accompanying training videotapes, and/or obtain training in motivational interviewing methods if possible. These methods are helpful for all types of mental health problems in which clients are often reluctant to engage fully in treatment. During this session, visualization exercises will help determine their level of insight and identify ambivalence about reducing clutter. We also recommend other motivation-enhancing strategies, including visits to group members' homes. In later sessions we will cover other strategies such as problem-solving and behavioral experiments (Session 9) that can also improve motivation.

Clients who flatly deny that they have a hoarding problem despite clear evidence to the contrary are not a good fit for group treatment and may interfere with the progress of other group members. For them, alternative strategies can be recommended to address the hoarding. For example, family members can consult with hoarding task forces if there is one in their area, or with regulatory or service agencies (e.g., public health, housing, elder abuse and neglect) that can help motivate clients by enforcing health and safety regulations.

Incorporating motivational enhancement strategies into the 20-week hoarding group is less about defining and teaching a specific lesson and more of a general approach by the leaders to help group members focus on achieving their personal goals. Walters, Ogle, and Martin (2002) point out that "unlike patient education, motivational interviewing is more a navigation process than a transmission of information" (p. 381). You can incorporate motivational principles into the group process by exploring both positive and negative experiences of the group members and focusing on potential solutions (Wagner & Ingersoll, 2013).

Sustaining motivation over the full course of the group CBT therapy is difficult for many people with HD, as motivation often wanes in the face of difficult discarding and non-acquiring decisions. Motivation to change depends on two things: the importance of the change and confidence that change is possible. "The importance of change" refers to the discrepancy between what life is like now and what we want our life to be. This discrepancy can be highlighted by using the visualization and other exercises described below. But the motivation to change created by discrepancy will be short-lived if the client lacks confidence that change is possible. Without that confidence, clients will seek to reduce the discrepancy by changing their perception of the problem rather than changing their behavior. Expect to hear comments like, "Well, the clutter is really not so bad," "I don't really mind the clutter," or "This is really my wife's problem, not mine." While these statements seem to reflect a lack of insight, they might well indicate a confidence problem. The job of group leaders is to help develop the discrepancy (importance of change) while also providing members with confidence that they can change.

Assumptions Behind Motivation-Enhancement Methods

Miller and Rollnick (2013) define motivational interviewing as "a collaborative conversation style for strengthening a person's own motivation and commitment to change" (p. 12). This method draws on clients' strengths and assumes they have the right and capacity to make informed choices. It is a person-centered intervention style aimed at resolving ambivalence about change. Some of the basic assumptions include:

- Motivation to change cannot be imposed by others. Clients who enter treatment because they are pressured by friends and family are unlikely to change their behavior unless they first decide they would benefit personally.
- If ambivalence about change is not addressed, non-compliance and a lack of common goals will undermine treatment.
- Clients must articulate the ambivalence, while clinicians help them express and explore all sides of it. Many group members recognize

their problems and want to change, but struggle to get rid of items as their emotions and beliefs get in the way. Encouraging them to voice their ambivalence helps clarify the impediments to their progress.

- Direct persuasion is rarely helpful, whereas expressing curiosity helps elicit the ambivalence and releases clients from having to defend their views.
- Developing a trusting relationship in treatment is essential, especially for clients who have had experiences in which others discarded their possessions.
- Therapy is a partnership, not a relationship between expert and recipient. Work side by side to understand the impediments and help clients learn to make wise decisions.

A variety of verbal and non-verbal examples of ambivalence and strategies to help resolve them are provided in the Appendix 21 for reference. This group session contains a selection of strategies to clarify motivation and address ambivalence and barriers to engaging fully in the treatment process. You may find the following two acronyms from Wagner and Ingersoll (2013, p. 33) helpful in recalling some of the main principles and strategies discussed in this chapter: DARN CAT and OARS.

DARN CAT refers to steps toward change:

- **D**esire for change
- **A**bility to change
- **R**eason for change
- **N**eed for change
- **C**ommitment to change
- **A**ctivation
- **T**aking steps

OARS refers to strategies for enhancing motivation:

- **O**pen-ended questions and encourage elaboration
- **A**ffirmations that foster positive feelings

- **R**eflections that show you understand
- **S**ummaries that extend reflections and build interest in change

Objective 1: Check-in

- Distribute and review the Group Session Form.
- Review one Brief Thought Record.
- Ask a couple of clients to note any additions to their personal general conceptual hoarding model.

Objective 2: Assess Motivation

To introduce the topic of motivation, ask clients to rate the following two questions on scales from 0–10 on their Session Form:

1. How important is it for you to resolve your hoarding problem?
2. How confident are you that you will be able to resolve your hoarding problem?

Briefly discuss members' ratings and note the range of scores. Be aware that scores of 6 or below on either of these scales may indicate the need for special attention with regard to enhancing motivation. For example, clients like Charlie, who was pressured into treatment by his wife, and Liz, who was mandated to treatment by the housing agency, are likely to report low motivation. Note, however, that they might also report high confidence in resolving their hoarding, believing that they could fix the problem quickly but don't see why they should. This type of discrepancy would indicate that motivational methods will be important in helping them arrive at a more realistic view of their situation and needs.

Objective 3: Visualization Exercises (Chapter 4 of the *Workbook*, pp. 44–45)

The exercises described below are intended to help understand the strength of group members' motivation for treatment. We recommend doing the clutter visualization task first, followed by unclutter visualization and imagining the ideal home. This sequence helps clients develop discrepancy between the current situation and what they want to accomplish, as well as help them realize that having a home they would enjoy is actually possible. Examples of completed visualization forms are given below, with blank copies included in the Appendix 19 and the client *Workbook* (p. 44).

Clutter Visualization

Begin the clutter visualization with the following instructions:

> *Since all of you have clutter as a central component of your problem, we're going to spend some time picturing it and talking about your reactions. We will start with a visualization task. During this exercise I'll ask you to complete the Clutter Visualization Form on page 44 of your Workbook. We will go over each part of the form together. First, think of the room in your home where you have decided to start working. Please write it on the form next to where it says "Room."*
>
> *Now try to visualize this room in its present cluttered state. Please close your eyes and imagine yourself standing in the middle of the room slowly turning around so you can see all the things in the room. Take notice of what you see around you.*
>
> *[Wait about a minute]*
>
> *How much discomfort do you feel right now on a scale from 0 (meaning "no discomfort") to 100 (meaning "the most discomfort you can imagine")? If it's easier for you to use a scale from 0 to 10, that's fine, too. Now please write that number down on the form in the space labeled "Initial Discomfort Rating."*

If clients have difficulty visualizing, suggest that they review the photographs of this room taken during the home visit to cue their reactions.

Clarify feelings (emotions) about clutter. Continue the exercise by saying: "Now let's go round and see how each of you felt (emotion) during this visualization." Help clients report on their emotions, rather than their thoughts and beliefs. As they identify feelings, ask members to record them on the Clutter Visualization Form. Their feelings might be negative (e.g., anxiety, embarrassment, fear, confusion, disorientation, comfort, hopelessness, depression, frustration, relief) and/or positive (e.g., happiness, pleasure, relief, comfort, hope, pride). If a member reported little or no discomfort and reported positive feelings about the presence of clutter, it is likely that he or she may lack the motivation for change. Some exploration within the group may be necessary to determine willingness to comply with the treatment, and if necessary, you may need to meet with the person outside of group before continuing.

Ask about thoughts. Help group members formulate their attitudes or beliefs and distinguish these from the feelings they just reported by asking: "What thoughts are you having that accompany these feelings?" Examples might be: "How will I find anything in this mess?" "I would be embarrassed for others to see this"; "This is going to take me forever to go through all my things"; and "These things are important to me." If clients have trouble identifying their thoughts, suggest ones that seem likely based on their model and formulation, as well as others that are quite unlikely ("Were you thinking that this is a really pleasant room?") as these contrary ideas offer a springboard to clarify thinking. Again, ask clients to record their thoughts on the form. An example of a completed Clutter Visualization Form is given in Figure 6.1.

Review and Summarize. Reviewing the feelings and thoughts recorded on forms during the group provides clients with a model for self-reporting as part of their homework. It also fosters interaction among group members. To insure that clients complete the form appropriately, look at group members' forms or have them work in pairs or triads. Summarize the connection between thoughts, feelings, and motivators of change. For example:

> *When you imagined your kitchen with its clutter, you thought that it isn't clean and you can't cook in there anymore. These thoughts left you*

Room: Kitchen

A. Visualize this room with all of its present clutter. Imagine standing in the middle of the room slowly turning to see all of the clutter.

B. How uncomfortable did you feel while imagining this room with all the clutter? Use a scale from 0 to 100, where 0 = no discomfort and 100 = the most discomfort you have ever felt.

Initial Discomfort Rating: 80

C. What feelings were you having while visualizing this room?

1. Overwhelmed

2. Frustrated

3. Anxious

D. What thoughts (beliefs, attitudes) were you having while visualizing this room?

1. This is going to take me forever to go through all my things. I can't deal with this.

2. I don't know what to do. They are going to evict me.

3. I used to love to cook. How could I have let this get so bad.

Figure 6.1

Example of Completed Clutter Visualization Form

feeling ashamed and frustrated. You also felt overwhelmed at the idea of cleaning up. Working on clearing the clutter would allow you to cook again, something you used to enjoy, and help you feel better about yourself. On the other hand, you are likely to feel overwhelmed and frustrated by the clutter and may want to avoid dealing with it. Does that sound right to you?

This review might lead to further discussion of clients' models for hoarding behavior and how to resolve potential barriers to working on the clutter during treatment. If clients report little discomfort and some positive feelings during the visualizing, explore their interest in treatment with questions such as: "Having these things around pleases you. Why would you want to change this?" or "You can see the benefits of keeping your home like this. Are there any downsides?" If a group member reports preferring to live in cluttered living spaces, help him or her generate realistic goals for treatment that balance the positive and negative feelings and thoughts about clutter.

Unclutter Visualization

This task is designed to help group members examine their feelings about possessions and the likely impact of removing clutter during treatment. For this exercise, ask members to use the Unclutter Visualization Form and give the following instructions:

> *Now, please visualize the same room as for the previous task, but this time without any clutter. Imagine that everything you wanted to keep is still in your home, put in a place where you can find it. Imagine that the furniture tops and the floor are clear of any clutter. It may be difficult to create this image, but please try. As you picture the uncluttered space, imagine what you can do with this room to make it a comfortable space. Think about the activities you can do there, ways you can decorate the room, having visitors over, etc.*
>
> *[Wait about 1–2 minutes]*
>
> *How much discomfort are you experiencing right now on a scale from 0 (meaning "no discomfort") to 100 (meaning "the most discomfort you can imagine")? Or you can use a scale from 0 to 10. Now please write down that number on the Unclutter Visualization Form in the space labeled "Initial Discomfort Rating."*

Ask group members to describe how they felt during this exercise. Focus first on what positive and negative emotions each person experienced before going on to their thoughts. As they identify their emotions, ask them to record these on their form. If they get stumped, try asking about specific negative and positive feelings such as loss, emptiness, loneliness, sadness, panic, fear, confusion, strangeness, disorientation, relief, pleasure, satisfaction, pride, joy, or comfort.

Next, help the clients identify the thoughts they had during the visualization. Have them consider why the uncluttered image produces the specific feelings for them. Use a Socratic questioning style ("That's interesting; I wonder...") and reflective listening strategies ("It sounds like...").

Then help clients connect their thoughts to their emotions. For example, a group member might realize that his thoughts about wasting things led to feelings of guilt. Do not challenge their thoughts at this stage, although it is fine to ask about thoughts and feelings previously reported during the assessment and model-building. Be sure your questions are genuinely curious (e.g., "Previously you mentioned ____, is that what you mean here?") so group members do not become defensive. To enhance motivation, you can ask open-ended questions such as "Are there ways your life would improve if this room were uncluttered?" or "How would it help you if your kitchen counter were cleared of stuff?"

Ask the clients to report their "Final Discomfort Rating" on the form and to note any conclusions they have drawn from this exercise. Figure 6.2 illustrates a completed Unclutter Visualization Form.

Room: Kitchen

A. Visualize this room with the clutter gone. Imagine that all the items are in a place where you can find them, and picture cleared surfaces and floors, tabletops without piles, and uncluttered floors with only rugs and furniture.

B. How uncomfortable did you feel while imagining this room without all the clutter? Use a scale from 0 to 100, where 0 = no discomfort and 100 = the most discomfort you have ever felt.

Initial Discomfort Rating: 60

C. What thoughts and feelings were you having while visualizing this room?

1. It's so not me. It looks so empty.
2. How am I going to find anything? I can't help but wonder where is all my stuff?
3. The inspectors will be happy.

D. Imagine what you can do in this room now that it is not cluttered. Describe your thoughts and feelings.

1. I can cook again. I really enjoy making bread.
2. I can make coffee, sit at the table and read the paper. I can put them down on the table and spread out the paper.
3. I can decorate a bit. Maybe put some flowers on the table and give the walls a fresh paint.

E. How uncomfortable did you feel while imagining the room this way?

(0 = no discomfort and 100 = the most discomfort you have ever felt)

Final Discomfort Rating: 30 *Some nervous excitement*

Figure 6.2

Example of Completed Unclutter Visualization Form

Ideal Home Visualization

Finally, ask group members to imagine their ideal (but not perfect) home, room by room, as this helps them clarify their goals for therapy and is especially useful if the unclutter visualization was somewhat disturbing. The ideal image should be of the home they currently live in, with rooms decorated in the manner they would find most satisfying. Ask them to picture details such as where the furniture would go, what items would be visible, where things are stored for easy access, and so forth; and then have them briefly describe their feelings and thoughts. A home assignment might be to draw out a floor plan for each room that illustrates the placement of furniture and other items to help clients focus on the positive aspects of decorating their rooms and increase their motivation to accomplish this goal. Later in treatment when significant clutter has been cleared, group members can be encouraged to engage in actual decorating of their new spaces.

Objective 4: Additional Strategies to Develop Discrepancy (Importance of Change)

One of the simplest ways to heighten discrepancy between the current state of the home and how the client wants to live is to ask who visits the home, as most clients with HD would experience shame about others seeing the condition of their home. A discussion about how group members feel when someone rings the doorbell or asks to stop by is a good starting point, or you can ask group members to visualize someone coming to the door now, followed by imagining someone coming over when the front room is cleared of clutter.

Another method for developing discrepancy is to focus on function—what would the group members like to do that they can't do now because of the condition of the home? Then ask them to visualize being able to do that activity (e.g., have friends or family visit) once their home is ready. For example, a grandparent who values family relationships but whose son or daughter will not allow the grandchildren to visit because of the condition of the home will be motivated to work on the clutter to accomplish a visit.

Table 6.1 Impediments to Motivation and Strategies to Intervene

Motivation Impediments	Intervention Strategies
Family member or partner pressured person into treatment Toxic levels of criticism from family members	Articulate personal goals, not family goals
No visitors to the home Lives alone and attachment to others is tenuous Social anxiety	Arranging regular home visits, initially by the clinician and/or coach, and as soon as possible by supportive family members and friends
Significant depression	Consider treatment for depression (e.g., medications, cognitive therapy) If needed, delay hoarding treatment until mood is sufficiently improved for client to work on clutter and homework
Complains of fatigue and health problems	Incorporate these vulnerabilities and avoidance behaviors into the general conceptual hoarding model Attend to scheduling and pacing of home tasks
Being at home is an unpleasant experience	Help clients develop strategies to spend more time at home doing things that are enjoyable

You can point out these discrepancies during group discussions, but avoid coming across as trying to convince group members of some conclusion, as only the client can explore and resolve ambivalence. They cannot be "convinced" by persuasion. This is a delicate balance that requires practice. Table 6.1 summarizes several factors that influence clients' motivation to engage in therapy, along with some strategies to consider using for each of these problems.

Objective 5: Recognizing and Addressing Ambivalence

Most hoarding clients feel ambivalent about changing their behavior. On one hand, they recognize the problems hoarding has generated for them, but on the other, they believe there are compelling reasons not to get rid of their treasured "collections." More than likely, group members will have had negative experiences from others' attempts to help them, often in the form of relatives' and friends' advocating, even arguing, to get rid of the stuff—"just throw it out." But this approach typically engenders an argument in which the helpers present reasons for getting rid of things and clients dig in their heels and counter with reasons to save them. Progress stalls quickly in this scenario. The motivational strategies used during group sessions are intended to disarm defensiveness by helping clients first articulate and then resolve their ambivalence.

Toward this end, Table 6.2 presents verbal and non-verbal behaviors that indicate that members are ambivalent about moving forward to address their hoarding problem. Examples include diverting the discussion to other topics, coming late or missing group sessions, and not completing home commitments. Non-verbal behaviors like turning away or rolling one's eyes are likely indications of ambivalence or disagreement with the group's focus. When you spot these behaviors at any point during this or other group sessions, consider how to directly address the ambivalence by using one or more strategies from Table 6.2.

Objective 6: Address Problems with Home Commitments

Failure to complete home commitments is especially common early in treatment and usually reflects some ambivalence about resolving their hoarding problem. Below are some possible solutions you can discuss in the group:

- Schedule particular times for doing the task.
- Link homework times to other routine activities that can serve as reminders.
- Ask someone to be present at home or in acquiring settings during practice.
- Play pleasant music or the radio during tasks.
- Find ways to interrupt self-defeating thoughts.
- Monitor the work completed (when, where, number of hours, etc.).

Table 6.2 Ambivalence and Interventions

Signals of Ambivalence	Examples	Intervention Strategies
Constant complaining; Diverting discussion to other topics	"I don't see why I can't just live like this; I'm really not bothering anybody." "The City has no right to do this." Repeatedly asking "Why do I have this problem?"	Assess motivation for working on the hoarding problem. Determine whether treatment for hoarding is appropriate at this time. Use broken leg analogy: Repairing the leg is the first priority and then clients can determine why it happened to prevent a recurrence.
Arguing	"That doesn't make sense to me. How am I going to remember what I want to get if I don't buy it right then?"	Re-establish collaborative spirit. Remind clients that they will make all decisions about possessions.
Non-verbal signals	Sighing; Not paying attention; Turning sideways	Stop and inquire what the sigh [or other non-verbal action] meant. Offer the hypothesis that the client was unhappy with the exchange.
Arriving late, canceling and "forgetting" appointments	Arrives late with a weak excuse; Cancels or forgets appointment; States that other problems are interfering with devoting time to working on hoarding; Reports dissatisfaction with the therapy or the clinician	Help clients articulate their ambivalence before using motivational strategies to strengthen their commitment and confidence in their ability to change. Use problem-solving method. Remove the client from the group and reschedule therapy for a later date. Routinely request feedback.
Not doing homework	"I haven't had time to go to any stores to practice." "I can't seem to find time to sort. I have things I need to do to get ready for the next day." "I don't want to get depressed or anxious so I keep busy with friends."	Use motivational methods and problem-solving before trying to move forward in treatment.
Discouraged despite progress	Discounts progress (especially when depressed) and holds high standards. Has so much clutter that small improvements are difficult to see.	Use updated photographs for comparison to recognize small changes. Emphasize importance of focusing work in one area, so progress is more evident.

- Arrange reminder calls by a coach.
- Plan brief phone contacts before and after homework.

Case Vignette

The following dialogue illustrates common group challenges in completing home commitment assignments between sessions—an indication of ambivalence among some members. Several motivation techniques used by the group leader are noted in italics.

CLINICIAN: So, let's review the home commitment. Does anyone want to state what it was?

CHARLIE: I don't know what it was—but I know I didn't do it.

JENNIFER: Okay, so the home commitment was to work on our model and do a Brief Thought Record. I don't think I did this right, but it occurred to me on the way home that I hadn't added to my model how worried I am about discarding certain clothes because I might not be able to replace the color—you know, matching the shades. Each color is unique and if I get rid of a green blouse, I can't just replace it.

CLINICIAN: Thanks Jennifer. What did others try out?

[*Silence*]

CHARLIE: I guess I'm not the only one who didn't do it. [*Chuckle*]

CLINICIAN: So for those of you who didn't do any of the home commitment or only did a little bit, what got in the way? [*open-ended question*]

GRACE: Well, I tried to put my *Workbook* where I said I would. But, then I don't think I ever brought it from the car into my home. And, I forgot about it. I did find my *Workbook* though—right before group under some pet supplies in the back seat of my car.

CHARLIE: My book was right where I left it after group last week. On my bed stand, next to my bed.

CLINICIAN: Charlie, how about we discuss you leaving your book there all week. Sound okay?

CHARLIE: Sure!

CLINICIAN: So, during the course of the week, was there ever a time that you noticed the book sitting next to your bed?

CHARLIE: Yes, I guess so. Yes, I saw it.

CLINICIAN: What led you not to pick up the book when you saw it? [*open-ended question*]

CHARLIE: I just figured I would do it later. I am a great procrastinator.

CLINICIAN: So, your thought was that you would actually use the book at some point, just not at that moment. [*reflective listening*]

CHARLIE: Yeah, I—I'm sure my wife would nag me at some point about doing it.

CLINICIAN: So, your wife wants you to use the book. What is her main concern? [*asking for elaboration*]

CHARLIE: Well, she's the whole reason I had to come here.

CLINICIAN: So, if you had it your way, you wouldn't use the book or come, as you don't need to be here? [*clarifying question*]

CHARLIE: Well, yeah. I mean, I'm not saying this is a bad group or anything or that I can't learn anything. I don't see my stuff as such a big issue.

CLINICIAN: So you see that there may be some things you might learn from the book and the group, but basically this is more of her problem than yours, and your stuff is your business. [*summarizing*]

CHARLIE: Yeah, I mean in my case it's my wife and she lives with me so I guess she has some right to complain about my stuff. But, I am coming here, so she should get off my back.

CLINICIAN: Do others of you feel pressured by others or by me to work on reducing your clutter?

LIZ: Yes, I get a lot of outside pressure from those housing managers. I mean, I know I have to reduce the amount of stuff in my house. But, all the pressure isn't helping.

CARL: My condo board is on my back, sending me letters.

CLINICIAN: You have all taken some steps to address your stuff by coming to group and need some space to actually work on it, but don't like feeling forced. Do you think this pressure has anything to do with whether you complete your home commitment?

CHARLIE: Yes. I can do the home assignment; it's not a big deal.

CLINICIAN: But, maybe it doesn't seem helpful or relevant? [*reflective listening*]

JENNIFER: Well, you did tell us that working at home could help us take what we learn and practice at home.

MARIA: I am just too tired to do anything.

CHARLIE: I am not sure what the point of this model is anyway.

CLINICIAN: Not understanding the home commitment or the point of the assignment, and feeling tired can get in the way of getting your home commitment done. [*summarizing, reflective listening*]

MARIA: I have to do it mid-afternoon because I am too tired at night.

CLINICIAN: So there may be better times to schedule the home commitment to increase the likelihood that you will do it. What is the worst thing that can happen if you go along as you have been and not do the work at home? [*using extreme contrasts*]

Charlie: My wife will nag me.

Liz: I'll be evicted.

Carl: Yeah, who knows what my condo association will do. They will probably drive up with a truck and take away all my things.

Joseph: For me, it's that my kids won't come visit.

Maria: Mine won't let me have my grandkids over.

Clinician: So on one hand, the home commitment is difficult to get done, and on the other hand, not doing your home commitment has negative consequences like eviction and other people nagging you. [*reflective listening*] How do these consequences fit with your own goals? [*developing discrepancy*]

Objective 7: Use Group Process to Enhance Motivation

Practicing motivational strategies may also facilitate positive group processes. During the visualizations, clients discuss their thoughts and feelings about the shame, isolation, and emotional attachment to items, providing rich opportunities to enhance feelings of universality, social interaction, and mutual aid. In some instances, however, negative group processes can undermine motivation. Below are some examples of group members' statements that can adversely affect others' motivation, and leader responses that might be helpful.

Example 1: Motivation Undermining

Jennifer: Well I really want to get rid of my pin that my grandmother gave me.

Sally: Oh, that is so beautiful. That would be really hard for me to just give away.

CLINICIAN: It sounds like Jennifer is taking a step here in making a difficult decision about her pin. Let's support her in achieving her personal goals. How about looking at the pros/cons of keeping this pin....

Example 2: Motivation Undermining and Group Enhancement

JOSEPH: This week I was actually able to get rid of that box of trade magazines that I had been procrastinating on.

MULTIPLE MEMBERS: That's great! Congrats!

LIZ: I don't know how you do it. I mean it's really great you did that. But, I can't imagine being able to do that. It's just so hard for me...and those housing people just don't understand.

Clinician: Nice work Joseph, working through your discomfort and getting rid of those magazines. Liz, you bring up an important point. Sometimes others successes are inspiring, but at other points they can feel overwhelming. [*reflective listening*]

GRACE: Just being here is a big step for all of us. It gives me hope that if you can do this that I may be able to do it too. [*group motivational enhancement*]

Objective 8: Home Commitment

- Make a list of the advantages and disadvantages (pros and cons) of addressing hoarding using the *Advantages and Disadvantages of Change Worksheet* in the Appendix 23.

Objective 9: Clinician Forms

- Clinician directs the clients to write their home commitment on the Group Session Form (see Appendix 12) and completes the Clinician's Group Progress Notes (see Appendix 15).

Chapter 7 *Session 4: Goals and Treatment Planning*

(Corresponds to Chapter 4 of the Workbook)

Materials Needed

- Advantages/Disadvantages of Change Worksheet (Appendix 23)
- Treatment/Personal Goals (*Workbook* Chapter 4, p. 42)
- Client's Model of Hoarding from Session 2 (*Workbook* Chapter 3, p. 33)
- Instructions for Coaches (Appendix 24)

Session Agenda

- Review advantages and disadvantages of changing.
- Establish treatment goals and set rules for treatment.
- Connect treatment methods to the general conceptual hoarding model.
- Review rules for coaches.

Objective 1: Check-in

- Distribute and review the Group Session Form.
- Each client checks in, listing one advantage and one disadvantage of hoarding (e.g., pros and cons of acquiring or having clutter in the home).

After discussing costs and benefits of hoarding identified by the group members during the check-in, extend this conversation so each client notes additional advantages and disadvantages. Comment on some of the similarities and differences across group members as they emerge. We recommend first identifying and discussing several advantages (noting each on the board) as they are mentioned by the group members, and then moving on to disadvantages. Encourage brainstorming to help clients present their ideas without fear of criticism. If clients have difficulty thinking of advantages and disadvantages or overlook obvious ones, suggest some possibilities based on previous conversations about their situations. For example, common advantages include a sense of identity, extra consideration from friends and family, and avoiding uncomfortable emotions and responsibilities.

Below are some advantages and disadvantages you might mention to facilitate the group discussion. During this discussion, keep in mind the group process and look for opportunities to foster the therapeutic factors and mutual aid.

CLINICIAN: Hoarding symptoms may have some benefits.

1. For instance, you may derive a sense of identity from being a collector of cookbooks. Ask yourself whether some of the possessions you save give you a sense of identity or reflect who you are or wish to be. What would it mean for you not to save those items? How could you still maintain those aspects of your identity? [*Open for discussion*]

2. Another possible benefit of having these symptoms is that sometimes they confer special privileges. For example, you may have more say over how your home is kept because of your hoarding. Maybe you receive extra consideration from family members, landlords, or others because your hoarding is considered a mental health problem. Think about what would change in your life if you were successful in resolving your hoarding problems. [*Open for discussion*]

3. Sometimes these special considerations allow you to avoid dealing with fears you have associated with your hoarding. For example, if you are afraid of losing important information, saving things is a way of avoiding dealing with that fear. Can you identify some of the things you fear that hoarding allows you to avoid? [*Open for discussion. If clients have difficulty thinking of fears they are avoiding, you can suggest fears of becoming upset, of making the wrong decision, of forgetting something important, of embarrassment or about the past, etc.*]

4. Sometimes hoarding may lead you to avoid and divert certain responsibilities. This can happen even though you don't intend to; it's not deliberate. But, hoarding can be very disabling and get in the way of being able to fulfill responsibilities. For example, it could lead people to avoid taking care of themselves, or their homes, and even supporting others. This can provoke feelings of shame and fear. [*Open for discussion*]

CLINICIAN: Hoarding symptoms probably have substantial costs.

1. For instance, hoarding can cause impairment in everyday life so you can't invite people to your home, your children may not be able to have friends over, you might be unable to work, there can be family tension, maybe you have creditors contacting you because you have not paid your bills. What problems in functioning has hoarding caused in your life, and which ones bother you most? [*Open for discussion*]

2. Hoarding is also associated with emotional discomfort. This discomfort can occur when you are trying to find an item, dealing with creditors, landlords, and family or friends. Perhaps you feel anxiety, anger, sadness, guilt, or shame. Although I'm sure you'd like to avoid these feelings, this discomfort will actually be helpful to you in treatment. Most people do not try to change problem behaviors unless they cause significant discomfort. We will ask you to remind yourself of the discomfort the hoarding creates often throughout treatment, especially when you feel tired or upset. Do you experience emotional discomfort because of your hoarding? [*Open for discussion*]

3. You may have had unpleasant interactions with other people—family members, landlord, co-workers, friends—about your hoarding. Can you give examples of conflicts you have had with others because of your hoarding? [*Open for discussion*]

4. Hoarding is also associated with financial costs. For example, you might be overspending, incurring late charges from unpaid bills, or paying for storage facilities. Perhaps you re-purchase items you already own because you can't find them. Those of you who own your home might put off calling the repair person for fear of what they will say, and this may have led to inconvenience and even a decrease in the value of your home. What have been financial costs to you of hoarding? [*Open for discussion*]

At this point, summarize the costs and benefits using various approaches. For example, you might say, "On one hand, you like having all this information around you. It helps you feel competent. But on the other hand, you also find that having so many books and papers is overwhelming, and you often can't find the information you are seeking and sometimes you don't even try." Paraphrase the group member's words so he or she can hear aloud the costs and benefits he/she has articulated. Avoid over-emphasizing costs as this can inadvertently encourage clients to defend the benefits.

Ask group members what conclusions they draw from this exercise. If the conclusions are in favor of change (*change talk*), reinforce this with mild agreement: "Given your lists, that makes sense to me, too." Avoid overemphasis on change as this can trigger ambivalence and defensive reactions. If clients focus on the advantages of their current behavior and the disadvantages of change, help them articulate their own values as these arise during the discussions. For example, "It seems like you really enjoy it when your things are organized, but it's hard to figure out how to do this."

Emphasize the need to keep these costs and benefits in mind, since they serve as treatment goals. When faced with distressing tasks, the short-term benefits of hoarding (e.g., avoiding emotional distress) may seem to outweigh the long-term costs. Accordingly, it is important to connect the moment-by-moment decisions to the client's larger goals.

Examining the costs of hoarding can also trigger negative emotions and depressive feelings. If so, attend to clients' needs in a sensitive manner to prevent the association of negative feelings with the therapy process. Table 7.1 provides examples of both advantages and disadvantages of hoarding behaviors.

Table 7.1 Examples of Advantages and Disadvantages of Hoarding (*Write out on the board as a group*)

Advantages of Hoarding Behavior	Disadvantages of Hoarding Behavior
Sense of identity	Feeling overwhelmed
Extra consideration from family and friends	Can't use parts of the house
Can avoid fears	Can't host visitors in the home
Can avoid responsibilities	Feelings of shame and guilt

Objective 3: Develop Treatment Goals and Rules (*Workbook* Chapter 4, p. 41)

Now that group members have completed the initial assessment, model-building, and worked on motivation, it is time to help them establish personal treatment goals and to describe treatment rules (these are different from the group rules established at the first session). During the previous session, several visualization exercises were used to help clients identify their thoughts and feelings about organizing, reducing clutter, and limiting acquisition.

Treatment Goals

Help group members develop their own personal treatment goals by directly asking,

- "What would you like to accomplish in working on your hoarding problem with me and the group?" or

- "When we are all done working together, what do you hope will happen? What are your goals?"

Below are some common treatment goals that might be relevant, but your client's own personal goals are even more important:

1. *Understand why I hoard.* A better understanding will help clients make progress and can enhance their awareness of early warning signs to prevent setbacks after treatment ends.
2. *Create living space I can use.* This goal is almost universal and suggests that early efforts should be devoted to clearing the most-desired living spaces. Help group members decide what they want to do most—cooking, dining, working on art projects, etc.—and work toward those ends.
3. *Reduce compulsive buying or acquiring.* The motivation behind this goal may be to reduce debt or save money, as well as to limit the amount of clutter. Because acquiring is usually associated with strong positive emotions like comfort and joy, developing alternative pleasurable activities is also an important goal of treatment (see Sessions 5 and 6).
4. *Get organized to find things more easily and make them more accessible.* Strategies for learning these skills are the focus of Sessions 10 and 11.
5. *Improve my decision-making.* Most hoarding clients struggle with decision-making, which is a focus of Sessions 8 and 9.
6. *Reduce clutter.* While this is a main goal for family members, it may not be a primary one for clients because it implies getting rid of things, and this is still an anxiety-provoking prospect. Do not add this to the list unless the client specifically states it. In fact, clutter will be reduced as other goals are achieved.

Below are a few personal goals listed by our clients:

- To have room to make my crafts
- To create a comfortable, pretty, and organized bedroom
- To have a living room where I could entertain my friends

- To clear the entrances and exits of my home
- To clear the kitchen so I can cook
- To clear my bath so I can take bubble baths

Ask clients to complete the Personal Goals section of the Goals Form (Chapter 4, p. 42 of the *Workbook*) to identify their own goals for the coming weeks and months. This may be started during the group session and completed as a home commitment.

Case Vignette

CLINICIAN: Now we are going to talk about our goals for treatment. We have already been discussing what contributes to your clutter problem. Some of you need to create more living space, while others need to improve organization. What are each of you hoping to accomplish in this group?

MARIA: That's my problem, I can't figure out where to put things and don't feel confident that I will remember where I put it, so I leave everything out so I can see it.

CLINICIAN: I see some heads nodding... it looks like some of you share that same problem. Sounds like you are hoping to organize your home and possessions. Are there certain types of items or areas of the home that you want to focus on?

GRACE: My bed is pretty messy. I haven't found a good way to organize my clean laundry, so it always ends up in the middle of my bed.

CLINICIAN: Would you like to add "cleaning off my bed" and "organizing my laundry" to your goal list?

GRACE: Yes, I haven't slept in my bed for months.

CLINICIAN: So it sounds like part of your goal is to "sleep in your bed."

When we were working on the model, some of you mentioned that you were still actively acquiring, bringing items into your home. What specific goals do you have for that?

Joseph: Well, I don't have any money to buy anything now. All that acquiring caused me to go bankrupt! Now I just need to figure out how to get rid of all that stuff that I bought.

Charlie: My house is filled with all my electronics, and I can't really afford to buy anything new. But it's all good stuff that can be used by someone. I don't think I could ever throw any of it away. That would be wasteful!

Clinician: Joseph and Charlie point out that acquiring not only adds to the clutter problem but it also can create a financial stress. What do the rest of you think? Does anyone else have a problem with acquiring and want to focus on reducing acquiring as one of their treatment goals?

Sally: I need to stop spending money on accessories and clothes. I just don't have any more room for all of it.

Liz: If I don't stop bringing all those flyers and containers into the house, I'll be in big trouble.

Clinician: Okay, so Sally, let's make your goals more specific. You stated that you want to stop spending money on accessories and clothes. Would it be reasonable to take a break from shopping for these items for a period of time?

Sally: No, that's too much. Maybe I could stop buying purses for a few weeks.

Liz: Wow, that's really amazing. Hmmm, I should do something about all the containers I have. During that exercise, I realized that I can't really prepare food on the kitchen counters because the containers are everywhere.

Clinician: So maybe your goals include "Clearing the kitchen counters so I can prepare food" and "Organize my containers"?

Liz: Yeah, I might have to get rid of some other stuff, too.

Clients' goals should be relevant and reasonable. It is important to discuss what each client values most in life and what goals and values will be gained by reducing their hoarding. Dividing large goals into sub-goals may help clients organize their steps, shape their behavior, and reinforce their progress.

Treatment Rules

The following therapy rules (see client *Workbook*, p. 43) are intended to ensure that treatment progresses in a way that is manageable for clients. The rules are specifically intended to increase client's confidence (self-efficacy) about managing their own hoarding symptoms. You can discuss these with the group as general rules for the treatment.

1. *Do not touch or remove any item without explicit permission.* Most people with hoarding disorder are extremely concerned that others will discard their possessions without consulting them. Misguided efforts to de-clutter by family members have heightened their sensitivity. An important aim of treatment is for clients to develop trust in a collaborative relationship with the clinician. This rule is not easy for home visitors, because the impulse to pick things up to help is powerful. Clients' initial fears often ease considerably as the therapy progresses.
2. *Clients make all decisions about possessions.* Group members must learn to make reasonable decisions about saving and organizing their possessions. You can occasionally offer advice when asked, but making decisions for clients interferes with their ability to acquire this skill. It is likely that past attempts to help by friends and family members have violated this rule and caused clients to be highly sensitive to other people's involvement.
3. *Treatment proceeds systematically.* Determine the plan for where, when, and how to sort cluttered areas. Most clients decide to work room-by-room because this produces highly visible progress that enhances motivation. You can blend this plan with sorting by types of items (e.g., all the books) from different rooms when this makes sense. Generally, work from easier to harder situations. Choose a method according to your client's preference

and tolerance, the likelihood of observable progress, and rapid learning of organizational skills. If clients insist on methods clinicians consider problematic, try an experiment to see if their preferred method works, and if not, consider alternatives.

4. *Establish an organizing plan before beginning the sorting process.* Develop a detailed plan for where to store kept items. Many clients tend to generate too many categories, becoming confused by the process. Establishing a limited number of categories at the outset of sorting will reduce this problem. For this reason, group members will learn to sort objects before paper, which requires many categories (Sessions 10 and 11).

5. *Clients think aloud while sorting (especially early in treatment).* This helps clinicians and clients understand the thoughts and emotions that determine acquiring, organizing, and saving (or removing) behavior. Speaking aloud helps clients become consciously aware of their reasons for saving and will be useful in learning how to alter problematic beliefs.

6. *Only handle it once (OHIO)—or at most twice.* The goal here is to prevent the churning of possessions that are merely recycled from one disorganized pile to another. Clients learn to make decisions quickly and firmly by handling objects minimally, although "once" may not be possible as items often must go to an interim location before space is cleared for the final destination. Allow some flexibility when clients are unable to make a final decision but are making clear progress.

7. *Treatment proceeds in a flexible manner.* Flexibility and creativity will help solve logistical problems associated with organizing a too-full home. When clients become stalled because organizing one area depends on having another space ready for storage, problem-solving may be needed.

Objective 4: Connecting Methods to the Model

It is important to help the group members connect treatment strategies they learn to their general conceptual hoarding model so they can see how the group activities and home commitments address their own problems. Throughout the 20 weeks of treatment, sorting clutter in the group and at home provides a basis for applying most of the therapy methods. "Sorting," as we refer to it here and throughout the sessions, means the evaluation and decision-making regarding what to do with possessions. This includes not only the decision about whether to keep or discard a possession, but also what to do next with the item. Kept items must go where they belong, and removed items should be recycled, sold, donated, or placed in the trash as quickly as possible. The treatment components to encourage non-acquiring and sorting include: (1) exposure practice to habituate strong emotions and reduce avoidance behavior, (2) learning skills for attention focusing, organizing, decision-making, and problem-solving; and (3) cognitive therapy to examine and correct faulty thinking. All of these methods rely on home assignments between sessions. Figure 7.1 illustrates the therapeutic strategies that will be applied to various elements of the general conceptual hoarding model for Sally (developed in Session 2; see Figure 5.1). A description of Sally can be found in Chapter 3.

Need for Social Support or Coaching (Steketee & Frost, 2013)

In our experience, many people with hoarding problems have great difficulty making progress on their own. The presence of someone else in the room, even if interaction is minimal, can provide emotional support that reduces uncomfortable feelings and helps distractible clients stay focused. Supportive people can also provide positive reinforcement, and just knowing that someone will visit can be a powerful motivator. The role of coaches is to help clients remain focused on their task, provide emotional support, facilitate decision-making by asking open-ended questions and expressing curiosity, help with hauling to remove unwanted items, and accompany clients on non-acquiring trips as needed. Ask clients if they know someone who might provide a calming presence while they work without interfering with their efforts. If a supportive family member or friend can assist as a coach, arrange a conversation with that person and the client to provide some information about hoarding and guidelines for what to do and what not to do. Ideally, the coach can observe you working with the client during a home session. Instructions for coaches are provided in the Appendix 24.

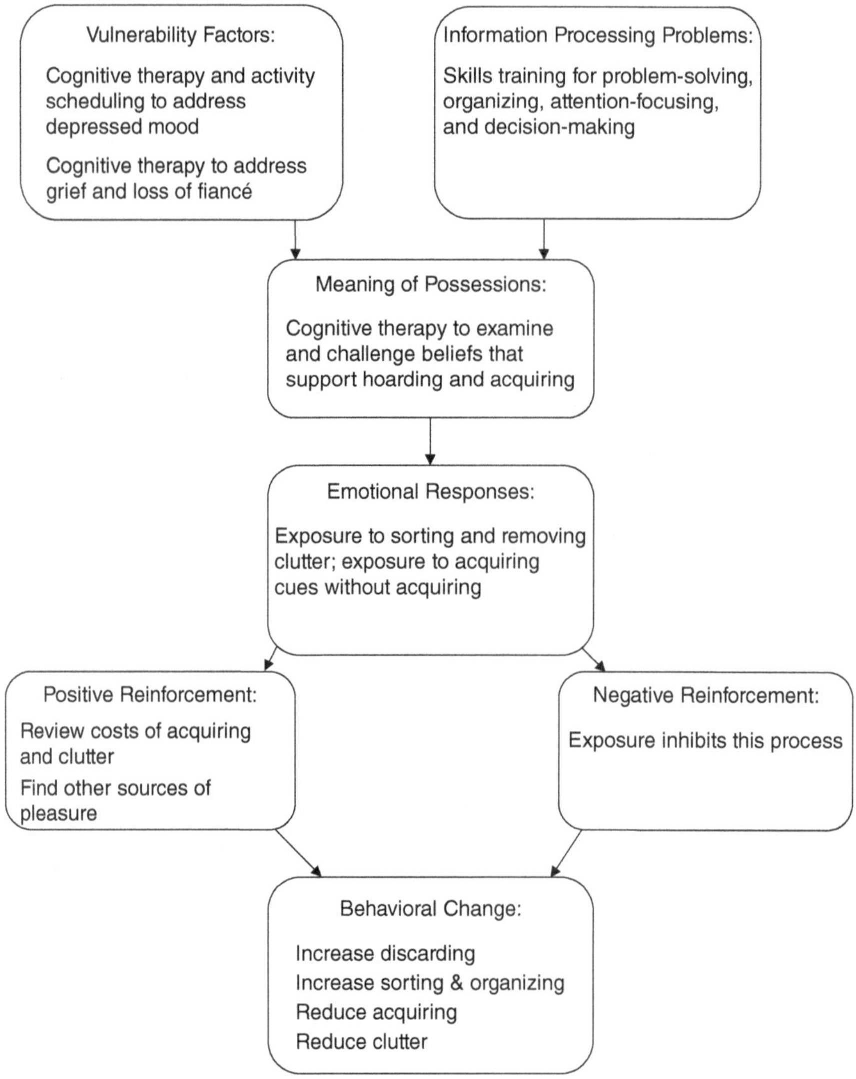

Figure 7.1

General Conceptual Hoarding Model with Treatment Strategies for Sally

A word of caution is in order here. Many family members do not make good coaches or helpers. Longstanding patterns of criticism and "taking control" are difficult to break, and even with explicit instructions and modeling appropriate behavior, some family members just can't resist handling and discarding the client's possessions. Work with group members to identify people they feel confident will be able to assist them, if only by being around when they are sorting and organizing.

Objective 5: Home Commitment

- Review Instructions for Coaches and arrange to share these with potential coaches.
- Read about acquiring (Chapter 5 in the *Workbook*).
- Begin to identify items that are acquired during the coming week using the Acquiring Form (Chapter 3 in the *Workbook*, p. 38).
- Bring an object that was acquired during the upcoming week to the next session.

Objective 6: Clinician Forms

- Clinician directs the clients to write their home commitment on the Group Session Form (see Appendix 12) and completes the Clinician's Group Progress Notes (see Appendix 15).

Chapter 8 *Session 5: Reducing Acquisition*

(Portions of this session correspond to Chapters 3 and 4 of the Workbook)

Materials Needed

- Acquiring Form (*Workbook* Chapter 3, p. 38, Appendix 25)
- General Conceptual Hoarding Model (*Workbook* Chapter 3, p. 33, Appendix 17)
- Acquiring Visualization Form (Workbook Chapter 4, p. 46, Appendix 26)
- Advantages/Disadvantages Worksheet for Acquiring (*Workbook*, Chapter 5, p. 53)

Session Agenda

- Complete Acquiring Form and discuss acquired items brought to the group.
- Complete Visualization Form and exercises.
- Discuss Advantages and Disadvantages and Worksheet.

Understanding Acquiring

As discussed in Chapter 1, the vast majority of clients with hoarding disorder have excessive levels of acquisition of purchased and free items that contribute to the clutter in their homes and storage areas. Most acquisition involves compulsive buying of items that are not necessarily needed or are duplicates of what is already owned. Often, the person has no plan for immediate use of the purchased items. A number of clients also have problems with acquiring free things, such as pamphlets, samples, and objects put in trash or recycle receptacles by others.

Intervention for acquiring should be based on the information collected during the initial assessment prior to treatment (see Chapter 2), on the client's General Conceptual Hoarding Model (see Session 2), and on the exercises conducted in this session to determine how and when acquiring occurs and how it is reinforced. Your goal in this session is to help group members become aware of how they acquire—whether they collect free things or accept items from others; have subscriptions; order from catalogs, on television, or on the Web; pick things out of the trash; buy in stores, yard sales, or flea markets; buy "extras"; or steal items. Stealing is deliberately mentioned in case group members wish to address it; group leaders do not directly assess who in the group is engaging in this behavior. As it is criminal activity, it must be managed carefully in group. If it comes to the group leaders' attention, it also may require a conversation with the client outside of group.

We recommend working on acquiring as soon as possible to avoid exacerbating the clutter problem. Some clients with hoarding disorder do not recognize an acquiring problem that becomes apparent over the course of treatment. Some have controlled their acquiring by avoiding places where they can't contain the urge. As noted below, avoidance rarely works in the long run. Keep these possibilities in mind during this session when asking group members about the possessions entering their homes.

Objective 1: Check-in

- Distribute and review the Group Session Form.
- Clients report on progress completing their Acquiring Form (*Workbook*, Chapter 3, p. 38)
- Clients discuss an object that they have acquired this past week and brought to group

While each group member was instructed to bring in an item that they acquired during the past week, there will only be time for a couple of people to talk in detail about their experience of acquiring and bringing the item to the group. Throughout the group sessions, group members will be encouraged to bring in items for sorting and discarding. This presents the challenge of balancing in-session discussion or decision-making around group members' personal possessions with covering the session content. From our clinical experience, we find it is helpful to rotate among members and assign two to three individuals per session to bring in items. This not only formalizes the commitment and sets a norm of accountability, it also insures that there is sufficient time to discuss and complete the decision-making process. During Sessions 5–12, we recommend splitting the group in half so each leader oversees a smaller group to support the decision-making of the clients who brought in items and to provide more time for the group to process the information. Later in treatment (e.g., Session 13), group members will be better able to divide into pairs and coach each other.

For this session, select two or three members to speak about the acquiring experience and item they brought in, commenting on shared experiences by group members as these arise. Indicate that, in subsequent sessions, you will be asking other members to talk about their experience so everyone gets an opportunity to process their own experiences.

Objective 2: Assessing Acquisition

Identifying Patterns of Acquisition

Ask each group member to use the Acquiring Form (*Workbook*, Chapter 3, p. 38) to identify the types of items that they commonly acquire and to rate the level of discomfort that they would experience if they didn't acquire it. Figure 8.1 illustrates an example of Sally's completed Acquiring Form. Encourage group discussion of the types of items and ask each client to identify one item they associate with the most discomfort if it is not acquired. The group should be entering the middle stage of group development when an increased level of trust and cohesion is developing among members. Remain attuned to

Instructions:

Make a list of the types of items you typically bring into your home and how you acquired them. Think about items you acquired in the past week and record what items you acquire during the coming week. Do not include groceries or other perishable goods.

Rate how uncomfortable you would feel if you didn't acquire this item when you saw it.

Use a scale from 0 (no discomfort at all) to 100 (the most discomfort I've ever felt).

Item and where you typically find it:	Discomfort if not acquired (0 to 100)
Purses for me, consignment shop	90
Clothes for me – dresses, skirts, blouses, pants	
consignment shop	80
on sale at department store	60
Other accessories (e.g., scarves), consignment shop	80
Decorative items for the house, figurines, pictures	
Dollar store	75

Figure 8.1
Example of Completed Acquiring Form for Sally

those dynamics and encourage continued sharing, support, and mutual demand for work.

At this time, you can also ask members what information from their Acquiring Form should be added to their General Conceptual Hoarding Model. Also ask about their attempts to resist or control acquiring and whether they use avoidance strategies. A discussion of the dangers of relying on avoidance to control acquisition (see below) may be warranted now or during the exercises following.

Visualizing Acquiring

Ask clients to imagine a typical situation in which acquiring contributes to their hoarding problem. Select one that they will encounter soon, preferably within the next week or two, and expect to have trouble resisting. Examples might include a yard sale, a store bargain, an item that looks pretty, or a free offer. In the image, ask the client just to look at the item, but not touch it or pick it up. Allow about a minute of silence and then ask, "How strong is your urge to get this?" using a scale from 0 (no urge) to 100 (irresistible). Then ask, "What thoughts do you have as you look at the item?" Ask the group members to record these thoughts on the Acquiring Visualization Form (*Workbook* Chapter 4, p. 46), along with a brief description of the scene they imagined.

Now ask clients to imagine leaving without acquiring the item, which they will not be able to get again (a lost opportunity). Allow about a minute of silence for visualizing, and again ask for a rating of distress for this new image and what thoughts they have about leaving the scene. Use examples to prompt the thoughts, such as, "Were you thinking that you'd miss a really good buy?" Some examples of thoughts might be, "I'll miss out on important opportunities" or "I won't feel complete if I don't get this." Comment on any aspects that seem especially important motivators for acquiring or important links to components of hoarding in the client's model. If they have trouble generating a distressing image, you can add elements that might prompt a more realistic image (e.g., seeing another shopper considering the item they were interested in).

Next ask members to list thoughts that are most likely to help them not acquire something. Examples might be:

- "I know I already own something like this. I will just wait until I find it during this treatment program."
- "I have plenty of reading material at home without adding this to the pile—it will just make me feel guilty anyway."
- "This would make a great birthday gift for Michael, but I know he would rather I stopped spending money I don't have."

Figure 8.2 illustrates an example of Sally's completed Acquiring Visualization Form.

Visualize a typical situation in which you have a strong urge to acquire something. In your image, don't actually pick up the item, just look at it. Please describe the location and item you imagined.

Inside my favorite consignment shop. Seeing a navy blue leather purse.

Rate how strong was your urge to acquire the item (0 = no urge to acquire, 100 = irresistible urge).

Acquiring Urge 100

What thoughts did you have while you imagined this scene?

1. This is gorgeous. I love the smell of leather. It's really good quality and in such great shape.
2. It's such a good deal. I can't pass it up. I can't believe I found this. Someone is going to grab it if I don't.
3. This blue is so pretty. It would match some of my blouses and shoes. I like the size.

Visualize this scene again, but this time, imagine leaving without the item. How much discomfort did you experience while imagining (0 to 100)?

Discomfort Rating 85

Please list any thoughts you think would help you to not acquire an object.

1. It's a great deal but still costs something. I really can't afford to spend extra money. I was here to look for a beach bag.
2. I have larger navy bags and others that are this size.
3. Someone else will feel really lucky and happy to get this.

Now rate how uncomfortable you feel about leaving without the item(s) from 0 to 100.

Discomfort Rating 60

Figure 8.2

Example of Completed Acquiring Visualization Form (Sally)

Avoiding Triggers for Acquiring

Sometimes clients can control their excessive acquisition by simply avoiding the triggers that begin their acquiring episodes. For example, they don't go out on Saturday morning so they won't see the tag sales in their neighborhood. This strategy may prove effective in the short term as long as their motivation remains high, but avoidance of acquiring cues is not likely to work over the longer term. Help group members discuss this issue to determine when avoidance is a wise decision and when it is unlikely to be effective. Ultimately, they will need to learn how to control their urges in the presence of common triggers for acquiring. This will require practice in acquiring situations, as discussed below.

Determining Advantages and Disadvantages of Acquiring

As for other components of hoarding, the general conceptual hoarding model (Session 2) helps clarify how acquiring benefits the client, as well as what they are avoiding by giving in to their urges. Often clients recognize that acquiring makes them feel better when they are distressed or depressed, but they don't always notice that this effect is short lived and that the long-term effects contribute to their unhappiness. Exploring the advantages and disadvantages of acquiring using the Advantages-Disadvantages Worksheet in Chapter 5 of the client *Workbook* (p. 53) can strengthen clients' desire to change.

Table 8.1 displays Sally's typical reasons for (advantages of) acquiring, examples of the disadvantages of acquiring, as well as the advantages and disadvantages of not acquiring. Help group members consider the weight of the evidence for the advantages and disadvantages to draw conclusions about their behavior.

Table 8.1 Sally's Advantages and Disadvantages of Acquiring Form

Advantages of Acquiring	Disadvantages of Acquiring
■ Feels good (kind of a "high") ■ Avoid feeling disappointment about not acquiring item ■ Reduces feeling a void in my life (temporarily) ■ Might lose an important opportunity if I don't get this	■ More financial debt ■ Feel anxious about the debt ■ Criticism from others about finances ■ Adds to the clutter because there isn't enough room for new items
Advantages of Not Acquiring	**Disadvantages of Not Acquiring**
■ Have more money for other things I need (or want even more) ■ Have more space for visitors ■ Have more space to cook and do other things I enjoy ■ Feel more in control of my life (I choose instead of feeling compelled to buy)	■ Anxious feelings ■ Disappointment of not obtaining item ■ Missed opportunity

Objective 3: Home Commitment

- Finish the Acquiring Form (*Workbook*, Chapter 3, p. 38) and indicate their degree of discomfort if the item is not acquired.
- Complete the Advantages and Disadvantages Worksheet (*Workbook*, Chapter 5, p. 53)

Objective 4: Clinician Forms

- Clinician directs the clients to write their home commitment on the Group Session Form (see Appendix 12) and completes the Clinician's Group Progress Notes (see Appendix 15).

Chapter 9 *Session 6: More on Acquisition*

(Corresponds to Chapter 5 of the Workbook)

Materials Needed

- Functional Analysis (*Workbook* Chapter 3, Figure 3.2, p. 39)
- Acquiring Questions Form (*Workbook* Chapter 5, p. 51)
- My Rules for Acquiring Form (*Workbook* Chapter 5, p. 52)
- My Pleasurable Alternative Activities (*Workbook* Chapter 5, p. 57)

Session Agenda

- Discuss acquiring and reinforcement.
- Demonstrate functional analysis of acquiring episode.
- Guide clients to generate acquiring questions.
- Work with the clients to develop rules for acquiring.
- Help the client identify and engage in pleasurable alternative activities.

Acquiring and Reinforcement

Excessive acquiring often results from difficulty in inhibiting urges to acquire that have been reinforced by positive emotions (pleasure, enjoyment). This is akin to the "high" people experience when they gamble or engage in other addictive-like activities, and warrants considering acquiring an impulse-control disorder. Sometimes acquiring occurs as an attempt to alleviate bad feelings like depression, distress, loneliness, and other unpleasant experiences. In these contexts it represents an attempt at self-regulation of emotion. Like interventions for sorting and discarding, treatment for this problem requires practice in situations that provoke acquiring and modifying acquiring beliefs. The goal is to increase tolerance for these urges. These practice exercises focus especially on cues that trigger strong urges to shop or pick up free things so clients can effectively resist these urges.

Objective 1: Check-in

- Distribute and review the Group Session Form.
- Identify one new advantage or disadvantage of acquiring and not acquiring from Advantages and Disadvantages Worksheet (Acquiring; *Workbook*, Chapter 5, p. 53)

Objective 2: Functional Analysis of Hoarding Behavior

You can help clients understand their behavior by developing models of the functional relationships between triggering situations, thoughts, feelings, and behaviors. This is especially useful to help clients understand what just happened; also, they can be used to develop treatment strategies. Because this is especially helpful for acquiring problems, we describe and illustrate this functional analysis model using acquiring as the target behavior. Start with information from the general conceptual model, and tie this to a recent situation the client recalls vividly.

Case Vignette

CARL: On the way home from work last week, I stopped at the music store and bought two new amplifiers that were such a good deal. Later that night I was really frustrated with myself. I spent money that I really don't have.

CLINICIAN: Had you planned to stop at the store?

CARL: No. I had a really bad day at work and I knew that stopping there on the way home would make me feel better.

CLINICIAN: So, it sounds like your bad day at work was a trigger for stopping at the store.

CARL: Yes, I mean music relaxes me. I was so stressed out. Nothing went right when setting up for the show, and a lot of the guys who were supposed to be there to help me set up didn't show up. The manager at the place was yelling at me.

JENNIFER: That sounds terrible. How were you feeling?

CARL: Just frustrated. You know, pissed off.
[*The immediate triggers for buying episodes for most clients are varied. Often they involve the sight of a "Sale" sign in a favorite store window, a newspaper or TV ad, a picture of a product, or seeing other people buying something. The list is endless. Once the trigger is identified, ask about the precursors.*]

CLINICIAN: The frustration due to what happened at work seemed to trigger your shopping trip.

GRACE: Shopping is definitely like an anti-depressant for me. Especially if I get a get a good discount with a coupon. It makes me so happy to see my pets playing with the toys I get them.

CARL: I sometimes get online and buy stuff when I am upset.

CLINICIAN: Do you also tend to buy things when you are in an especially good mood?

CARL: Probably less. It depends. But, I tend to buy things when I am alone, and when I am in a good mood I like to be around people.

[*Now a pattern begins to emerge. Clients frequently acquire when they are in a highly emotional state—in this client's case the emotion was generally negative. From here we move on to the thoughts and beliefs about the buying and the immediate consequences.*]

CLINICIAN: So, tell us what happened when you entered the store.

CARL: I know that store so well, and it was Thursday night, when they stay open later. So, I had time to talk to one of the guys and find out about the new equipment that just came in. He showed me a couple of new amplifiers that they'd just brought off the truck.

CLINICIAN: Do you remember what thoughts went through your mind when you saw them?

CARL: Yeah, I thought to myself, "These are awesome. They have the latest technology and the quality is amazing. They are so reasonably priced!" I couldn't believe it. I just couldn't pass it up.

CLINICIAN: Then what happened?

CARL: Well, I told the guy, I think his name is Stuart, I said, "Stuart, don't even set up the display. I'm taking them home."

JENNIFER: You look so happy.

CARL: I felt like my luck had turned. I mean an hour earlier, I was having the worst day. I felt really good when I bought them.

CLINICIAN: So this was kind of a "high" for you.

CARL: Yeah, for sure.

These types of acquiring thoughts are outlined in a general way in Figure 5.1 (see Chapter 5, Session 2). For this client, the thoughts had to do with opportunity and validation. Other common thoughts associated with acquiring include control, uniqueness, availability, low cost, and so forth. People who hoard often work hard to control their acquiring, but strong emotions and beliefs allow free rein to the impulse to acquire. The immediate consequences of acquiring are usually a positive mood and even a sense of euphoria. After identifying these immediate reactions, continue and ask about the long-term consequences.

CLINICIAN: Were you still feeling good when you arrived home?

CARL: Well, things changed when I got home. My partner Michael was in town. And he looked at the stuff I bought and walked away from me. I started to regret buying them. Here I am trying to save money so we could visit each other more often, and I go and blow hundreds on two amplifiers that I really don't need.

CHARLIE: But they made you happy, and they were the latest technology.

CARL: Yeah, but I felt like such a loser.

SALLY: Carl, I know what you mean about the regret. It's so painful.
[*At this point, summarize what you and the client have learned about the episode, and review the sequence of events. From a group process perspective, notice the mutual aid that occurs as Sally empathizes with Carl.*]

CLINICIAN: Let's keep going, okay? Let's see if we can review what we just discussed to help us understand what happened. So, you left work feeling frustrated and pissed off. On your way home you passed the music store and thought to yourself, "I am so stressed out and need to relax. Music will make me feel better." Then you saw two amplifiers and made the decision to buy them. This felt really good, but, as soon as you got home, you felt guilty when Michael questioned your purchases. You not only felt bad about the money you spent, you also felt bad about yourself as a person. Do I have that right?

CARL: Yes, that sounds right.

CLINICIAN: You have mentioned that when you are experiencing intense negative emotions you are more likely to make expensive purchases.

CARL: I think it's also when I am beat. When I am upset and tired, that's the worst combination because I don't hold myself back and I'm looking for a quick way to feel better. But then I feel worse afterwards—a lot of guilt and regret.

CLINICIAN: So, let's draw out this situation. At the top are your negative emotions "angry, pissed off, tired." Then you saw the music shop, which was a trigger for you. Next came the thoughts that you needed to relax and feel better. These thoughts took over, drowned out your rational thoughts about not having extra money to spend, and led you to buy the amplifiers. Does this sound accurate?

CARL: Yes.

CLINICIAN: So, immediately after the purchase, you felt good. You thought about how it was the latest technology and you couldn't wait to use them. But as you return home, your pleasure turns to guilt when you see Michael. This triggers thoughts about not being able to afford the equipment and the need to save money so that you and he can visit each other. How does the conflict with Michael affect your mood and acquiring behavior?

CARL: It makes me feel awful and guilty, which sometimes triggers more buying. I mean not really expensive stuff. But, getting online and buying trains and stuff also relaxes me. I tend to get online after our fights, which of course just makes things worse with him.

CLINICIAN: Sounds like you get into vicious cycles.

SALLY: Wow, this sounds exactly like me. "Shopping therapy," right?

Figure 9.1 displays this functional analysis model sketched out during the therapy session. You can point out places in the model where the behavior is positively reinforced (by immediate pleasure and excitement) and negatively reinforced (by relief from frustration and anger). Also be sure to highlight how this process actually increases

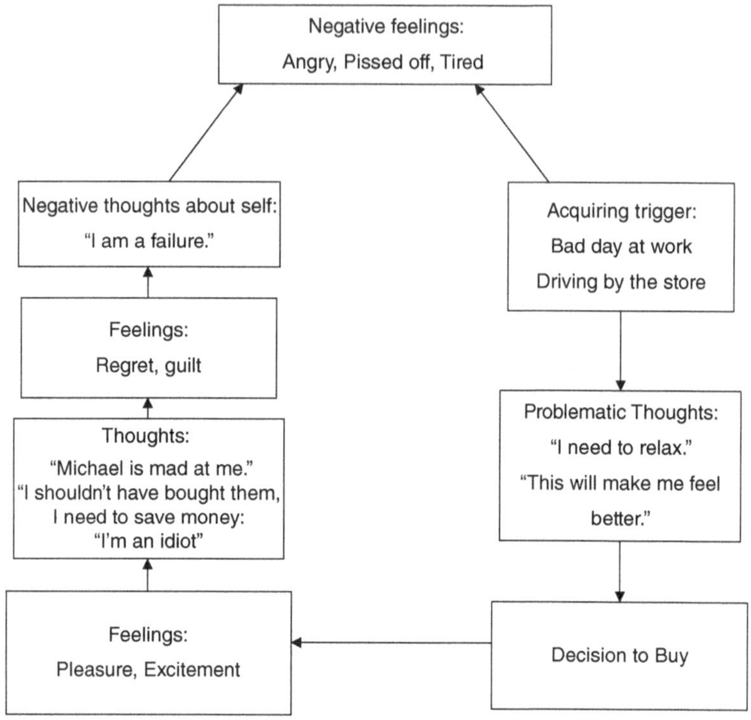

Figure 9.1
Functional Analysis of an Acquiring Episode

the likelihood of the episode happening again. Once you've laid out the functional analysis, ask the client about events and thoughts that typically lead to decisions to buy. Ask whether they can think of any alternative ways of coping with the emotions that triggered the episode. This is important, as avoiding the triggering stimuli (e.g., avoiding specific stores or not using the Internet) can help in the short term, but eventually clients will need to find other ways to manage their strong emotions.

Objective 3: Questions and Rules for Acquiring

Questions for Acquiring

One thing we have noticed about acquiring episodes in clients with hoarding disorder is that their focus of attention can narrow so much that they are not aware of what they are doing when they acquire. They focus so exclusively on the desired item and its attractive features that they don't think about the fact that they don't have the money, room, or need for the item, or that they already have a dozen similar items. A very simple yet effective strategy is to ask clients to generate a set of questions they consider reasonable to ask themselves before acquiring something (see the Acquiring Questions Form in Chapter 5, p. 51, and the Appendix of the *Workbook*). We ask them to fill out this form and carry it with them wherever they go so they can pull it out when faced with an acquiring situation. If, after answering the questions, they still want to acquire the object, they are free to do so. This procedure brings the broader picture of the acquiring process into play to reduce impulsive acquiring.

Several common acquiring questions from the form are listed below; encourage clients to use questions from this list and others they find helpful.

- Does it fit with my own personal values and needs?
- Do I already own something similar?
- Am I only buying this because I feel bad (angry, depressed, etc.) right now?
- In a week, will I regret getting this?
- Could I manage without it?
- If it needs fixing, do I have enough time to do this, or is my time better spent on other activities?
- Will I actually use this item in the near future?
- Do I have a specific place to put this?
- Is this truly valuable or useful, or does it just seem so because I'm looking at it now?
- Is it good quality (accurate, reliable, attractive)?
- Will *not* getting this help me solve my hoarding problem?

Establish Rules for Acquiring

Once clients agree they need to acquire fewer things, help them establish rules to accomplish this goal, especially for items or activities (e.g., going to tag sales) that contribute heavily to the problem. For example, clients might decide not to acquire unless they:

- Plan to use the item in the next month.
- Have sufficient money (not credit) to pay for the item.
- Have an uncluttered place to put the item.

Some rules may be temporary. For example, clients could eliminate all magazine and newspaper subscriptions for the short term and place a limit on how many of these they will purchase until the clutter is reduced below a certain level. The advantage of this strategy is that it feels less upsetting for the client while also giving them practice in curtailing acquiring.

Some people with acquiring problems can get into a cycle of buying items with the intention of returning them.

Case Vignette

CLINICIAN: Maria, you mentioned during check-in that you have this pattern of continuously buying with the intention of returning items.

MARIA: I do that. I go to the store and buy a bunch of stuff, and I do plan to return them. I save the receipts. In fact, the items typically stay in the bag. I might look at them. It's exciting to buy things and when I return them it feels great, too. But looking at the pile of bags that sits in my dining room makes me feel terrible. Plus, I really can't afford to do this. I need to return the items for the money.

Grace:	I buy things all the time for the dogs that I really think I will use, but then I can never find them. When I do find them, the time limit for returning has passed.
Clinician:	What type of acquiring rules might be helpful here?
Jennifer:	I always carry a list of items that I am going to purchase before I go to the store so that I don't buy "impulse purchases." And, can I just say that I hate those items around the cashier—the hand sanitizers, ChapStick, magazines, candy, tissues. I always feel like I need them.
Clinician:	Anyone else have a strategy that works for them?
Liz:	Because of all my debt, I cut up my credit cards, so that has worked for me. I don't really buy much. But I still acquire containers from the recycling bins near my building.
Clinician:	Maria, let's consider what rules you could set for yourself with regard to buying and returning things.
Maria:	Well, I mean I probably shouldn't buy things unless I plan to use them.
Clinician:	Is that a reasonable rule for you?
Maria:	I am not sure I could do that.
Sally:	Maybe you could make a rule for yourself that you could only buy something after returning three other items.
Maria:	I probably need to practice just returning items without actually looking at anything new.
Clinician:	Do you think you could commit to that?
Maria:	I am going to try that this week. I'll let you know how it goes.
Clinician:	How difficult do you think it would be to do this?
Maria:	Maybe I should try returning items to one of the stores that is less tempting for me. I have one in mind.

SALLY: That's a good idea. Do you think you need someone to go with you?

MARIA: No, I think I can do this. Knowing I have to report to all of you helps.

Observe the mutual aid and support that is occurring in this case vignette. Try to ensure that all members have equal time to share their thoughts and draw out the quiet members.

Objective 4: Alternative Sources of Enjoyment and Coping

In Session 5, clients visualized one or more of their most common acquiring situations to clarify what provokes and reinforces their acquiring. Because acquiring is accompanied by pleasurable feelings, helping clients resist their urges will also require finding alternative sources of enjoyment. This is like helping people with alcohol problems find other places, activities, and companions besides going to the local bar to join their drinking buddies. Similarly, because acquiring sometimes serves as a coping or mood-regulation strategy, alternative methods of dealing with unpleasant emotions must be sought. Be sure to spend sufficient time identifying equally enjoyable and fulfilling replacements for the pleasure and distress-relief associated with acquiring. Failing to do so is an invitation for failure and relapse.

Ask clients to brainstorm a short list of likely alternative activities, especially those that can be done spontaneously, alone or in the company of friends, and inside and out of the home. (See below for suggestions.) This activity creates an opportunity for increased support and socializing. Try to ensure that all members have equal time to share their thoughts about this, drawing out the quiet members.

List of Pleasurable Alternative Activities

- Take a walk or a hike.
- Dance to music.
- Do yoga.

- Read a book or a magazine.
- Feed birds in a park.
- Cook a meal.
- Draw, sketch, or paint a picture.
- Play with your pet.
- Paint your nails.
- Do some gardening or plant a flower.
- Soak in the bathtub.
- Watch a movie at home or at a theater.

Then ask group members how pleasurable they expect each activity to be, using a 0 (none) to 10 (maximum) scale. Select two or three activities that seem most feasible, enjoyable, and consistent with personal goals and interests, and assign these as homework during the coming weeks. Discuss when they will engage in these activities, and ask them to keep a record of how much enjoyment (0–10) they expected to experience beforehand and how much they actually experienced during the activity. Often there is a discrepancy, with lower expectations of enjoyment than actually occurs. This is an example of a behavioral experiment, as it enables clients to test whether non-acquiring activities can actually provide enjoyable alternatives to acquiring (see Chapter 12, Session 9, for discussion of behavioral experiments).

Equally important is providing clients with alternate ways to relieve distress or low mood. Some of the activities listed above may serve this function, and others can be generated and tested to determine how well they work to reduce negative moods.

Objective 5: Home Commitment

- Carry Acquiring Questions Form during outings.
- Work on a Functional Analysis (Figure 3.2 in Chapter 3 of the *Workbook,* p. 39) after an incident of acquiring or inability to

discard, to capture the sequence of triggering events, thoughts, feelings, and actions.

- Plan enjoyable activities as alternatives to acquiring during the week, and record the expected and actual degree of pleasure experienced.

Objective 6: Clinician Forms

- Clinician directs the clients to write their home commitment on the Group Session Form (see Appendix 12) and completes the Clinician's Group Progress Notes (see Appendix 15).

Chapter 10 *Session 7: Exposure Practice for Non-Acquisition*

(Portions of this session correspond to Chapter 5 of the Workbook)

Materials Needed

- Habituation Graph of Acquiring (*Workbook* Chapter 5, Figure 5.1, p. 54)
- Practice Exposure Hierarchy for Non-acquiring Form (*Workbook* Chapter 5, p. 55)
- Acquiring Questions Form (*Workbook* Chapter 5, p. 51)
- Questions About Possessions Form (*Workbook* Chapter 7, p. 80)

Session Agenda

- Discuss the role of avoidance in acquiring and discarding.
- Discuss rationale for non-acquisition exposure practice exercises.
- Describe habituation.
- Work with the clients to develop a practice hierarchy for non-acquisition.
- Discuss plans for non-acquisition practice.

Objective 1: Check-in

- Distribute and review the Group Session Form.

- Each client summarizes a functional analysis of an acquiring episode or identifies the pleasurable activity that they participated in and the actual degree of pleasure experienced.

Objective 2: Understanding Avoidance in Acquiring and Discarding

Because this session will focus on exposures to non-acquiring and be followed next week by exposures to discarding, it is important to help group members understand the role of avoidance behavior in acquiring and discarding. Begin by noting that people with hoarding problems often acquire to avoid the distress associated with the idea of missing out on important opportunities (e.g., a sale, a special item) and the pleasure associated with the process. As described in the general conceptual hoarding model in Session 2, acquiring behavior is positively reinforced by the immediate enjoyment of acquiring the item and negatively reinforced by the relief from unpleasant emotions such as sadness, guilt, anger, or fear.

Despite their intense attachment to possessions, most people with hoarding disorder spend little or no time *using* the things they acquire and save. In fact, they spend less time with their possessions than most people do. Decisions to save appear to be based on relatively brief initial interactions with possessions (acquisition, bringing them home), which then go onto a pile of disorganized objects, often remaining there for years. After that, consideration of these possessions (i.e., decision-making) tends to be brief or avoided all together, so most people save the item without further deliberation. This avoidance behavior is designed to escape unpleasant emotions that occur when contemplating discarding possessions. The strategies in the next few sessions are designed to reduce avoidance behavior and increase the amount of time clients spend processing information and making decisions about possessions.

Ask clients to review the General Conceptual Hoarding Model to remind them of what they avoid and to show how such avoidance maintains their fears and their clutter. For example, keeping items in a disorganized way helps them avoid distress about making decisions that might be wrong (mistakes), worries about memory and about losing an opportunity or information, feelings of loss and vulnerability, and embarrassment about clutter and inviting people home. (Of course, some forms of avoidance are actually adaptive. For example, not allowing anyone into the home protects clients from ridicule, scrutiny from authorities, or eviction.) Indicate that clients' strong negative reactions to not acquiring or getting rid of possessions trigger strong urges to avoid these feelings, fitting the pattern of most anxiety problems. Unfortunately, the more people avoid facing their fears, the more entrenched their discomfort becomes, so that emotions, rather than rational thinking, soon control what they acquire, keep, and discard. Suggest that today's session will help reduce avoidance that leads to excessive acquiring.

Objective 3: Describe Non-Acquisition Practice Exercises

Indicate to group members that treating acquiring problems requires practice in situations that expose clients to their urges to acquire. Repeated practice without acquiring helps clients learn to tolerate discomfort about not getting desired items and facilitates changes in the meanings associated with this (e.g., making mistakes, not having extras in case of need, etc.). Non-acquiring practices will be arranged hierarchically, beginning with easier experiences and progressing to more difficult ones. Usually, this means increasing their proximity to favorite acquiring locations and items.

You can show the graph below (Figure 10.1) to encourage clients to face their discomfort about not acquiring things they want. This figure reflects the reduction in urges to acquire and in discomfort on a scale from 0 (none) to 100 (maximum) for a group of eight people with hoarding and acquiring disorder who volunteered to participate in small groups in a non-shopping practice session with a clinician after one of our workshops. These individuals noticed substantial reductions in discomfort within a few minutes after leaving the store where they resisted buying something they typically would have acquired. Approximately 20 to 30 minutes later when leaving the mall, their urges to acquire and discomfort were only mild to moderate—a 50% reduction in intensity. Many were surprised by how rapidly their discomfort declined. Remember to use Motivational Interviewing techniques from Session 3 when group members have difficulty resisting their urges to acquire.

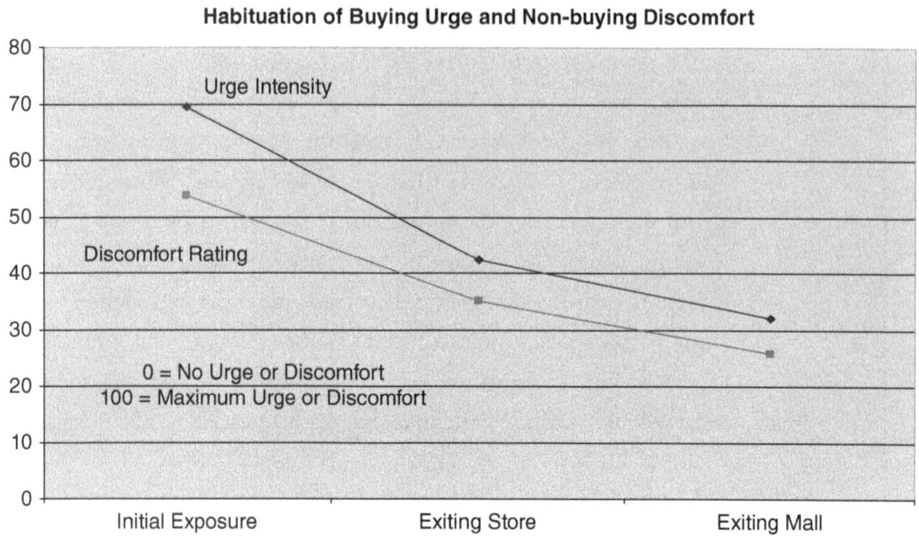

Figure 10.1

Reduction in Urges to Acquire and Discomfort Ratings for 8 People with Acquiring Problems During a Non-shopping Exercise at an International OCD Foundation Workshop.

Objective 4: Developing a Practice Hierarchy for Non-Acquisition

Clients who acquire possessions through store purchases can begin their practice with what we call "drive-by non-shopping," followed by walking through shops without touching things, and then handling objects without buying anything. Clients should select their hierarchy situations based on information from the Session 5 Acquiring Form (*Workbook*, Chapter 3, p. 38) and from the Acquiring Visualization Task (*Workbook*, Chapter 4, p. 46). After developing a list of possible practice situations with clients, help them order the items from "least" to "most distressing," or you can assign this as homework. An example of a practice hierarchy for Sally is given in Table 10.1.

Case Vignette

We recommended guiding the initial hierarchy development during the group session to illustrate with one or two members how to do this. Acquisition hierarchies should include all of the contexts in which members acquire, including Internet shopping. Developing hierarchies

Table 10.1 Example of a Practice Hierarchy for Sally

Situation	Discomfort (0–10)
1. Driving past a consignment shop in which I've bought things	1
2. Standing outside a discount shop with a good sale	2
3. Standing near a consignment shop in which I've bought things	3
4. Walking around at a discount shop without buying anything	4
5. Walking into my favorite consignment shop and not buying anything	5
6. Walking into my favorite consignment shop with a sale and not buying anything	6
7. Seeing accessories at a good price at the discount shop and not buying them	7
8. Returning a clothing or accessory item I spent too much money on	8
9. Finding a purse that I like on sale at my favorite consignment shop	8
10. Trying on sale clothing and accessories in my favorite consignment shop and not buying anything	9
11. Finding a purse in the color and style I've wanted for a long time at a terrific price and not buying it	10

in the group setting also creates an opportunity for nurturing therapeutic processes such as universality, cohesion, and mutual aid. Below, you will see that group members help problem-solve, empathize, and report similar feelings, helping others feel less alone with their problem.

CLINICIAN: Let's start working on our hierarchies. For this work, let's use ratings from 0 to 10 to indicate how hard it would be for you not to acquire in that situation. Who will start?

CARL:	Well, as I said during check-in, I just bought eight more trains this week that were such a good deal. I couldn't pass it up. But I know I need to stop doing this.
CLINICIAN:	Carl, thanks for volunteering. Could you remind us where you acquired these trains?
CARL:	I find most of the best deals online—like Craig's List and places like that. It's amazing what people give away.
CLINICIAN:	Ok, let's create practice steps of not acquiring the trains.
CARL:	I can't pass up buying any trains.
CLINICIAN:	Well, let's test this hypothesis while building our hierarchy. Let's figure out which situations create the least distress and the most distress. In what situations is it easier to not acquire trains? For example, when the computer is off or the Internet is not working, what would be your level of discomfort about not acquiring?
CARL:	Generally, if it's off, I'm busy with other things, so that would be a "1." And if the Internet is not working, I would be frustrated, but there's nothing I could do.
CHARLIE:	Well, you could go to the library.
CLINICIAN:	Continuing with our hierarchy, what would be the most difficult scenario for you to tolerate in not acquiring a train?
CARL:	[*Chuckling*] Well, if the train was part of a limited edition, and it was a great deal, I couldn't pass that up. That would be a 10.
CLINICIAN:	Let's everyone take a moment and consider what would be your least distressing and most distressing scenarios for your own hierarchy.
LIZ:	Passing by the dumpster down my block—it's magnetic. I just can't walk by without finding something. There was this lampshade yesterday that was so beautiful, an antique.

CLINICIAN: So walking by the dumpster and spotting something beautiful, would you rate that as a 10?

LIZ: A 10 would be finding nice furniture or decorative items for my home. Beautiful free stuff is so hard for me to resist.

CLINICIAN: Good. What would be a 1?

LIZ: On Tuesdays after the dumpster has been emptied, it's usually no big deal to walk by.

CLINICIAN: So, let's all consider what is between the 1 and the 10. Returning to you, Carl, what comes to mind between your 1 and 10?

CARL: I don't really know. It's just really hard.

CLINICIAN: You mentioned that you work on the computer and need to use word processing software for work. If you are working on a document on the computer and the Internet browser is not open, what would be your distress level?

CARL: Then it's a 4. But I usually open it.

CLINICIAN: Ok, do you use the Internet for anything else besides acquiring trains?

CARL: Yes. I read the paper.

CLINICIAN: What is you distress level then?

CARL: Then it's a 5.

CLINICIAN: Let's move ahead to Craig's List. If you are on the Craig List's site and search for trains and observe that there are postings (without clicking on them, reading through them, and viewing pictures), what would your distress level be?

CARL: If I couldn't open the posts, just looking at lists of posting headers for trains, I would be pretty stressed. My rating would be a 6.

CLINICIAN: What if you clicked on a posting for your favorite train, read through it, looked at the photos, but didn't buy it?

CARL: Wow. That would be really hard. Probably an 8.

CLINICIAN: What if it was part of that limited edition you mentioned and was a great deal, but you didn't buy it?

CARL: That would be really difficult. I don't think I could stop myself from buying it. That would be a 10.

Carl's hierarchy for exposure practices after further discussion in the group is given in Table 10.2.

Objective 5: Planning Non-Acquisition Practice

Once the hierarchy is developed, help members decide which exercises they can do alone and which ones should wait until they have support from a coach or a clinician because the urge to acquire may be too difficult to resist. For example, driving by and standing outside shops may be relatively easy for group members to accomplish alone, but going into shops is likely to be harder. In Session 15, the entire group will have the opportunity to practice non-acquisition exposures with the group leaders, as they learn to use coping skills that are taught in Sessions 4, 8, and 12 (e.g., using acquiring questions, advantages/disadvantages). We recommend covering the coping skills, coaching practice, and fostering sufficient group cohesion prior to the group non-acquisition trip and before encouraging group members to practice in pairs outside of group.

In the meantime, if group members want to arrange a non-shopping trip with a partner, they need to identify a coach (see Session 14) who can be a willing and helpful family member or friend. Whether you speak to the helper first to agree on the task and a plan for exposure practice depends on your confidence that the client can explain the task accurately and the client's confidence in the helper's ability to follow the instructions. When in doubt about either of these, arrange to speak to the task partner and the client together in person or by phone.

Table 10.2 Example of a Practice Hierarchy for Carl

Situation	Discomfort (0–10)
1. Walking by the computer when it is off	1
2. Walking by the computer when it is on	2
3. Being on the computer with no Internet access	3
4. Being on the computer with Internet access with browser closed, working on a Word document	4
5. Being on computer with Internet access and using the Internet for reading the newspaper	5
6. Being on Craig's List (or like site) and not looking at train stuff	6
7. Being on Craig's List (or like site) and observing train sale postings (but not clicking on them to open them up)	6
8. Being on Craig's List (or like site), clicking on and reading through train postings	7
9. Being on Craig's List (or like site) and reading through a posting for my favorite types of trains	7
10. Being on Craig's List (or like site) and finding my favorite train and not buying it	8
11. Being on Craig's List (or like site) and finding my favorite train at a really great deal and not buying it	9
12. Being on Craig's List (or like site) and finding the limited edition trains that I have been hoping to find at a great price	10

When members undertake a step on their hierarchy, ask them to record their discomfort level about every 10 minutes, or whenever they notice a change. This can be done on a small card carried by the client or task partner. Work out how long to remain in the setting, depending on how quickly discomfort abates. The goal is to have clients experience a noticeable reduction in their discomfort and their urges to acquire items while still in the shop. However, this may not be possible early on, when visual cues provoke strong urges that clients can resist only because of the presence of the accompanying partner. Urges will decline with increasing practice in not acquiring despite cues and in the use of coping strategies for managing discomfort. Effective coping skills may include the advantages/disadvantages (Session 4), acquiring questions and alternative sources of enjoyment and coping (Session 6), questions about possessions (Session 8), and other cognitive strategies (Session 12). Ask clients to record not only the level of discomfort during practice, but also their coping methods, in order to discuss how well these worked.

Note that clients who have serious acquisition problems will need to practice non-acquiring hierarchy steps throughout treatment until they can easily resist acquiring in all problematic situations. This can become part of their home commitment plan for most weeks.

Identifying a Site for Group Non-Acquisition Exposure in Session 15

The site for the group non-acquisition trip for Session 15 will need to be determined in advance. Choose a location and meeting spot that is accessible for everyone in the group (i.e., via public transportation, accessible for those with physical disabilities). Ideally, the location will be as private as possible (e.g., a private room in a bookstore; a shop where the owner agrees to be open only to the group); otherwise, you can meet at a local coffee shop or nearby park before entering acquiring locations in the area. The site should have a sufficient variety of items (e.g., food, clothing, office supplies, books, newspapers) so all group members can identify items of moderate difficulty (4 or 5) on their hierarchies.

Propose a few locations to the group as possible non-acquisition sites. During the discussion, it is common for group members to request different locations, and disagreement and conflict can erupt. View conflict as an opportunity for growth within the group and address it by talking about the disagreement, supporting each member's opportunity to have a say, and pointing out areas of agreement (e.g., easy access, parking, sale items). This will help move the discussion toward a plan that offers an opportunity for everyone to practice not acquiring.

Objective 6: Home Commitment

- Practice a non-acquisition exercise that is lower on the hierarchy and that the client is confident that they could do on their own (e.g., client drives by or stands outside store).
- Use selected thinking strategies (advantages/disadvantages, Acquiring Questions, Questions About Possessions) when considering acquiring an item.
- Bring a possession to Session 8 for thought-listing exercise.

Objective 7: Clinician Forms

- Clinician directs the clients to write their home commitment on the Group Session Form (see Appendix 12) and completes the Clinician's Group Progress Notes (see Appendix 15).

Chapter 11 *Session 8: Decisions about Saving and Discarding*

(Corresponds to Chapter 7 of the Workbook)

Materials Needed

- Habituation Graph (*Workbook* Chapter 7, p. 77)
- Thought Listing Exercise Form (*Workbook* Chapter 7, p. 78, Appendix 27)
- Questions About Possessions List (*Workbook* Chapter 7, p. 80)
- My Rules for Saving Form (*Workbook* Chapter 7, p. 81)

Session Agenda

- Review the process of habituation.
- Conduct a Thought Listing Exercise.
- Develop a Thought Listing Exercise hierarchy.
- Help clients develop Questions About Possessions and My Rules for Saving.
- Briefly discuss types of items to bring to the next session for sorting.

The next few sessions will guide treatment for the discarding portion of the intervention. The exercises in Sessions 8–11 are aimed at facilitating discarding decisions, while cognitive therapy (CT) methods described in Session 12 will help clients evaluate problematic thoughts and beliefs about possessions that interfere with discarding. Remember to use Motivational Interviewing techniques from Session 3 when clients hit emotional roadblocks that impair their resolve.

Objective 1: Check-in

- Distribute and review the Group Session Form.
- Briefly discuss whether group members practiced non-acquisition and used a specific strategy (e.g., Advantages/Disadvantages, Questions About Possessions) when considering whether to acquire an item during the past week
- Report what possession they brought in for today's Thought Listing exercise. Make sure this item seems appropriate for the Thought Listing exercise below.

Objective 2: Introduce Thought Listing (TL) Exercise and Discuss Habituation

A recent study by Frost, Steketee, Tolin, and colleagues showed that simply asking people with hoarding disorder to spend a few minutes talking about a possession enabled many of them to discard the item; in fact, they did so at about the same rate as people without hoarding problems. Furthermore, their emotional distress about discarding decreased over the course of the 30-minute exercise. The Thought Listing exercise also led to a decrease in emotional attachment to the object, beliefs about its usefulness, and judgments of its attractiveness. This exercise worked as well as, if not better than, attempts by a therapist to use cognitive restructuring. We therefore recommend the Thought Listing exercise described below as a good starting point for practicing discarding decisions. The purpose of this exercise is fourfold:

- to help clarify the nature of attachment[s] to a possession
- to increase the amount of time spent thinking about the value of possessions
- to increase exposure to discarding and to reduce avoidance
- to provide a mechanism for practicing sorting and organizing

Explain to the group that in a few minutes you will be asking them to engage in a Thought Listing exercise with regard to the possession they brought in today. This will help them better understand how they think and feel about this object. This exercise will help prepare them to make decisions here in the group and at home about whether to keep or not keep items they are sorting.

Next, remind group members of the process of habituation described in the previous session (Session 7) on practicing non-acquiring. The Habituation Graph (Figure 11.1) below illustrates the gradual drop in discomfort experienced by a client during exposure.

Describe it this way:

> *When we are uncomfortable in a situation in which there is no actual danger (for example, encountering a friendly dog), our discomfort declines over time as a natural process—we habituate. This is what happens to people who live near a train track or a subway line. When they first move in, they hear the noise whenever it occurs, and it keeps them awake at night. But soon, they barely notice the sounds and sleep through it easily. The same process of habituation happens when we are exposed to situations that make us anxious. Initially, we are very uncomfortable, but with time we become used to it, and it no longer disturbs us. For example, children with dog phobias can overcome their fears through gradual exposure to dogs of increasing scariness, starting with puppies, then little dogs, and eventually larger dogs, and even barking dogs. Fearful children are initially uncomfortable, but this discomfort gradually declines until eventually they can pet and play with the dog without discomfort. Let me illustrate what happens on a graph.*

Indicate that not everyone follows exactly the same pattern. Some people habituate slowly, others quickly, and others have up and down reactions that are gradually reduced over time. Remind clients that discomfort is not something they can control or talk themselves out of. It is a physiological process that requires repetition to be reduced. Emphasize that the experience of some discomfort is necessary for habituation to occur, and that this is part of the process of learning how to control their hoarding problem.

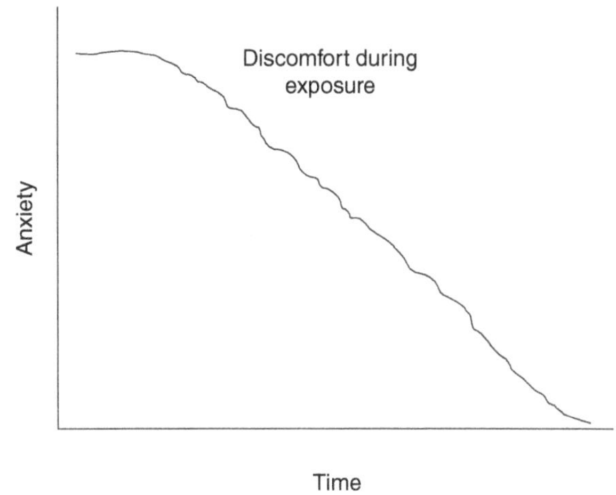

Figure 11.1
Habituation Graph

Objective 3: Conduct Thought Listing Exercise

This simple exercise can have a big impact on how clients with hoarding disorder make decisions about discarding. It is a good one to do in two smaller groups, each with one of the co-leaders; it can also be done in the larger group, but that takes more time, as ideally all members should practice Thought Listing.

Ask clients to write down their stream-of-conscious thoughts associated with discarding an item they brought from home, for 4 to 5 minutes. Ask them not to filter out any of their thoughts, even if they feel embarrassed or uncomfortable about them. Remind them that there are no right or wrong answers and that the more honest and open they are about their thoughts and feelings, the more they can learn about this process. Ask clients to write down how much distress they expect to feel if they actually discard the object. Ask them to indicate where the item would fit on the hierarchy (e.g., at what level of distress), and after that, ask them to write down how long they think they the distress would last.

At the end of the five minutes, ask each person one at a time to make a decision about whether to keep or discard the item. Do not try to influence their decision. Decisions to save are as informative and valuable as decisions to discard. If the decision is to discard, ask the client to put the item directly into a trash or recycle bin. Now ask the client how much distress they feel at this moment. Go on to another member of the group, and repeat the process. When each member has made a decision, go back to the first person and ask for a new rating of distress (about 10 minutes later) and note whether this has changed from the previous report. Repeat this question after about 30 minutes, so each group member can track the habituation process for themselves.

The *Workbook* contains a Thought Listing Exercise Form (Chapter 7, p. 78 and Appendix 27) which was designed to be completed individually by clients who are rating their distress every five minutes. As this is less feasible for a group context, we recommend using only three rating periods: initial, 10–15 minutes, and 30 minutes. An example of Sally's Thought Listing is given in Figure 11.2.

Between these ratings, use Motivational Interviewing strategies to help explore their ambivalence about discarding the possession. Be careful not to advocate for discarding, since you want clients to explore reasons

Initials Sally Date 6/15/13

Selected Item: tote bag

Anticipated Distress (from 0=none to 10=maximum): 7

Predicted Duration of Distress: two weeks

Thoughts about Discarding: I can't imagine getting rid of it. This tote is the perfect size and shape for everyday use. It is of great quality. It's an expensive brand but was a bargain. It's versatile, it matches everything. I never actually use it. I have others that are somewhat similar.

Discarding Decision: Discard

Distress after Decision: 8

Distress after 15 minutes: 5

Distress after 30 minutes: 3

Notes from Discussion: Initially I wouldn't consider discarding the tote. After thinking about it I realized that maybe it wasn't perfect after all because I never actually use it. Talking this out was helpful and I didn't feel pressured. My distress started to go away much sooner than I anticipated.

Figure 11.2

Example of Thought Listing Exercise Form

for saving as well as reasons for discarding. If the decision is to save the object, ask the client where they plan to put it (see Session 10 on Organizing). At the end of the 30 minutes, ask the client what they learned by the exercise—was it easier than they thought? Harder? Why?

Be sure to comment on habituation when this occurs for group members. Keep in mind that one of the goals of the exercise is to teach about attachments to possessions, so even if habituation did not occur, the exercise will have taught group members something about their attachment to this object. Also, the exercise will have provided a strategy to use in making decisions about possessions.

Objective 4: Developing a Thought Listing Exercise Hierarchy

Exposures using the Thought Listing Exercise are easiest to accomplish by helping clients develop a hierarchy of possessions that are increasingly difficult to discard. For example, papers with unidentified phone numbers may be easier to discard, whereas getting rid of newspapers is harder. Help clients create their own list of types of items and locations in the home, ranked from "easy" to "hard." This need not be a formal list, but it serves as a general plan for sorting, moving, and removing clutter as they work from easier to harder items. Remind clients that they will undoubtedly experience some discomfort, and the intention is to increase their tolerance gradually for making decisions and getting rid of items. To make progress on the clutter, clients must learn to tolerate some discomfort, because removing things that cause no discomfort will not help them manage their anxiety and learn new skills to prevent future hoarding. In Session 12, you will be introducing various cognitive therapy techniques to help them deal with beliefs that have been reinforcing hoarding problems.

Case Vignettes

CLINICIAN: Let us start by identifying the items that are the least and the most difficult to discard.

CARL: Well, I collect trains and tools.

CHARLIE: Tools are at the top of my list, too.

SALLY: The most difficult for me are clothes and accessories.

CLINICIAN: What are the least difficult?

MARIA: Magazines and mail are much easier for me.

JOSEPH: Well, trade magazines are at the top of my list... and I don't care about clothes.

CLINICIAN: What would be your rating for clothes, using a 0–10 scale?

JOSEPH: That's a 1.

CLINICIAN: What items are in between a 1 and 10? Picture a room in your home. What items do you see?

JOSEPH: Well, I have tools, electronics, office items, flashlights, luggage...

CLINICIAN: Good, so rate each of those you listed.

JENNIFER: Accessories are the hardest for me, but I don't understand. I have so many types of accessories—earrings, scarves, hats, umbrellas, purses. Do I write all of them at the top?

CLINICIAN: Would all accessories be rated the same?

JENNIFER: Not exactly the same, but all are at least an 8.

CLINICIAN: So if they are all generally an 8 or above, list accessories as an 8 for now. We will discuss item-based and category-based hierarchies in a few minutes.

JOSEPH: The trade magazines are hardest for me. Though I have piles of other magazines, they are not all that difficult for me.

CHARLIE: I have a lot of electronics. I suppose if I think about it, some of those electronics would be easier for me to let go of than others. Like the old broken printers I may consider letting go of, but not wireless routers.

CLINICIAN: Consider creating hierarchies for specific categories, such as magazines. These hierarchies will help you create your decision rules.

Example of Joseph's Hierarchy

Item	Distress
Clothes	1
Office supplies	2
Old toys	3
Tools and flashlights	4
Electronics	4
Luggage, bags	5
Books	6
Mail (financial documents, papers)	7
Photos	8
Children's' art projects	9
Trade magazines	10

Example of Joseph's Hierarchy for Magazines

Item	Distress
Catalogues	1
Sports Illustrated	2
National Geographic	4
Car and Driver	5
Consumer Reports	7
Time magazine	8
Trade magazines	10

Planning Sorting at Home

Discarding exercises in the home should mimic the work done at the group sessions. Assist clients in planning their sorting and discarding practice at home, particularly in deciding where to start. Help clients create their own list of types of items and also locations in the home (e.g., area next to the bed, versus stairwell), ordered from easier to harder ones. This need not be a formal list, but it serves as a general plan for structuring sorting exercises at home. Remind clients that they will undoubtedly experience some discomfort while they make these decisions, and the intention is to gradually increase their tolerance for making decisions and letting go of items. Indicate to clients that to make progress, they must learn to tolerate some discomfort, because discarding things that cause little or no discomfort will not help them reduce anxiety and learn new skills to prevent future hoarding.

Objective 5: Generating Questions About Possessions

After doing the Thought Listing exercise, ask group members to generate a list of questions they feel might help them speed up the process of making decisions about saving or discarding. Have them write the questions down on the Questions About Possessions Form from the *Workbook* (Chapter 7, p. 80). Be careful not to direct them too much in coming up with this list so they do not feel pressured and become defensive.

Objective 6: Establishing Rules

Guide clients in making decisions about saving and discarding by creating a set of general rules that remove the necessity of deliberating over each separate object. Based on their experience with the Thought Listing exercise, ask clients to start generating rules they believe will be useful in determining when to save and when to discard items, and record these on the Rules for Saving Form in the *Workbook* (Chapter 7, p. 81). For example, items not used in the past year and those with more than one copy could be discarded. Another example is to get rid of all items of clothing and jewelry that are not flattering.

Because recycling, selling, and giving away items is easier for many clients than discarding, it is wise to have rules for these categories as well, especially when clients overestimate what can be sold or recycled. Ask clients to obtain their community's recycling specifications and review them so they know what can be recycled and what cannot. If needed, these specifications can be discussed in the group to further members' understanding and compliance. In addition, develop general definitions or rules to guide members who want to sell or give away items. These rules will help members better understand what types of items are not acceptable for sale or as gifts, as well as to think about the cost in time and effort to clean up or repair something that cannot be sold as is. Cognitive therapy methods from Session 12 such as Socratic questioning and taking another perspective may help clients recognize what items would or would not qualify.

Objective 7: Preparing for In-Session Sorting Exercises

Have your group members to bring in boxes or bags of things from home, especially items that they think will be hard to make decisions about. One strategy is to sweep off the corner of a cluttered counter top or table into a box and bring it in without sorting through it. The point is to bring in a wide range of items, including items they do not intend to discard, as some clients may otherwise bring only items that are easy for them to discard. Remind clients that in-session sorting exercises will be helpful only if the items they select are challenging.

Objective 8: Home Commitment

- List items to be saved if the home would be demolished by a disaster soon.
- Take home items to be saved from the Thought Listing exercise and store them where they belong.
- Bring in a box or bag of items to group for sorting and decision-making exposures in the next session. Items may be collected from one area like the surface of a table or desk, or a

stack of things on the floor. Bring a wide range of items, including possessions that you do not intend to discard.

Objective 9: Clinician Forms

- Clinician directs the clients to write their home commitment on the Group Session Form (see Appendix 12) and completes the Clinician's Group Progress Notes (see Appendix 15).

Chapter 12 *Session 9: More on Decisions about Saving and Discarding*

(Corresponds to Chapter 7 of the Workbook)

Materials Needed

- Behavioral Experiment Form (*Workbook* Chapter 7, p. 83, Appendix 28)

Session Agenda

- Discuss challenges in bringing items for sorting.
- Review and practice behavioral experiments.
- Teach clients how to use a systematic strategy for problem-solving.

Objective 1: Check-in

- Distribute and review the Group Session Form.
- Clients report where they stored the item from the Thought Listing exercise (*Workbook* Chapter 7, p. 78, Appendix 27).
- A couple of clients note the top items that they would save if their home would be demolished by a disaster soon.
- Clients report what they brought in for sorting and decision-making (saving/discarding) exercise.

Objective 2: Discuss Challenges in Bringing Items for Sorting

Discuss with group members that clients with hoarding sometimes struggle to decide what to bring to session for sorting. Describe how clients may struggle at home, and link the decision of what to bring with the decision about keeping or discarding an item. If group members bring only items that they have already decided to discard, this interferes with the group experience of working through the decision-making process and practicing skills. The exchanges below illustrate this discussion. Emphasize throughout the session that the most efficient way to identify items to bring is to take a small box to a target area and put in a random assortment of items without looking through them.

Case Vignette

For this exercise, the group was divided into two smaller groups. This first subgroup included Charlie, Maria, Carl, and Grace:

Maria: It was tough to bring in items to sort. I brought in some of my late-husband's tools and hardware.

Grace: Good for you. How hard was that?

Clinician: How did you decide what to bring in today?

Maria: I felt pressure last night, knowing I had to bring something in for the group. I was not going to bring in his ties or clothing, or my art supplies. The tools seemed like a good choice. Besides, a few were already in this box, so it was convenient. I have been thinking of getting rid of them for a long time and just couldn't bring myself to do it. But I think I am ready now.

Charlie: So you already decided to get rid of them?

Maria: I guess so. It seemed wrong to just throw them in the trash. I just don't want to regret doing this. I feel queasy about it now that we are talking about it.

CLINICIAN: How about considering doing a behavioral experiment? Let's look at the form together.

[*This subgroup included Sally, Liz, Joseph, and Jennifer*]:

JENNIFER: It was my turn to bring things in today. I had a really difficult time deciding what to bring in. But then I thought of what you said about not making decisions about the items I am bringing in before coming to group.

JOSEPH: What did you bring in?

JENNIFER: I brought some of my silky scarves.

SALLY: Oh, those are really pretty.

JENNIFER: I know. I am feeling very anxious about having to make a decision about them.

CLINICIAN: How do you think you would feel if you decided to discard them?

JENNIFER: I am afraid that I will want them and feel upset and guilty for letting them go. I spend a lot of time searching for the perfect scarves that match my outfits. It may sound silly, but scarves make me feel like my outfits are complete. As you all know, I always wear them.

LIZ: You are so put together. They always look nice.

JENNIFER: Thank you. This is really hard. I am not sure I want to get rid of them.

CLINICIAN: This is your choice. Let's consider how keeping them fits with your goals.

JENNIFER: Well, it's true I do have a lot of them, and they are taking over my bureau and falling out onto my bedroom floor. I am not sure what's worse—feeling bad because I am getting rid of them, or bad because I am taking such poor care of them.

CLINICIAN: Well, let's take a look at your questions about possessions. Are any of them relevant to this decision?

JENNIFER: Let's see.... One question asks "how many do I already have?" It's really too many to count.

JOSEPH: How many scarves does one woman need?

LIZ: I never wear scarves. They don't look good on me, but they really do look well on you.

SALLY: I think we are making it harder for you. Do you think they are all equally beautiful?

JENNIFER: No. I definitely have my favorites. Like this one [*holding up a blue paisley scarf*] which I wore to a special dinner last year.

SALLY: It sounds like there are ones you favor more than others.

JENNIFER: I guess so.

CLINICIAN: Would you consider discarding some of the other scarves besides the blue paisley?

JENNIFER: It would be hard, but I could part with these three, but I want to keep the blue one and this orange one, too.

SALLY: You said the blue paisley one was your favorite, but are also keeping the orange one. Do you like the orange one equally?*

JENNIFER: Well, not equally. The blue one is a 6, and I guess the orange one is a 5. The other ones are more like a 3 on the hierarchy. I do like the blue one the most. But it's really hard to think of parting with the orange one, too. It's such a unique color. I don't think I would find one like it again. I am afraid that if I get rid of any of my scarves, then I won't stop thinking about them. What if I feel guilty and regret my decision?

CLINICIAN: Would you be willing to do a behavioral experiment and discard the three scarves that you described were a 3 on the hierarchy?

JENNIFER: Yes, I could do that.

*Here in this middle stage of group development, Sally tries out a mutual aid strategy in coaching Jennifer to use her own information to support CBT skills.

Objective 3: Review and Practice Behavioral Experiments

Describe a behavioral experiment as a more targeted version of the Thought Listing exercise in Session 8 with the added feature of testing a hypothesis or belief. When clients express reluctance to proceed because they fear intense anxiety will overwhelm them or are concerned they will be unable to perform some task, you can recommend a behavioral experiment to test their concern by framing it as a hypothesis. The testing of beliefs is often about the severity of clients' discomfort after removing or not acquiring an item. In the two vignettes above, the clinician suggests an experiment to test Maria's belief that she will regret getting rid of her husband's tools, and Jennifer's belief that she won't be able to stop thinking about the discarded scarves.

We suggest using the Behavioral Experiment Form from the *Workbook* (Chapter 7, p. 83 and Appendix 28) for each experiment. Clients first state the context and record in writing their hypothesis about what will happen, and then rate the strength of their belief and initial discomfort. After the experiment, clients record what actually happened and their actual discomfort. Then they state whether their prediction came true, their explanation for what happened, and their conclusion about whether their original belief and estimated discomfort were correct. Obviously, this experiment is intended for situations in which clinicians believe there is a high likelihood that clients will learn that dire predictions do not come to pass and that their beliefs are mistaken. Behavioral experiments can be used throughout the therapy to test and modify clients' thinking.

Figure 12.1 illustrates Maria's and Jennifer's completed Behavioral Experiment Forms.

Initials M

Date 4/12/13

1. Behavioral experiment to be completed: Getting rid of piles of my late husband's tools
2. What do you predict (are afraid) will happen? I will feel regret and won't be able to tolerate it. I will miss him more or feel like I am forgetting what a hard worker and great provider that he was.
3. How strongly do you believe this will happen? (0-100%) 80% feeling regret and missing him
4. Initial discomfort (0-10) 80%
5. What actually happened? I felt sad and thought a lot about the sacrifices that he made to provide for me, our children, and my sister's family too. I started to feel better a couple of days after I discarded the tools. I also realize that there are many more tools around the house.
6. Final discomfort (0-10) 30%
7. Did your predictions come true? No, they weren't as bad as I thought they would be.
8. What conclusions do you draw from this experiment? That I will miss him whether I hold onto all his belongings or not. I was petrified to even start sorting his things. I still have many items and memories to keep him close.

Initials J

Date 4/12/13

1. Behavioral experiment to be completed: Discarding silk scarves
2. What do you predict (are afraid) will happen? I will want a scarf that I discarded and won't be able to find the exact one again. I will feel guilty for letting it go.
3. How strongly do you believe this will happen? (0-100%) 85% will want it again; 75% guilt.
4. Initial discomfort (0-10) 80%
5. What actually happened? I thought about the scarves for a couple of days and then realized that I still have my favorite ones.
6. Final discomfort (0-10) 20%
7. Did your predictions come true? No, I didn't think about them as long as I had thought I would. I didn't feel the urge to replace them. I didn't feel as guilty as I thought I might for not choosing or saving some of them.
8. What conclusions do you draw from this experiment? I believe that I will miss things more than I actually do. Perhaps my scarves are less unique than I thought they were. Maybe I don't love all of them the same.

Figure 12.1

Example of a Completed Behavioral Experiment Form

Complications with Behavioral Experiments

Be aware that not all behavioral experiments will turn out as planned. Accordingly, indicate to the group that beliefs and behavior patterns in hoarding are notoriously rigid and resistant to change, and not everyone will benefit from each strategy tried. Behavioral experiments allow clients to "try on" new behaviors or beliefs without yet having to give up their old ones. Because these patterns are so persistent, clients sometimes alter behavioral experiments to avoid discomfort. For instance, a client may go shopping just before a non-shopping exposure is planned. One of our clients arranged for a friend to rescue an object she was supposed to discard as part of an experiment to test her beliefs about waste. Thus, as much as possible, clinicians should anticipate these complications and plan accordingly. When such events happen, they can be used as valuable learning experiences; for instance, by examining how much the fear of "wasting" something has control over the client's mood and behavior.

Gaining Distance

When the sight of a possession evokes strong emotions and memories that increase its perceived value, ask clients to distance themselves physically and temporally from the item and then see if they can part with it. This may be incorporated into a behavioral experiment. Suggest that clients give the item to a friend or to you to hold for one week or more if needed. At the end of the time period, ask clients to decide whether to keep or dispose of the item without seeing it again. The initial hypothesis is that the client will be unable to part with the object without careful scrutiny, and hopefully the final conclusion is that they find it easier to get rid of things that are not in sight, suggesting that the importance they attach to objects they are looking at is disproportionate to their actual value. It is important, however, to shape clients' behavior so they can eventually discard objects that are in sight.

Objective 4: Practice Problem-Solving Steps

As described in Chapter 5 most clients with hoarding problems exhibit information-processing deficits that interfere with their ability to engage in effective problem-solving. For example, they find it difficult to figure out how to move items around within the home, how to get unwanted items out of the house, and how to deal with everyday issues such as time management, paying bills on time, making and getting to appointments, and identifying people and organizations who can help with various needs.

Introduce the simple steps for problem solving outlined in Table 12.1 to group members so they can begin to think of some of the challenges that crop up during sorting and organizing efforts as "a problem to be solved" using a series of steps they can learn to apply systematically.

Case Vignette

JENNIFER: I have been really struggling with staying focused on sorting.

JOSEPH: I have that problem also. I always get distracted.

CLINICIAN: How about we use the problem-solving steps to think through this?

Table 12.1 Problem-Solving Steps

1. Define the problem and the contributing factors.
2. Generate as many solutions as possible (be as creative as you can before judging whether they would work).
3. Evaluate the solutions and select the one or two that seem most feasible.
4. Break the solution down into manageable steps.
5. Implement the steps.
6. Evaluate how well the solution worked.
7. If necessary, repeat the process until a good solution is found.

JENNIFER: That would be helpful. So, I see the steps. First, we need to define the problem. It's a problem with distraction. Then what?

JOSEPH: I have had ADD for most of my life.

CLINICIAN: So, the next step is to brainstorm all possible solutions for this problem. Let's all try to come up with suggestions for solving this problem. Have fun with this, and be as creative as possible. Your ideas can be silly, too. For example, you could glue your feet and shoes to the ground so you don't wander away. I will write all ideas on the board.

SALLY: Maybe you could use a timer when sorting. I tried that, and it was helpful.

MARIA: I use music to help me stay focused. I put on a CD and work until it is done.

JOSEPH: I like the idea of listening to music.

GRACE: I sort while I watch my favorite soap operas. It keeps me in front of the TV where I can sort.

CARL: I watch the news sometimes, but it doesn't always work for me. I sometimes spend more time watching and don't really sort.

JENNIFER: One therapist told me to tape off the area where I am sorting. I even hung up a sheet so that the other huge piles didn't distract me.

CLINICIAN: Great ideas—any others?

SALLY: It can be really helpful when someone is sitting with me. Just having someone there is a big help.

[*Several group members nod.*]

CHARLIE: Maybe I should put up a big sign that says "Stay!"

[*Leader encourages clients to brainstorm as many potential solutions as possible and adds a few silly ones to spark creativity.*]

Clinician:	So, here is our list [*see below for a more exhaustive list*]. It's time to determine which ideas are the most feasible ones for each of you.
Carl:	Well, like I said, watching the news isn't always helpful. I think a timer may be better for me.
Joseph:	I am not sure which one.
Maria:	Didn't you comment that the music idea may work for you?
Joseph:	Right—I guess I could try that.
Clinician:	Joseph, how likely are you to try that out this week?
Joseph:	Um...I would like to find my old Stones albums.
Clinician:	It sounds like that may need some additional preparation. What might be easier to do this week?
Joseph:	I have some CDs around, like Jimi Hendrix. I could listen to them.
Clinician:	So let's think this through. Do you know where the CDs are, and do you have a CD player that you could use that is readily accessible?
Joseph:	Actually, yes. The CDs are in my car, and I just pulled out my player for something else last week. So it's still on my kitchen counter.
Clinician:	Excellent! Everybody, please think through the steps for trying out one of the solutions that you brainstormed. Breaking down potential solutions into more manageable and practical steps will help you try this out. Each of you, please write down at the bottom of the Group Session Form, which solution you are going to try and any steps you need to do to accomplish this. Joseph, you stated you will bring your Hendrix CDs into your home first, and put them into your CD player so they are available when you sort. Next week, we will check in about how this went. Any questions?

Once a situation is identified as warranting problem-solving steps, begin by helping the client label the "problem to be solved" (e.g., the *distraction during sorting*) in order to short circuit self-blame and guilt and free clients to focus on new ideas. This statement defines the problem and the goal (e.g., *staying focused so I can get my sorting done).* Then, help clients identify the factors they think could be responsible for their distraction during sorting sessions. At this point, the leader encourages the group to come up with as many potential solutions as they can that address each contributing aspect, and adds a few silly ones to get the creative juices going. The silly ideas often help generate new thoughts that might not otherwise occur to clients. Be sure to add ideas clients haven't mentioned, and list all of them on the board. The list of ideas can eventually include both global and specific ones, as well as ridiculous and reasonable ones that address the sources of the problem (see Table 12.2). As illustrated in the dialogue above, clients should make a specific plan that becomes a home commitment. During next session's check-in, members report on the outcome of their plan (e.g., did listening to music improve Joseph's ability to stay focused and sort for a longer period of time?). If a client reports that the plan did not work, the

Table 12.2 Problem-Solving Example

***Problem*: Being distracted while sorting**
Possible solutions
1. Glue my shoes to the floor so I don't wander away.
2. Use a timer when sorting.
3. Listen to music.
4. Watch a favorite soap opera on TV.
5. Watch the news.
6. Tape off the area where I am sorting.
7. Hang up a sheet so that the other huge piles don't distract me.
8. Have someone [name] sit with me.
9. Use a Hula hoop to define the target area.
10. Make a game out of it (Boxes are like basketball baskets).
11. Hang a poster on the wall that says "Stay"!

group should help the client consider trying one of the other ideas that might work better. Needless to say, group members' support in joining the problem-solving efforts and the mutual expectation that everyone will work on this fosters mutual aid and the group process therapeutic factors.

Uses for Problem-Solving Method

The problem-solving approach described above can be used to deal with a variety of stressful life situations that come up during treatment. Below is a short list of the types of problems for which it is well suited:

- Being unable to make myself start the work on sorting
- Can't figure out how to move items around inside the home because there is no place to put them
- Haven't been able to get unwanted bags and boxes out of the house
- Running out of time to get tasks done
- Not paying bills on time
- Not making medical appointments when I need health care
- Don't know who to call to fix my plumbing
- Don't understand the legal notice I got in the mail, so I haven't done anything about it

Considering the Use of Extensive Cleanouts

Although cleanouts are a temporary solution for hoarding, we do not recommend a forced cleanout except in rare cases where it is essential for health and safety reasons. Forced cleanouts temporarily change the living situation, but not the problem behavior. Cooperation and motivation for seeking help will be seriously impaired after forced cleanouts, which are invariably traumatic. However, within the context of therapy, cleanouts for very severe clutter can be effective if they are timed and structured properly with the client's full cooperation.

In our experience, cleanouts work best when the volume of clutter is simply too large for clients to manage easily, and a substantial portion of the material is destined for the trash or recycling rather than for donation or sale. A well-timed and planned cleanout can result in rapid improvement that encourages clients' renewed efforts to sustain and increase the reduction in clutter. Clients must first have practiced discarding extensively so they can make decisions quickly and with relatively little discomfort, and have established written rules for what items to keep and what to remove. The timing and planning of cleanouts are crucial, as holding a cleanout before the client is ready can frustrate everyone involved and set back the course of treatment.

Typically, cleanouts are day-long affairs in which carefully chosen helpers (e.g., family, friends, clinic staff, neighbors, paid students) are enlisted and trained to help sort and remove clutter. These extended sessions expose clients to a variety of situations they typically avoid, such as allowing others into the home, letting others touch and make decisions about items (always following the basic rules established by the client), making decisions quickly, and, of course, discarding or removing a large number of items.

Cleanout sessions require advance planning to determine who will participate, establish the rules for discarding and keeping items, set ground rules for how volunteers will remove objects from the house, and determine the method of getting rid of unwanted items. Arrangements must be made to coordinate dumpster delivery and pick-up or other trash-hauling plans to ensure that discarded items are removed from the property on the same day to prevent clients from retrieving or searching through items again. Volunteers follow the client's rules for decision-making. When they encounter items for which the decision is unclear, workers bring these items to the client and clinician, who work together to make rapid decisions about those objects. As this process can be very challenging for clients, do not schedule it until the client feels ready and you or a trusted assistant are able to work closely with them during the process.

Objective 5: Home Commitment

- Conduct a behavioral experiment.
- Try out the problem-solving plan identified during the session and record the outcome.
- Bring in additional items (e.g., photos, mail, items from a particular area) to group for decision-making and organizing practice. Bring a wide range of items, including items that you do not intend to discard.
- Make arrangements for trash removal. In the case of a major cleanout, arrange for dumpster delivery and removal.

Objective 6: Clinician Forms

- Clinician directs the clients to write their home commitment on the Group Session Form (see Appendix 12) and completes the Clinician's Group Progress Notes (see Appendix 15).

Chapter 13 *Session 10: Skills Training for Organizing*

(Corresponds to Chapter 6 of the Workbook)

Materials Needed

- Decision Tree for Sorting (*Workbook* Chapter 6, p. 70)
- Organizing Plan (*Workbook* Chapter 6, p. 66)
- Personal Organizing Plan (*Workbook* Chapter 6, p. 68)
- Preparing for Organizing Form (*Workbook* Chapter 6, p. 69)

Session Agenda

- Identify organizational goals.
- Guide clients to develop and implement a personal organization plan.
- Help clients use a "decision tree."
- Discuss transfer of sorting and organizing skills from group sessions to home.

Objective 1: Check-in

- Distribute and review the Group Session Form.
- Clients report on the outcomes of their problem-solving plans.
- Clients report what they brought in for decision-making and organizing practice.

Objective 2: Identifying Organizational Goals

In addition to problem-solving, most clients with hoarding disorder have difficulty categorizing and organizing objects, as well as sustaining attention on overall goals and during sorting tasks. This session focuses on helping clients utilize a step-wise organizing method. Strategies for managing attention challenges will be covered in Session 16.

Ask group members to identify specific organizing goals. These might include:

- Define categories for items to be kept
- Decide on an overall organizing plan with locations for each category of saved items
- Develop a plan for sorting and moving items to interim and final destinations
- Decide on categories for unwanted items (e.g., give to people, give to charities, recycle, trash)
- Plan how to dispose of unwanted items
- Develop a plan to routinely put newly acquired or recently used items where they belong
- Decide how to make the organizing and de-cluttering process as pleasant as possible

Objective 3: Developing Organizing Skills and a Personal Organizing Plan

As you can see from the Decision Tree (Figure 13.1), the initial decision is whether to keep or discard an item. Once that has been decided, the number of categories and where they belong need to be determined. To help group members learn to sort effectively and efficiently, the first step is to teach them to categorize and organize possessions. To train them in these skills, we recommend working first on objects and later on paper items (Session 11), which require more complex thinking. Begin by defining the categories for items that will be removed from the home, and then work on categorizing the items that will be saved. This

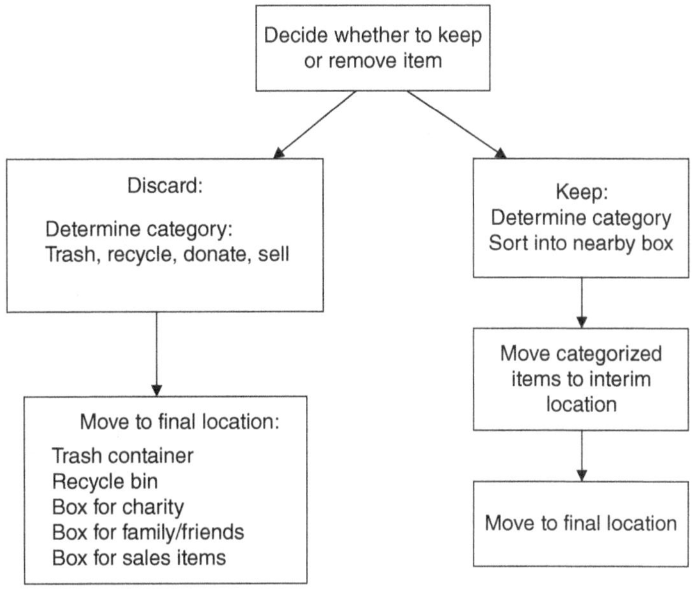

Figure 13.1
Decision Tree for Sorting

sequence helps clients feel more comfortable that their strong wish to avoid waste by recycling objects or giving them to a worthy cause will be respected. During the actual sorting process, use decision-making skills and cognitive strategies (see Session 12) to help reduce unreasonable urges to keep, give away, or try to sell worn-out or useless objects that few people would want and are better put in the trash.

Categorize Discarded Items

Introduce clients to the following categories for disposing of items they want to remove from their homes:

- Trash
- Recycle
- Donate (e.g., charities, library, friends, family)
- Sell (e.g., yard sale, bookstore, consignment shop, Internet sales)
- Undecided

Discuss what belongs in these categories and develop a short list of ways to donate or sell things that are relatively easy to accomplish and apply to the types of items likely to fit this category (e.g., books, clothing, toys, small appliances, kitchen items). This helps plant the idea that many items will be removed but may be usefully recycled, sold, or given away. For those especially concerned about being wasteful, this discussion may increase their willingness to remove items. There is no need to suggest what proportion of possessions should be placed in these categories, but the process of determining them helps clients think differently.

Develop an action plan for how and when to remove items in each of these categories. This is essential, as many clients set items aside for removal but have difficulty actually getting them out of the home. Determine when items can be put out for trash pickup or recycling or other methods of removal. Ask clients to identify local charities that could benefit from their unwanted items (e.g., donated books), and find out how to give these away. Local charities that come to pick up unwanted items are especially helpful. We strongly recommend that clients (who can afford it) give away items instead of selling them, as the latter action requires considerably more time and effort, which can derail the sorting and de-cluttering process. However, when items are valuable and their sale helps generate needed income, problem-solve ways to sell the items (e.g., local consignment stores, online methods) as conveniently as possible. Homework assignments can include Web searches to identify locations, calling charities and sales outlets, and scheduling removal of the unwanted items.

Select Categories for Saved Objects

As noted, the plan for organizing paper items requires a finer-grained approach that will be addressed in the next session. For non-paper items to be saved, help clients define a limited number of categories for each type of possession to decide where the item goes. This can be accomplished by creating an organizing plan. Table 13.1 contains an example of a completed Personal Organizing Plan including categories of saved items (e.g., mail, photos, clothing, newspapers, office supplies), and typical locations where people might keep them. A similar example (i.e., Organizing Plan) is given in the *Workbook* (p. 66). Review these examples with clients,

Table 13.1 Example of Completed Personal Organizing Plan
Target Area: Kitchen

	Item Category	Final Location
1.	Dishes	Cupboards above kitchen counter
2.	Pots and pans	Cupboard underneath stove top
3.	Spices	Small cupboard above counter
4.	Food—boxes, cans, etc.	Pantry closet
5.	Tea, coffee, and cups	Middle cupboard above coffee pot
6.	Dish towels, aprons	Drawer
7.	Bowls and baking pans	Corner lazy Susan
8.	Silverware	Large top drawer—get dividers
9.	Cooking utensils	2 drawers—large and small
10.	Household cleaning products	Cupboard under sink
11.	Paper supplies	Desk drawers
12.	Odds and ends, hardware	Bottom drawer in kitchen
13.	Glasses, stemware	Cupboard above counter
14.	Trash and recycle bins	Pantry floor
15.	Recent magazines	Shelf near table, move to recycle after 6 mos.
16.	Newspapers	Recycle bin when 2 days old
17.	Current financial papers and bills	Upright file on top of small desk
18.	Older financial papers, tax papers	Small file cabinet
19.	New mail, advertisements	Desktop "to do" pile or recycle bin for junk mail
20.	Dog food	Pantry bin

noting that each household may have different types of items and may choose different locations for keeping them. Convey the need to keep similar items together in one main place in order to find them easily.

Next, introduce the blank Personal Organizing Plan from the *Workbook* Appendix (p. 162). Help clients determine what kinds of items clutter their homes and need to be categorized and organized. Using a random mix of items brought from home may be helpful for this purpose. Group members can also review their own photos of their homes (but are not expected to share photos with the other group members). Ask clients to list each category in the left-hand column and write down the final location where these items belong (room, piece of furniture, etc.). Some clients have difficulty naming the categories for possessions but are more effective at deciding where they go. In this case, begin by asking about rooms (e.g., living room, dining room, bedrooms, basement) and storage locations within these rooms (e.g., desk drawers, closets, shelves, bookcases) to find out what items belong where. Try to keep the task manageable (non-frustrating) by finding a method that works best for your group of clients. For example, members with homes with similar types of rooms (e.g., group members who live in single-family homes) might pair up to work together on this. Assign the form as homework if the client is comfortable using it.

Pick Locations for Categorized Items

Clients must eventually have an appropriate storage or filing location for all of their things. Filing cabinets, bookshelves, and other storage furnishings will be needed, and some clients may decide to make structural changes to the home (e.g., built-in bookcase, added closet) to help them get organized.

Ask group members to trade off deciding aloud about the category and location for items they brought with them to the session. Use the Personal Organizing Plan to record these details. To help clients make organizing decisions, use a questioning style (e.g., "What category does this belong to? Where should that go?") and comment positively whenever their ideas seem reasonable. If some ideas seem unfeasible, prompt gently ("Interesting; how did you decide it belongs there?" "Can you think of any alternatives?"). Encourage clients to develop and try out their own ideas and to support each other with suggestions.

Specific organizational information may be helpful. For example, when a client has difficulty organizing office supplies, he or she may consult the website of a large office supply company to see the categories this company uses for organizing their products. For broader categories, clients might consider which aisle in the supermarket certain items are typically found. Group members can use these sources of information to develop their own plan.

Preparations for Sorting and Moving Saved Items

Use the Preparing for Organizing Form from the *Workbook* (Chapter 6, p. 69) to help clients determine what preparations are needed before undertaking major sorting tasks. These are likely to include choosing and obtaining:

- storage furniture—filing cabinet, bookcase, desk
- containers—clear plastic bins, cartons, large and small boxes, kitchen containers
- supplies—colored labels, markers, tape

If necessary, help clients problem solve where to find these things, how to transport them home, and other practical concerns. Encourage mutual aid in the group, inviting group members to help each other by coming up with ideas. Clients who agonize over purchasing decisions may require help to address their fears about making the wrong choices; these can be addressed using behavioral experiments or other cognitive strategies (see Session 12).

Because many final destinations are already full of clutter when treatment starts, you'll need to help members decide on interim locations or "way stations" to store things until the final location is available. This process usually requires (1) clearing space that serves as a staging area for sorting; (2) clearing temporary storage areas (e.g., porch, spare room); and (3) several large boxes labeled with the appropriate destination and contents. You might want to warn clients and family members that some sections of their home will look worse temporarily while they sort.

Objective 4: Implementing the Personal Organizing Plan

Decision Tree for Sorting

Once the Personal Organizing Plan, equipment, and storage locations are in place, help clients begin sorting their things using the Decision Tree (Figure 13.1), which summarizes the sorting and organizing process. To implement the initial decision, we often use three boxes labeled "Keep," "Discard," and "Don't Know" (temporary). Sometimes, we include a fourth pile labeled "Trash," so that if the decision is to discard into the trash, then this can be done immediately without revisiting and possibly reversing the decision. To speed up the decision-making process, the Don't Know pile is used for more difficult items (higher on the hierarchy) that need additional time and attention. Prior to the end of the session, ask clients to re-sort the Don't Know box into either Keep or Discard, unless this box contains items that are high on the hierarchy and need to be held for later sorting. Label this box "Hold for Later." Encourage clients to minimize the number of items in the Don't Know box, and if this proves challenging, eliminate this category to ensure the client gains skills in making difficult choices.

Case Vignette

CLINICIAN: We recommend starting with four boxes when you begin sorting your target area items: Keep, Discard, Discard into Trash, and Don't Know, which is a temporary category. The first decision is whether you are going to keep or get rid of the item. If you choose to discard the item as trash, please put it in the Trash receptacle.

JENNIFER: Well, that will be really hard! I don't really understand! I mean, how could I do that? When I am sorting through my clothing, I think I would need to have a category for each color or maybe for each type of clothing. Does it really make sense for me to put sweaters in the same box as pants? [*Talking faster and louder*]: I need more categories, I need categories for winter clothing, summer clothing, season changes, right? I can't do this!

CHARLIE: Yes you can. But with a category for everything, you'll have too many boxes. In my house, I just need one box—Electronics.

CLINICIAN: You both raise important points, and Charlie, it's great that you believe in Jennifer's capabilities! It's true that you can have many categories or only one. But, for now we are making the decision to keep or discard each item.

Jennifer: What's the purpose of limiting the categories? It seems to me it will be more efficient to have everything organized as we sort.

Sally: I really want to get a handle on this, and I want to take your advice. I don't think I would have room in my home to have so many categories. I mean there just isn't space to have more than three or four sorting boxes. And besides, all the clothing goes into the closet, so I can put things away once I have the clothing together. I just need to get the clothing separated from the newspapers and other items that are mixed in with them.

Clinician: Yes, this is important. Someone like you has two major categories of possessions in her bedroom—clothes and newspapers. So when sorting the newspapers and clothes, we would use two separate Keep boxes, one for each category. The newspapers and clothes would not be separated when the decision is to discard them. For now, they would go into this one discard box. Adding categories needs to be considered carefully. What do you think the barrier to progress would be if we had many categories?

Joseph: I guess it would take a long time, is that right?

Jennifer: I suppose it would take more time, but I think this will be really hard for me. I'm already sweating just thinking about it!

Clinician: This is hard work, indeed. After you decide whether to keep or discard, you can categorize "Keep" items and decide on the interim or final location. You can also re-categorize Discard items to Trash, Recycle, etc.

The processes happening in this vignette highlight the instilling of hope and mutual aid when Charlie comments that Jennifer can minimize her categories. The group leader notices his support of Jennifer and validates both Charlie's and Jennifer's concerns. Jennifer demonstrates the anxiety that can emerge due to the process of deciding whether to keep or remove items. Cognitive strategies for working on these are described in

Session 12. For now, keep the focus on helping clients select useful categories, plan the organizing process at home, and practice sorting items brought from home into categories.

Objective 5: Sorting and Organizing at Home

Discarding exercises at home should be combined with organizing skills. Help the group members plan the specific tasks and decisions to be made as they prepare for a sorting session. Highlight the importance of beginning in areas and with objects that are relatively low on the discomfort hierarchy. Proceed with the following general steps to integrate organizing with decisions about discarding.

- Select the target area.
- Determine the types of possessions in the target area and eventual storage locations for items that will be saved.
- Assemble the necessary organizing materials to facilitate moving the items.
- Determine which items will be easiest and hardest.
- Select a type of possession to begin with (e.g., clothing, newspapers).
- Use categories and filing systems created earlier to select interim and final locations for saved items.
- Allow a temporary Don't Know category when clients are unable to decide, and place those items in a designated location for later decision-making.
- Continue until the target area is clear.
- Plan appropriate use of cleared target area immediately.
- Plan how to prevent new clutter in this area.

As skill in decision-making improves, their discomfort gradually habituates, and progress increases. But progress is rarely entirely smooth, and many clients, especially those with traumatic histories connected to their hoarding, move forward in fits and starts. Help group members sustain hope and motivation by noticing incremental progress when they describe successes during the check-in. Emphasize the goals of making decisions, organizing possessions, creating living space, and the necessity for experiencing some discomfort in order to make progress.

Objective 6: Preparing for In-Session Paper Sorting

Ask your client to bring in mail and other paper to the next session (Session 11). Mail is often an excellent thing to bring to office sessions if clients have problems opening and sorting mail every day. Likewise, newspapers, magazines, or other saved paperwork that is not filed can be the focus of decisions about sorting and discarding.

Objective 7: Home Commitment

- Ask clients to time how long they can sort their possessions at home until they become distracted or confused.
- Complete the Personal Organizing Plan for items remaining in the target work area.
- Take home items sorted in the group and put them in an interim or final location where they belong.
- Bring in items that were difficult to categorize.
- Bring in a few days' worth of mail or other papers for use in the organizing paper session.
- Call charities and sales outlets to make plans to remove discarded possessions.

Objective 8: Clinician Forms

- Clinician directs the clients to write their home commitment on the Group Session Form (see Appendix 12) and completes the Clinician's Group Progress Notes (see Appendix 15).

Chapter 14 *Session 11: Organizing Paper*

(Corresponds to Chapter 6 of the Workbook)

Materials Needed

- How Long to Save Paper list (*Workbook* Chapter 6, p. 70)
- Filing Paper Form (*Workbook* Chapter 6, p. 72)
- Questions About Possessions Form (*Workbook* Chapter 7, p. 80)
- File folders and labels
- Filing box (an accordion filing box works well for this activity)

Session Agenda

- Help clients develop paper-organizing skills.
- Teach strategies for organizing paper and creating a filing system.
- Conduct group sorting activity.

Objective 1: Check-in

- Distribute and review the Group Session Form.
- Each client reports on progress with Personal Organizing Plan (*Workbook* Chapter 6, p. 68), putting items from the previous group session into the interim or final locations, and solicits help with items that are difficult to categorize.

Objective 2: Developing Skills for Organizing Paper

Filing System for Documents

People who hoard often intermix important and unimportant things, such as checks and bills intermingled with grocery store flyers and newspapers, most likely because everything seems important and therefore is put in the same pile. Clients may also be concerned about filing away important papers and wish to keep them in sight for fear of forgetting them. Others create overly complex or perfectionistic filing systems that are challenging to maintain.

Help clients establish a filing system for bills and other important documents (insurance papers, tax papers, personal medical matters), as well as places to store informational materials, upcoming events of interest, pictures, etc. Establishing a filing system at the outset enables clients to sort items throughout the home. A common sense approach to creating this system is best; encourage clients to consult with friends or family members if they feel stuck deciding how and where to file papers. Many decisions are straightforward, but some difficult ones require extra thought. Examples include what to do with old bills and how long to keep financial and tax documents. We provide some suggestions for how long to keep papers in Table 14.1 (also found in the client *Workbook,* p. 70).

If clients balk at developing a filing system and putting papers out of sight, remind them of their goals to create usable living space and be able to find things easily. To accomplish this goal, they will need to create and use a paper filing system. You can expect that fearful beliefs (e.g., putting items out of sight means losing them) and emotional attachments will intrude as you develop the filing system with clients. Consider a behavioral experiment to examine clients' fears regarding a filing system (e.g., filing several items and asking whether clients remember where to look when the item is needed). The next session covers other cognitive strategies that may be useful here.

Table 14.1 How Long to Save Paper

Keep for One Month

- Credit-card receipts
- Sales receipts for minor purchases
- Withdrawal and deposit slips (discard after verifying them against monthly bank statement)

Keep for One Year

- Paycheck stubs/deposit receipts
- Monthly bank, credit card, brokerage, mutual fund, and retirement-account statements

Keep for Six Years

- W-2's, 1099s, and tax return information
- Year-end credit card statements, brokerage and mutual fund summaries

Keep Indefinitely

- Tax returns
- Receipts for major purchases (furniture, art, etc.)
- Real estate and residence records
- Wills and trusts

Keep in a Safe-Deposit Box at the Bank

- Birth and death certificates
- Marriage license
- Insurance policies

Planning the Filing Process

After agreeing on the need for a filing system, use the following questions to encourage planning:

- When is the best time to work on filing?
    - Usually when clients are alert and less likely to be distracted
- Where will you start?
    - Typically the area that makes the most difference to clients

- How frequently should you file, and for how long?
    - New mail should be sorted daily.
    - Organizing other items several times a week helps clients become comfortable with their new filing system.
- Where will files be stored? Do you need receptacles for storage?
    - If storage space is not readily available yet, consider storing files temporarily in cardboard or plastic file boxes that can be stacked in an interim location and moved later to the appropriate place.
- What materials do you need in order to file papers now and in future?
    - Possibilities include filing cabinets, file folders, labels (especially color-coded ones), pens, Rolodex or electronic methods for address and phone information, boxes for temporary sorting.
    - Consider adding shelves or bookcases.
    - For categories with many items, consider large file folders or clear plastic storage bins, available cheaply at discount stores.

Case Vignette

CLINICIAN: Okay, so now that we've discussed the categories and the filing system, let's practice together before we break into pairs. Who would like to volunteer?
[*Joseph raises his hand.*] I guess I'll be the guinea pig today.

CLINICIAN: Okay, let's set up the file box.

JOSEPH: Okay, got my pile, got my pen, and I have a list of categories: I'm ready! [*smiling*]

JENNIFER: You probably need different-colored pens to indicate importance, don't you?

CLINICIAN: What do the rest of you think about that idea?

SALLY: Sounds complicated to me.

LIZ: ...and time-consuming

MARIA: Wouldn't you have a special folder for very important items?

CLINICIAN: Jennifer, can you say more about your idea?

JENNIFER: Well, I think financial papers are more important than my receipts.

JOSEPH [*raising his voice*]: My receipts are important, too! This is going to confuse me. I'm just going to use one color pen for my labels.

CLINICIAN: Joseph, are you okay?

JENNIFER: I'm sorry that I upset you. I guess you'll still be able to find the important papers even if they aren't in a different color. I know I get too particular sometimes.

JOSEPH: Sorry I raised my voice. I guess this is getting me anxious.

CLINICIAN: Joseph, thank you for verbalizing how this makes you feel. This is a tough process. And I'm really impressed how you and Jennifer worked this out. How is everybody else right now? Anybody need to say anything?

GROUP MEMBERS: [*clients shake their head no*]

CLINICIAN: Okay, let's keep going then.

The above dialogue demonstrates the dialectical process and the cohesion that can happen in groups. Joseph is anxious and becomes agitated. The clinician notices and checks in. Jennifer apologizes and acknowledges her perfectionism, which leads Joseph to apologize. The group moves on to the task at hand.

File Categories

Ask clients to review the Filing Paper Form in the *Workbook* (p. 72) to determine which of the listed categories are relevant for their own filing systems. Each category will need its own file folder, and some categories

Table 14.2 Common Filing Categories for Paper

Addresses and phone numbers	Humor
Archives: Wills, insurance policies, other important papers	People: One file for each household member
Articles (e.g. Gardening, Cooking, etc.)	Instruction manuals/warranties
Automobile	Medical
Catalogs	Personal/sentimental
Checking account(s)	Photographs
Computer	Product information
Correspondence	Restaurants
Coupons	Savings account(s)
Diskettes	School papers
Entertainment	Services
Financial	Stamps
– Credit cards	Stationary
– Bank statements	Taxes
– Retirement	Things to do—lists
– Savings account(s)	Things to file (things that have to be reviewed)
– Stocks	Calendar items (reminders for that specific month)
	Trips/vacation information

may need to be subdivided. A list of several common categories can be found in Table 14.2.

Group Filing Activity

Discuss strategies for sorting and filing paper items, especially daily mail. Ask how clients currently handle mail and if they avoid it; if so, suggest that they pick a certain time each day to sort new mail. Invite one of the group members who brought in mail to sort, and facilitate a group sorting activity.

Ask the volunteer to begin as usual by deciding which items to keep and which ones to get rid of (in this case, recycle). Help the client talk aloud about their thoughts and feelings about mail. At this stage, do not point out faulty logic or correct cognitive errors; simply ask for a decision. The Questions about Possessions from Session 8 (*Workbook* Chapter 7, p. 80) may be helpful here. For discarded mail, ask whether it should go into the Trash or Recycle bin. If clients want to save an item, ask what category it belongs to, and help them decide where to put it. Most people have a bin or small pile of items of current interest (e.g., upcoming events to attend, travel plans for the near future, current sales flyers). Even these should be sorted into type, but they can be kept in view rather than filed because of their short-term nature. This group of papers should be examined weekly or monthly and out-of-date ones discarded.

A number of websites may assist group members with what to shred (see, e.g., http://www.bbt.com/bbtdotcom/financial-education/security/shredding-personal-documents.page and http://fraudpreventionunit.org/2010/01/21/document-shredding-what-should-you-shred-and-when-should-you-shred-it/). Some clients may become obsessive about the shredding process and display paranoid thinking. Refocus on paper-filing. Shred papers that have personal and financial information.

Another common problem concerns the accumulation of magazines and newspapers. A similar decision process can be used here with the newspapers or magazines from the past couple of weeks. Ask clients which ones to keep or remove from the house. If one is kept, does the client want the whole thing, or just a part (e.g., an article)? Determine where to put each item and for how long. Encourage group members to develop their own rules for these decisions, such as keeping newspapers only until the next recycle day and magazines only for a few months or perhaps a year. Some magazines can be kept as resource material if clients truly use them for this purpose, but remind clients that most published material is now available on the Web through a search engine, so it may actually be much easier to find it online than by hunting through stacks of old magazines. Consider canceling subscriptions to magazines and newspapers that clients rarely read. Remember that the initial focus of these exercises is to develop the organizing and filing systems without too much concern about clients' decisions to keep too many items.

Case Vignette

Liz: I brought in mail today. It's probably been sitting on my stairs for five years. I'm not kidding—five years.

Maria: Good for you for bringing it in today.

Liz: I needed to bring something in. This is really hard for me and embarrassing. I have a lot of mail that I have never opened.

Joseph: I avoid opening the mail, too. I know what it's about. The collectors are contacting me.

Liz: It is the collectors for me, too. I have a hard time paying my bills. But I know it's not just the bills.

Clinician: It sounds like the mail is relevant to those avoidance patterns that you described when each of you was working on your models. To avoid the distress, some of you mentioned not opening your mail. Liz, would you be willing to open a piece of mail and talk through the experience with us?

Liz: Yes. I randomly picked this pile so I don't know what's in there. [*She empties out a plastic bag with several sealed envelopes inside.*] Okay, well, I see here an envelope from the electric company. It's postmarked July 23, 2007. [*Opens it.*] It's a bill. I don't need this.

Charlie: Did you pay it?

Liz: Well, I don't remember. It's so old, it doesn't really matter at this point. It feels good to hear myself say that it doesn't matter.

Clinician: Good, should we move on to the next envelope.

Liz *[Picks up another envelope and notices that it is a personal note]*: Hmm . . . I don't recognize the return address. [*Opens it and reads it. She becomes tearful.*]

Jennifer: Are you okay?

Liz: It's from a cousin who was inviting me to her my niece's college graduation. I am so embarrassed but also touched that she invited me. I never expected that she would think of me and want me there. I hadn't spoken to that part of the family in years.

SALLY: What are you going to do with it?

LIZ: Of course, I am going to keep it.

CLINICIAN: Do you have a place for personal letters?

LIZ: No.

CLINICIAN: Would you like to create a file for such personal cards and other correspondences?

LIZ: I feel uncomfortable putting this in a file folder. I will forget I have it, and it means a lot to me.

CARL: Will you really forget you received this if you put it away?

MARIA: How about putting it in a card box instead of a file folder?

LIZ: That would feel better to me.

Observe that by this stage of the group process, members are able to come up with suggestions that are quite helpful in solving the problem of where to keep personal correspondence.

Objective 3: Home Commitment

- Identify appropriate filing space for paper and non-paper items, and assemble necessary materials.
- Generate file categories, label file folders, and put papers in an interim or final location for filing. This could be for mail or other papers.
- Read about "Errors in Thinking" (*Workbook* Chapter 8, pp. 86–89).

Objective 4: Clinician Forms

- Clinician directs the clients to write their home commitment on the Group Session Form (see Appendix 12) and completes the Clinician's Group Progress Notes (see Appendix 15).

Chapter 15 *Session 12: Cognitive Strategies*

(Corresponds to Chapters 5 and 8 of the Workbook)

Materials Needed

- Faulty/Problematic Thinking Styles list (*Workbook* Chapter 5, pp. 56, 58–59, for acquiring; *Workbook* Chapter 8, pp. 86–89, for discarding; Appendix 29)
- Questions about Possessions (*Workbook* Chapter 7, p. 80)
- Acquiring Questions Form (*Workbook* Chapter 5, p. 51)
- Downward Arrow Form (*Workbook* Chapter 8, p. 61)
- Thought Record Form (*Workbook* Chapter 8, p. 93, Appendix 30)

Session Agenda

- Help client identify and reduce problematic thinking styles in discarding and acquiring situations.
- Practice the Downward Arrow strategy.
- Use Socratic questioning to examine the evidence.
- Work with client to apply cognitive therapy techniques while practicing sorting and discarding.

Commentary on Cognitive Strategies

The cognitive therapy methods for hoarding described here are best used while clients are actively sorting, organizing, and getting rid of clutter. In other words, you will interweave cognitive methods as they fit the context of skills training and behavioral practice. Help clients learn how to observe their own reactions and become aware of their thinking in hoarding contexts as a first step toward changing those reactions. Once you identify the important beliefs that maintain hoarding by using strategies such as the Downward Arrow and thought records, help clients evaluate their accuracy using methods such as Socratic questioning to examine the evidence. A few commonly used cognitive therapy methods are described and illustrated in this chapter.

Cognitive strategies take time and cannot be rushed, as clients can only change their thinking at their own pace. Gradually, as they get the hang of using these methods, they will pick up speed, but the going will be slow and can seem painstaking during the initial phases of treatment. If clients do not seem to be gaining skills in decision-making about discarding by using these methods, consider whether ambivalence is still a central problem and requires motivational interviewing.

Due to limited group time, we focus on only a couple of cognitive strategies in this session. However, we also recommend additional cognitive strategies such as taking another perspective, using the Perfectionism Continuum Scale, metaphors and stories, and valuing time. For additional information about these techniques, see the individual treatment guide for hoarding by Steketee and Frost (2013) and the cognitive therapy manual for OCD by Wilhelm and Steketee (2006).

Objective 1: Check-in

- Distribute and review Group Session Form.
- Each client identifies their filing space for paper and reports on their progress in creating file categories, labeling files, and/or filing their documents.

- Poll group members to find out who read about Problematic Thinking Styles in the *Workbook* (Chapter 8, pp. 86–89).

Objective 2: Changing Thinking about Acquiring and Discarding

Introduce the session topic by explaining that the session will address cognitive strategies that focus on the thoughts and beliefs that make it difficult to discard possessions as well as to resist urges to acquire. These are the ones they identified in their General Conceptual Hoarding Model. Indicate that you will be providing instructions for using cognitive therapy methods to reduce problematic thinking in acquiring and discarding situations. Explain that the cognitive methods you will cover are designed to help clients step back and take a different perspective on their hoarding problems during the process of sorting within the group session and at home, and making decisions about acquiring, keeping, or removing possessions.

Note that people who hoard engage in problematic thinking styles in relation to decision-making about discarding possessions as well as acquiring. An important goal is to identify these patterns in order to avoid habitual (automatic) mental traps. Direct clients' attention to the Problematic/Faulty Thinking Styles list in the client *Workbook* (Chapter 5 for acquiring, pp. 56, 58–59; and Chapter 8 for discarding, pp. 86–89). A table (Table 15.1) combining these concepts is provided below; you may prefer to distribute this one to group members so they do not need to flip between chapters during the session. (The chart is also included in the Appendix 29.) Reviewing this list will help clients notice their problematic thinking styles when they occur during office, home, and non-acquisition sessions. Emphasize to clients that determining the particular category of thinking is less important than becoming aware of the unhelpful patterns.

Problematic Thinking Styles

Table 15.1 provides a list of various problematic thinking styles and examples. These will assist you in helping group members identify their own patterns of thinking.

Table 15.1 Problematic Thinking Styles and Examples

Problematic Thinking Styles	Definition	Acquiring Examples	Discarding Examples
All-or-nothing thinking	Black-and-white thinking exemplified by extreme words like "most," "everything," "nothing"; often reflects perfectionist standards	"This is the *most* beautiful teapot I have ever seen." "I won't remember *anything* about this if I can't bring home this reminder."	"It seems like *everything* in this box is just so important."
Over-generalization	Generalization from a single event to all situations, using words like "always" or "never"	"I always regret not buying things like this." "I'll never have another opportunity if I don't get this now."	"I will *never* find this if I move it." "If I don't keep this, I'll *always* regret it."
Jumping to conclusions	Predicting negative outcomes without supporting facts; akin to catastrophizing	"I'll need something just as soon as I walk away without getting anything."	"You know I'll need this just as soon as I decide to get rid of it."
Catastrophizing	Exaggerating the severity of possible outcomes	"If I don't buy it now, I'll regret it forever."	"If I throw it away, I'll go crazy thinking about it."
Discounting the positive	Positive experiences are not counted	"Yeah, I suppose I resisted the urge and saved some money, but what if I can't stop thinking about it?"	"Creating a filing system isn't really progress because there is so much more to do."
Emotional reasoning	Using emotions instead of logic so feelings substitute for facts	"I feel uncomfortable walking away without this, so I should just get it."	"If I feel uncomfortable about throwing this away, it means I should keep it."
Moral reasoning:	Statements with "should," "must," "ought," and "have to" accompanied by guilt and frustration; often driven by perfectionistic standards.	"I must get this magazine or I won't know all the facts."	"I have to keep this health information in case something happens to my husband."

(continued)

Table 15.1 Problematic Thinking Styles and Examples *(continued)*

Problematic Thinking Styles	Definition	Acquiring Examples	Discarding Examples
Labeling	Attaching a negative label to oneself or others	"I'd be an idiot not to take advantage of this great sale."	I can't find my electric bill. I'm such a fool." "She's just greedy and wants all my stuff."
Under- and over-estimating	Under-estimating the time to accomplish a task or one's ability to cope; over-estimating one's ability to complete a task and/or the emotional costs of doing so	"I know I have a lot of magazines, but I'll be able to read them all eventually." "If I don't get this, I won't be able to handle it."	"I'll be able to read those newspapers eventually."

This list is adapted from D. Burns, *Feeling Good Handbook* (New York: Morrow), 1990, 8–11.

Exercise for Problematic Thinking Styles

After the problematic thinking styles are introduced, engage in an exercise that may help group members understand and remember the different styles. Make the following statements while group members identify the appropriate problematic thinking styles. You also may consider writing each statement on an index card, distributing the cards to the group, and after each client reads their card, having the other group members identify the relevant thinking style. This exercise also helps create a playfulness in the group and can help develop mutual aid.

- *Client*: "If I get rid of this, I will need it." [*jumping to conclusions or mind reading*]
- *Client A*: "You did such a great job discarding the pile of newspapers." *Client B*: "I really didn't do much. I didn't do any of my other home commitments!" [*minimizing the positive*]
- *Client*: "If I throw this out, I will never find that information again and I don't know what I would do then." [*catastrophizing*]
- *Client*: "I'm never going to make any headway with my clutter." [*fortune telling*]

- *Client*: This is the most beautiful shade of green I have ever seen. There is nothing like it. [*all-or-nothing*]
- *Client*: "I'm an idiot! I should have bought that purse while I had the chance." [*labeling*]
- *Client*: "Whenever I put things away, I can never find them again." [*over-generalization*]
- *Client*: "I feel like such a failure, so I guess I am one." [*emotional reasoning*]
- *Client*: "Clearing this space would take years." [*overestimating*]
- *Client*: "If I put this away, I won't remember that I have it." [*jumping to conclusions*]

After reviewing these statements and other thoughts and identifying the thinking styles, invite clients to identify potential alternative thoughts (or "replacement" thoughts) by asking, "What's another way of thinking about this?" If clients have trouble coming up with a replacement, suggest one (for example, "Even if I feel uncomfortable about getting rid of this, I might get used to it," when clients catastrophize about their likely reaction) and discuss. Replacement thoughts should be flexible and promote tolerance of some uncertainty. Continue this exercise during sorting tasks or other group exercises, by commenting on problematic thinking styles that you notice, asking group members which one it might be, referring to the list, and asking about alternative or replacement thoughts.

Managing Automatic Thoughts, Interpretations, Beliefs, and Core Beliefs

Remind clients that during the assessment and in building their General Conceptual Hoarding Model, they identified relevant thoughts about the meaning of possessions from the Saving Cognitions Inventory, the List of Reasons for Saving, and/or by completing a Thought Record. These cognitive elements included automatic thoughts (e.g., "Oh no, I need that!") and interpretations or beliefs that justify hoarding behavior (such as, "I might never be able to find this again," or "It would be wasteful to get rid of this"). These interpretations often contain cognitive errors (problematic thinking styles) discussed above, and the beliefs typically concern one or more of the topics listed in Table 15.2.

Explain that automatic thoughts are like the top layers of an onion, and if we delve a little deeper and peel away layers of our thoughts, we usually find some catastrophic fears and core beliefs. Core beliefs are more fundamental to the person's self and can be positive or negative. They have a global, generalized, and absolute quality and can usually be very simply stated. In some cases, core beliefs may also refer to other people. Not surprisingly, these beliefs derive from important early experiences in the person's life. Examples of positive core beliefs are: "I'm capable," "I'm a good person," "I'm likable," and "Other people mean well." In the context of hoarding, we focus on negative core beliefs, because these are the ones that cause problems. Examples are: "I'm bad," "I'm a failure," "I'm inadequate," "I'm unlovable," "I'm unworthy," "People can't be trusted," and "People are mean." Often these core beliefs are negative labels that clients apply to themselves. When activated, core beliefs drive clients' interpretations of events and elicit powerful negative emotions. For this reason, it is helpful to figure out what the core beliefs are in order to evaluate whether they make sense.

Table 15.2 Types of Hoarding Beliefs

Value of Objects	Responsibility for Objects
Objects representing personal identity	Responsibility to people
Objects representing safety	Usefulness, avoid waste
Need for objects	Confidence in memory
Ability to tolerate discomfort	Need for control over objects
Perfectionism	

Objective 3: Downward Arrow Method

The downward arrow method illustrated in Figure 15.1 helps identify catastrophic fears, as well as strongly held (core) beliefs about oneself

"I am not interested in getting rid of the boxes of trade magazines"

↓

In thinking about getting rid of this, what thoughts occur to you?

"I may start up a business again. I may need them. I haven't read them yet. I have gotten a lot of really good info from them in the past."

↓

If you got rid of this, what do you think would happen?

"I would miss some really important information for my work."

↓

If this were true, why would it be so upsetting? What would it mean to you? Why would that be so bad?

"I may not be prepared."

↓

If that were true, what's so bad about that?

"I need to stay on top of the ideas."

↓

What's the worst part about that?

"I wouldn't be an expert."

↓

What does that mean about you?

"I'd be a failure."

Figure 15.1

Example of a Downward Arrow for Discarding

and others. Label and describe the downward arrow as a "cognitive technique that helps clarify thoughts and beliefs." For example, during a discarding practice, ask clients to select an item that would provoke moderate discomfort if they discarded it, and list this on the Downward Arrow Form (*Workbook* Chapter 5, p. 61; and *Workbook* Appendix, p. 154). Ask how distressed (0–10) they feel about discarding this item, and continue with a series of iterative questions after each response:

- "What would that mean?"
- "If that happened, what would that mean?"

- "What would be the worst part about that?"
- "Would anything else happen?"

Use this method to better understand clients' reasons for saving and strong urges to acquire. Complete the Downward Arrow aloud with one or two clients in order to introduce the strategy to all group members and clarify any confusion about how to use it to uncover strong beliefs. If clients state thoughts that seem irrelevant to the discarding task, ask: "Do you have any other concerns about this?" Do not press it if clients have trouble identifying deeper meanings. After reaching the client's "bottom line" (no further thoughts occur), connect the final belief or catastrophic fear to the original premise to help clients understand their own assumptions. In the example below, Joseph had difficulty discarding a stack of trade magazines, because they represented his professional identity and provoked anxiety about his professional competence.

Case Vignette

CLINICIAN: Today, we are going to apply a specific technique called the Downward Arrow method. We will focus on one person to start, but would like all of you to follow along in your *Workbooks* and think about your own responses. As mentioned, the exercise includes a series of questions to help us figure out your beliefs that get in the way of making decisions about your items. While you all may have a lot of responses, I am going to try to keep us focused on the specific questions that are included in the exercise. Our initial conversation will be more structured, and we will have time for more discussion after we complete it. Joseph, you had mentioned briefly during check-in, that you had difficulty completing your home commitment of sorting and discarding a stack of trade magazines. Would you be willing to explore this further using a Downward Arrow?

JOSEPH: All right.

CLINICIAN: Looking at the form, the "items" under consideration are trade magazines. [*Writes this down on the board.*] Others of you can write down on your worksheet the item that you are considering discarding, recycling, selling, or giving away.

JOSEPH: Yes, I know I have held onto those boxes for a long time, but I'm not interested in getting rid of them.

CLINICIAN: [*Writes Joseph's thoughts on the board. To the group members*]: Please write your own thoughts on the lines below the first question, "In thinking about getting rid of this, what thoughts occur to you?" Joseph, could you say more about why you are not interested in getting rid of the magazines?

JOSEPH: Well, I may start up a business again. I am not really sure, I may need them. And I haven't had a chance to read them. I have gotten a lot of really good info from them in the past.

CLINICIAN: *[Recording Joseph's thoughts on the board]:* If you got rid of the item, trade magazines in your case, Joseph, what do you think would happen?

JOSEPH: Happen? Um.... Well, I wouldn't be able to find information that is so important to my work. I would miss some really important information. Besides, I like them.

CLINICIAN: *[Writing on the board]:* You think you would miss information, and you like them. If you miss out on some really important information when discarding these magazines, why would that be so upsetting?

JOSEPH: I'd be upset that I don't have the information.

CLINICIAN: What would it mean to you, not to have that information?

JOSEPH: Well, it might mean that I may not be prepared. That I would be missing out on important ideas for my work.

These are tough times and you have to be on top of stuff. The technology changes so fast.

CHARLIE: Yeah well, if the technology is changing so fast, would those magazines really be of use at this point?

CLINICIAN: Before, you answer that, let's focus on the next question. Why would it be so bad to possibly miss out on ideas for your work?

JOSEPH: This is what I do. I need to stay on top of the ideas. I will never be able to start the business if I am not on top of all these ideas. I am supposed to be an expert in this.

CLINICIAN: If you are not on top of all these ideas, what is the worst part about that?

JOSEPH: I wouldn't be an expert in that... That's what I am good at....

CLINICIAN: So if you are not an expert in that, then what does that mean about *you*?

JOSEPH: Then what's left? A failed marriage, failed business... I am not sure; what else is left for me? I'd be a failure [*trails off*...].

JENNIFER: That is sad. You are not a failure. Those magazines don't define you.

CARL: Yeah, because those magazines have been sitting there, but you have still been working, right?

JOSEPH: [*Looking down, holding his head*]

CLINICIAN: Okay, the idea of failure seems pretty important for you. Are you saying that discarding the trade magazines means that you are not an expert but instead a failure in your area of work? Is that how you see it?

JOSEPH [PAUSES]: No, I know some things about my work.

CLINICIAN: But discarding the magazines means that you would fail?

JOSEPH: Well, not necessarily. It seems that way sometimes. But I guess I may not need all of them.

CLINICIAN: Are you sure?

JOSEPH: Yes.

CLINICIAN: Should we set some rules to sort them?

JOSEPH: Okay.

In the next vignette, the leader identifies the specific relationship between the core belief at the bottom of the Downward Arrow and the automatic thoughts at the top from the start of the exercise for Joseph. The leader then moves on to help group member Grace complete the exercise.

Case Vignette

CLINICIAN: Let's go back to the top of the Arrow. Your initial automatic thought was that you don't want to get rid of the trade magazines. These thoughts and the anger that you described during check-in are directly tied to these underlying fears about yourself [*pointing at the core belief at the bottom of the arrows*].

JOSEPH: I don't understand how they are connected.

CLINICIAN: Sometimes decisions about possessions, in this case deciding whether to keep or discard trade magazines, are connected to and trigger deep beliefs, core beliefs, in ourselves. We all have core beliefs about ourselves, others, the world, and the future. They shape how we perceive and respond to situations—how we feel at the time (our emotions) and what we do (our behaviors). Considering getting rid of the trade magazines seems to activate your fears of being a failure. This Downward Arrow exercise helps us identify core beliefs that may be getting in the way of progress. [*Turning to the group*]: How was it for you all?

GRACE: For me, the items I was thinking of were the brushes and things for my animals. So I wrote that "I just have too many but can't seem to let them go." And I got lost doing this. I don't know what it means. The worst part is I have too many.

CLINICIAN: So if you got rid of them, what would be so bad about that? Why would it be upsetting?

GRACE: Well, I could use them. They are still good, you know.

CLINICIAN: So, if you discarded them and did not use them, what would that mean about you?

GRACE: It would mean that—um ... I am wasting something good ... and I already paid for them.

CLINICIAN: So if we buy into this idea that you are wasteful, what is the worst part about that? What does that mean about you?

GRACE: Well, I'd be a bad person if I wasted things ...

CLINICIAN: So, are you saying that discarding the brushes for your animals means that you are a bad person? Is that true?

GRACE: I guess not; it's very difficult though.

CLINICIAN: Yes, I hear that. Our thoughts can get in the way, but there are a number of strategies to help work through those thoughts. Would you be willing to more closely examine this thought that you are a bad person?

GRACE: Okay.

Because many clients are unaware of the beliefs that drive their hoarding, clearly stating them aloud makes them more accessible and easier to evaluate. Recommend that group members practice using the Downward Arrow procedure several times until the beliefs become clear (e.g., "I'll be stupid for not buying this"; "As soon as I get rid of it, something terrible will happen and I'll need it"). Then, help clients strengthen positive core beliefs about themselves while examining and disputing the negative ones using one or more of the cognitive strategies suggested below (e.g., Socratic questioning to evaluate the logic; designing a behavioral experiment). A video located at www.ocfoundation.org/hoarding/videos.aspx provides an example of the use of the Downward Arrow method during a behavioral experiment by Dr. Frost with a client who is working on discarding. We recommend showing it to the group and discussing their reactions to it.

While the examples provided earlier were focused on Joseph and Grace's difficulties discarding, the Downward Arrow technique can be applied to an acquiring episode as illustrated in Figure 15.2. The group leader

"I have to have this. It's right there for me to take."

↓

If you did not acquire this, what do you think would happen?

"I would miss out on a great opportunity. It was meant for me."

↓

What would it mean to miss out on an opportunity?

"I mean I guess, someone else would get it."

↓

If that were true, what's so bad about that?

"Well, I needed it. I don't have a lot of money. It would mean I missed out."

↓

What is the worst part about that?

"I would be really disappointed. I might never find that again."

↓

And what is the worst part about that?

"I would never have the chance to have it."

↓

What would that mean about you?

"Maybe I didn't deserve it to begin with. Maybe, I'm not good enough."

Figure 15.2

Example of a Downward Arrow for Acquiring

begins the downward arrow by asking, "In thinking about not acquiring this item, what thoughts occur to you?" (see *Workbook*, p. 61). From this point, the clinician can continue the line of questions to help the client understand how not taking advantage of a free lamp sitting outside a dumpster became connected in the client's mind to not being deserving of it. For example, this might derive from early experiences of deprivation and/or low self-esteem, although this is certainly not always the case.

Objective 4: Socratic Questioning to Examine the Evidence

Introduce the Socratic questioning method, which involves asking clients a series of questions about their beliefs to clarify the logic they are using. Your main aim is to point out the obvious holes in clients' reasoning by asking questions that highlight discrepancies in their assumptions. This method relies on open-ended but directive questions. Because the style of Socratic questioning is not forceful or argumentative, avoid phrases like "Yes, but ____ " and " ____, right?" as these reflect efforts to convince clients rather than asking for clarification within their own belief system. The goal is to help group members develop alternative ways of appraising situations. Use exploratory questions to help clients review the evidence they are using to draw their conclusions. Encourage them to think of themselves as scientists or detectives and to state their beliefs in the form of hypotheses. For example:

> *You have been trying to hold on to everything so as not to be wasteful. Let's call this a hypothesis, that "Keeping things means you are not wasteful." Would you be willing to examine the truth of this hypothesis and see if there are any alternative viewpoints? For example, an alternative might be that "Keeping everything may be wasteful." Then we can determine whether there is evidence to support either hypothesis.*

Ask "curiosity questions" to elucidate ideas and rephrase clients' statements in slightly different words to verify that they understand correctly. These questions are generally focused as follows:

- What evidence supports your hypothesis? Is there any evidence that doesn't?
- Is there another way of looking at that?
- What is the most likely outcome?
- Are you using any problematic thinking styles?

To help examine the meaning of and the evidence for the need to acquire, Socratic questions can focus on whether clients actually think that not purchasing the item means that an unfortunate consequence will follow (e.g., "I'll never feel good again," "My life means nothing," "I won't be accepted by others"). For example, if the Downward Arrow questioning led a client to say, "If I don't buy this, I'll feel stupid" (emotional reasoning), consider the following types of questions to examine the evidence. Notice that some techniques are used more than once, with a slightly different focus.

- Are other people who don't acquire this also stupid? [*double standard*]
- Would you consider me stupid if I did not acquire this? [*taking a different perspective by using the clinician as example*]. Why not?
- What would be the most accurate way to describe what it would really mean if you didn't buy this?
- Do you usually feel stupid when you don't buy something? [*generalizing to other situations*]
- Doesn't everything you touch represent an opportunity? Shouldn't you buy them all? [*devil's advocate*]. Why not?
- When we discussed the advantages and disadvantages of acquiring, I think you concluded that taking advantage of all the opportunities to acquire things would interfere with your ability to live your life the way you want to. [*recalling incompatible information*] If that is true, how does that fit with the idea that you are stupid if you don't get this?" [*evaluating the logic*]
- I am curious to know whether making any kind of mistake means that you are stupid? [*generalizing to other situations*]

- What about other people or me? Should we feel stupid if we made these same mistakes? [*taking another perspective*] Why not?

When clients begin to question their assumptions routinely and challenge the usefulness and accuracy of labeling of themselves as stupid (or "missing out" or some other conclusion), ask where they think these ideas originated (e.g., influential past experiences). This helps consolidate a different perspective in which the original assumption ("I should buy this or I'm stupid") has become questionable. Such changes typically occur gradually rather than all at once, so you will need to repeat these methods of questioning before a strongly held belief is relinquished.

Socratic questioning (and some other cognitive strategies that we have covered such as Questions about Possessions, Advantages and Disadvantages, Thought Records) are intended to promote rational alternative viewpoints that fit the facts and are more plausible to clients than the original interpretation. Remind clients to keep in mind the alternative belief that they are aiming for, such as, "I'll be able to find the information if I need it," or "These are just things; they don't represent me as a person," or "Putting things away where they belong means I can find them when I want to."

Although these exercises are focused on individual clients, encourage interaction between the group members during these activities. While it is essential to demonstrate the techniques clearly, take care not to preclude opportunities for group process. Consider asking the group members to hold their questions until the end of the demonstration. After working through the technique with one client, be sure to encourage group members to share their reactions and ask questions of you and the other group members.

Objective 5: Home Commitment Agreement

1. Complete Thought Records and/or a Downward Arrow form to identify beliefs associated with letting go of possessions.
2. Complete the bottom half of the worksheet to evaluate the advantages and disadvantages of getting rid of a specific item (*Workbook* Chapter 8, p. 90).

3. Apply the Acquiring Questions and Questions about Possessions when sorting or considering acquiring an item.
4. Bring in to group a wide range of items to sort.

Objective 6: Complete Clinician Forms

- Clincian directs the clients to write their home assignment on the Group Session Form (see Appendix 12) and completes the Clinician's Group Progress Notes (see Appendix 15).

Chapter 16 *Session 13: Cognitive Therapy Skills for Letting Go*

(Portions of this session correspond to Chapters 3, 5, 7, and 8 of the Workbook)

Materials Needed

- Questions about Possessions (*Workbook* Chapter 7, p. 80)
- Acquiring Questions Form (*Workbook* Chapter 5, p. 51)
- Need Versus Want Scales (*Workbook* Chapter 8, p. 94)
- Thought Record Form (*Workbook* Chapter 8, p. 93, Appendix 30)
- Advantages-Disadvantages Worksheet (*Workbook* Chapter 8, p. 90)
- Downward Arrow Form (*Workbook* Chapter 8, p. 92)
- Functional Analysis (*Workbook* Chapter 3, Figure 3.2, p. 39)
- Box of items brought in by each client to sort

Session Agenda

- Complete the Need Versus Want exercises.
- Review Questions about Possessions and Acquiring Questions.
- Work with client to apply cognitive therapy techniques while practicing sorting and discarding.

Objective 1: Check-in

- Distribute and review the Group Session Form.
- Ask one or two group members to review their completed Thought Records.
- Ask group members to each briefly state whether they completed the Advantages/Disadvantages worksheet and if they are applying their Acquiring Questions and Questions about Possessions at home during sorting exercises.
- Determine which group members brought in items to sort.

During this session, you will work with clients to apply several of the cognitive and behavioral therapy techniques they have learned while they practice sorting possessions in pairs. Prior to dividing the group into pairs for the sorting exercise, introduce the Need versus Want cognitive strategy to the group. If you did not cover all the cognitive strategies from Session 12, please do so before starting the sorting exercise.

Objective 2: Defining Importance: Completing the Need versus Want Exercise

For this exercise, explain that thinking styles reviewed in the previous session such as magnifying, over-generalizing, and emotional reasoning lead people to magnify the importance of possessions to such a point that it seems crucial to save them. This exercise helps group members clarify the true value of a possession based on their personal goals and rational thinking. The Need versus Want Scale helps them distinguish what they truly need from what they merely want, and can be applied to acquiring as well as discarding decisions.

To begin, use the Need versus Want Scales for discarding in the client *Workbook* (Chapter 8, p. 94). Ask group members to select one of the possessions they brought to the session that would be moderately difficult but appropriate to discard. If someone chooses an item you believe is reasonable to keep, ask the person to choose another one that most people would probably discard. Lead the group through the exercise by reading each question aloud while clients record their responses in the client *Workbook*. Ask clients for an initial rating of "need to keep" and "want to keep" using the scales from 0 to 10 (see Figure 16.1). Then review the questions shown below and in the client *Workbook* to see if clients alter their ratings after thinking about the true value of possessions in relation to their other important goals in life. Ask clients to reflect on what they have learned from this exercise and to make a decision about keeping or getting rid of the item. You can conduct this exercise by focusing on one group member while the others observe, or by having all group members participate simultaneously in pairs.

Next, ask clients to complete the Need versus Want Scales focused on acquiring (*Workbook* Chapter 5, p. 60). Help group members refine the

Need to Keep Scale

0 ------- 1 ------- 2 ------- 3 ------- 4 ------- 5 ------- 6 ------- 7 ------- 8 ------- 9 ------- 10

No need Required to survive

Want to Keep Scale

0 ------- 1 ------- 2 ------- 3 ------- 4 ------- 5 ------- 6 ------- 7 ------- 8 ------- 9 ------- 10

Don't want Desperate for

Questions to evaluate importance and value of objects

- Would you die without it?
- Would your safety be impaired without it?
- Would your health be jeopardized without it?
- Is this critical to your work or employment?
- Is it essential for your financial records (e.g., tax or insurance records)?
- Is there some other reason why you need the item?
- To what extent do you want the item more than you actually need it?

Figure 16.1

Need versus Want Scales for Discarding

scale by asking them to think of things they cannot live without (e.g., food, water). Next, ask them to think of something they might like to have, but know they do not need or expect to acquire, like a luxury car or a diamond necklace. Then ask clients to select an item that they are considering acquiring and rate their need for it on a scale from 0 (not needed for survival) to 10 (required for survival) by circling the appropriate number on the scale (see Figure 16.2).

Want to Keep Scale

0 ------- 1 ------- 2 ------- 3 ------- 4 ------- 5 ------- 6 ------- 7 ------- 8 ------- 9 ------- 10

Not needed (for survival) | Required (for survival)

Want to Acquire Scale

0 ------- 1 ------- 2 ------- 3 ------- 4 ------- 5 ------- 6 ------- 7 ------- 8 ------- 9 ------- 10

Don't want | Desperate for

Figure 16.2

Need versus Want Scales for Acquiring

Ask the following questions to help clients re-evaluate their desire for the item:

- How much do you need to get this item?
- Would you die without it?
- Would your safety be impaired without it?
- Would your health be jeopardized?
- Must you have this for your work?
- Do you need it for financial purposes? (e.g., tax or insurance records)
- Is there some other reason why you need the item?
- To what extent do you want the item more than you actually need it?

It may be useful to specify different dimensions of need, such as safety, health, employment, financial affairs, or recreation. Also ask about items that might be designated as moderate need—spoons and forks, bed sheets, a suitcase, and so forth. Be careful that the level of need takes into account how many of the same items are already available in the home (that is, the value of the tenth set of bed sheets is considerably lower than that of the first set). Now ask clients to re-rate their need for the original item they want to acquire on this scale. The rating for the item is likely to go down, now that they have expanded their view of needed items and their purpose.

Now, ask clients to create a Want Scale and rate the item on this scale as well. For example, a least-favorite food (lima beans) and a most favorite food (chocolate cake) will not receive the same Want rating, but they might receive a similar Need rating depending on the client's hunger.

After discussing the true value of possessions in relation to other important goals in life, ask clients to re-rate their desire for the item. If this has been reduced, discuss what aspect of this exercise was useful and how they might use this method during non-acquiring homework practice.

Objective 3: Sorting Exercise

Next, prepare the clients to practice several of the cognitive and behavioral therapy techniques they have learned while sorting their possessions. First, divide the group into pairs. Request that group members select one of the items that they brought to session that would provoke moderate discomfort if discarded. Make sure the item is appropriate for discarding. Ask clients to rate and record their level of discomfort (0–10) about discarding the item.

Next, write on the board at least four cognitive and behavioral strategies (e.g., Questions about Possessions, Thought Record, Advantages/Disadvantages, Downward Arrow, and/or Functional Analysis), including the page numbers in the *Workbook* for the corresponding information and worksheets. Copy the name of each skill onto separate pieces of paper, and then fold them so that each technique is not visible. Ask each pair to select one technique and to practice their assigned skill while sorting, with one client making the decision of whether to keep or discard their item and the other client assisting with the decision-making. Each pair should switch roles mid-exercise so that both clients have practice with decision-making and providing support. Clients who decide to discard the item should re-rate their level of discomfort (0–10) about discarding the item and then decide whether to put it in the trash, recycle, etc. Clients who decide to keep the item will need to decide what category it belongs to and where it will go in the home. Following this exercise, prompt each pair to share with the other group members what skills they practiced and their experiences working on the skill together.

If time is available, ask the client pairs to continue to sort and make decisions about the possessions that they brought to group. Emphasize the goal of discarding (or when kept, categorizing) as many items as possible and the necessity for experiencing some discomfort and observing its change over time.

This activity creates an opportunity for socializing, behavioral rehearsal, and instilling hope, among other therapeutic factors and mutual aid. As the pairs are engaging in the activity, walk around and observe the interactions in a non-judgmental way. Ask if anyone needs help or direction. Be available to support them as needed.

Case Vignette

Pair dialogue: Charlie and Sally

CLINICIAN: We have divided you up into pairs so you can practice skills together. One of you is a coach, while the other is a client. Then you will switch roles. I wrote a list of techniques on pieces of paper in the hat. Each coach will select a technique to work with your partner. Please take a moment and select your technique.

CHARLIE: I am not sure I am ready to be the coach. Sally, would you want to go first?

SALLY: Sure. What did you bring in?

CHARLIE: I didn't bring in anything.

SALLY: Is there anything that we might work with in your bag?

CHARLIE: I have so many receipts, I can't even close my wallet.

SALLY: Okay [*unfolding the small piece of paper and reading the technique aloud*]: so our technique is Need versus Want. Pick one of the receipts.

CHARLIE: So this one is for fast food.

SALLY: On a scale of 0–10 (0 = "no need" and 10 = "required to survive"), rate your need for the receipt.

CHARLIE: I guess it's a 3 for survival. But, I need some of the receipts for my electronics. I might need them for the warranty.

SALLY: Okay, but let's stay focused on this receipt.

CHARLIE: It's from a fast food restaurant, but I like to keep all of my receipts.

SALLY: How would you rate how much you want this restaurant receipt (0 = "don't want" and 10 = "desperate for")?

CHARLIE: It's a 7.

SALLY: Would you die without it?

CHARLIE: Obviously not.

SALLY: Would your safety be impaired?

CHARLIE: No.

SALLY: How about your health?

CHARLIE: No problem there.

SALLY: Is this important for your work?

CHARLIE: Not really.

SALLY: Do you need it for tax reasons?

CHARLIE: No, I can't deduct this.

SALLY: Okay, how would you rate your need for the fast food receipt now?

CHARLIE: It's about a 1.

SALLY: According to the *Workbook*, need is different from want. So, I am going to ask you more questions about it. Do you keep it because you like it?

CHARLIE: No.

SALLY: Are you keeping it for sentimental reasons?

CHARLIE: No.

SALLY: How much do you actually use it?

CHARLIE: Never. But I still want to keep it.

SALLY: Hmmm. I am not sure this is working. Maybe we should check in with the group leader.

CLINICIAN: How's it going over here?

SALLY: We seem to be stuck with Want versus Need.

CHARLIE: I don't see the point. I know I don't need this receipt for survival, but I want to keep it.

CLINICIAN: Charlie, could you tell us why it is important to you to hold onto this receipt?

CHARLIE: I like to know where I spend my money. I was always told to save my receipts.

SALLY: I thought you said earlier that you don't need it, but you want it.

CHARLIE: Yes, I don't need it for survival.

CLINICIAN: What makes you want it?

CHARLIE: Its mine. I don't see the reason not to keep it.

CLINICIAN: Let's consider the reasons to keep it.

SALLY: Wait! How is this relevant to Needs versus Want?

CLINICIAN: You ask an important question. It sounds like this strategy may not be so helpful right now, as Charlie has concluded that he still wants the receipt. So I'm trying out another strategy.

This exercise illustrates the need for flexibility in approach. In this case, Charlie does not seem interested in reducing his desire for the receipt and is not committed to working on changing that. It will be unproductive to continue with this strategy, which does not match his pre-contemplative stage of change. Thus, another strategy is needed, perhaps one that uses more open-ended questions that focus on his reasons for saving and the larger goals he articulated early in treatment.

Objective 4: Homework Commitment

- Take home items to be saved from the sorting exercise and store them where they belong.
- Practice Need versus Want for keeping or acquiring.
- Identify a sorting goal (e.g., target items or areas) for the week.

Objective 5: Complete Clinician Forms

- Clinician directs the clients to write their home commitment on the Group Session Form (see Appendix 12) and completes the Clinician's Group Progress Notes (see Appendix 15).

Chapter 17 *Session 14: Coaching and Letting Go*

Materials Needed

- Instructions for Coaches (Appendix 24)
- Dialogue of coaching episode
- Acquiring Form (*Workbook* Chapter 3, p. 38)

Session Agenda

- Discuss the role of a coach.
- Discuss a coaching episode.
- Practice being a coach.
- Practice sorting items brought by members.
- Enhance communication with coaches.
- Prepare for and discuss the upcoming non-acquisition trip.

Objective 1: Check-in

- Distribute and review the Group Session Form.
- Clients report if they put away in the appropriate place the items that they decided to keep during last session's in-session sorting exercise.

- Each client notes whether they reached their sorting goal for the week.
- Each client reports if they used Need versus Want or another cognitive strategy while sorting over the past week.

Objective 2: Discuss the Role of a Coach

Continuing the discussion from check-in and from Session 4, suggest that coaching support may be important to helping hoarding clients address their saving and acquiring problems and achieve progress. Note that there are many types of coaches, and peers (e.g., fellow group members) may be one type of coach. Coaches can be friends or family members whom clients view as calm, supportive, helpful, and reliable; echo any positive characteristics that group members described during check-in. Reiterate that clients may also hire students, professional organizers, neighbors, acquaintances (e.g., a local church member) for home-based support and encouragement.

Review the types of support a coach can provide. For example, coaching may focus on assisting with reducing clutter, transitioning the skills from the group sessions to the home, and enhancing attention and motivation (Davidow & Muroff, 2011). More specifically, coaches can assist with reviewing much of the content covered throughout the sessions, such as:

- Goal setting and motivational enhancement
- Skills training (problem-solving, categorizing and organizing systems, scheduling sorting, decision-making rules)
- Non-acquiring practice
- Sorting, organizing, and moving wanted and unwanted items; applying basic cognitive strategies (e.g., evaluate pros and cons, needs versus wants)
- Completing assigned homework

- Identifying and accessing social supports for hoarding and related needs

Also, coaches who have specialized skills in case management can assist with other life needs such as:

- Obtaining financial help (e.g., helping clients apply for food stamps)
- Housing needs (e.g., appointments and meetings with housing agencies and staff, rental property management, condo association, advocating for reasonable accommodations, scheduling and attending inspections)
- Medical needs (e.g., scheduling medical appointments)
- Transportation needs
- Addressing safety hazards
- Connecting clients to additional services and resources (e.g., cleaning services, elder services, community supports).

Additionally, coaches can serve as a bridge between clients and other potential support persons (e.g., human services or cleaning staff, professional organizers, family members, friends) in order to help them understand the client's general conceptual hoarding, model effective support strategies, and develop plans for maintaining gains. Noting these diverse roles helps broaden group members' perceptions of "a coach" and their potential usefulness. This may be especially important for clients who experience social anxiety and tend to be socially isolated.

Objective 3: Discussion of a Coaching Episode

To build on the check-in discussion of examples of helpful peer-based coaching, you can role-play the following dialogue of helpful and unhelpful coaching episodes. Alternatively, these can be provided as a handout for discussion.

Case Vignette

Helpful coaching:

CLIENT 1: I have this box of my kids' stuffed animals from when they were young that I can't figure out what to do with.

CLIENT 2 (COACH): Oh, they are cute. So let's use the "questions about possessions." What do you think?

CLIENT 1: Okay, well, looking at the questions: They don't use them anymore, and they have obviously been loved a lot. These are not in great shape, although I suppose a few are. But they really remind me of when my kids were young.

CLIENT 2: So you answered two questions already. How about, "Does this seem important to you because you are looking at it right now?"

CLIENT 1: Hmmm...Well, I did just come across this box. I hadn't looked at it in a while. Though I knew I had it. It made me think about the fun times when my kids were little.

CLIENT 2: It sounds like these stuffed animals remind you of nice memories. Do you think your kids might want them?

CLIENT 1: No, I already tried to give them to my kids.

CLIENT 2: Is there a way to hold on to these memories but consider not keeping the stuffed animals?

CLIENT 1: I don't know. How could I do that?

CLIENT 2: What if we took a photo of the stuffed animals as a keepsake?

CLIENT 1: Oh, I never thought about that. That is a good idea. I want to remember that they had them.

CLIENT 2: If you take photos of them, do you think that you could let them go?

CLIENT 1: Yes, I am going to try that.

Unhelpful coaching:

Client 1: I have this box of my kids' stuffed animals from when they were young that I can't figure out what to do with.

Client 2: Oh those are cute but are kind of dirty.

Client 1: They make me think about the fun times when my kids were little, but my kids don't want them.

Client 2: I can see why. So since they don't want them, you really should get rid of them.

Client 1: Well, they mean a lot to me. It would be like throwing away all those memories.

Client 2: You are not throwing away the memories. You are trying to deal with your hoarding problem and these are cluttering up your house. Name one advantage of keeping it.

Client 1: Well, they make me feel good.

Client 2: Okay, so what are the disadvantages of keeping it?

Client 1: It's adding to my clutter.

Client 2: So, it sounds like you should get rid of it. They are old and dirty and your kids don't want them anyway.

Client 1: I am just not ready to make this decision.

Encourage group members to provide their reactions to these two dialogues and to describe their thoughts about using a coach. To contain conversations about negative experiences with coaches, consider framing the discussion around the following questions:

- What have been barriers in the past to identifying and working with a coach?
- What characteristics are important to you in a coach (e.g., well trained, flexible, good listener, trustworthy)?

- What would you like the coach to help you with most (e.g., physical moving or removing objects, emotional support, organizing skills, staying focused)?

- Whom would you use or hire as a coach (e.g., student, professional organizer, peer with hoarding issues, family member, friend, acquaintance, case manager)?

- Where to locate a coach?

    - National Study Group for Chronic Disorganization
    - National Association of Professional Organizers
    - Faith communities
    - Job boards/Craig's List
    - Contractor/home cleaning companies
    - High school/college community service volunteers
    - Fellow support group member
    - Family and friends

- After a coach is identified, what are the next steps?

    - Identify specific goals and objectives
    - Decide on primary role of the coach (e.g., physically moving/removing items, emotional support, helping you stay focused, motivation)
    - Establish cost per session
    - Decide on schedule (frequency of sessions, duration of each session, how many sessions)

Objective 4: Practice Being a Coach

Divide group members into pairs to sort items they have brought to the group. Working in pairs or smaller groups increases the opportunities for social interaction and encourages mutual aid in a coaching role (support, pushing for work, problem-solving). After practicing sorting together, discuss these questions in your coaching pairs.

- What coaching strategies were used?

- What did your coach do or say that was helpful?

- What could you have said or done to communicate more effectively with your coach?
- How can a coach help you most? How can you set clear goals and communicate clearly (e.g., assert your needs, receive assistance)?

Emphasize the importance of communicating effectively with a coach. The following is an example of incorporating problem-solving skills within the group when addressing the coaching relationship.

Case Vignette

Grace: I need some advice on how to manage something with the coach I started working with.

So, as I mentioned, I have this helper from the senior center who has come to my house to help me de-clutter. She doesn't charge me anything, which I am so thankful for. The problem is she has much more energy than I do, and she wants to stay and sort for hours. It's too much for me, and I don't know how to tell her that; after all, she *is* doing this for free. I also don't want to disappoint her.

Clinician: This sounds like a good scenario to apply our problem-solving skills. Does anyone remember the first step?

Carl: Identify the problem.

Grace: Okay, I did that. The problem is she wants to sort for a very long time. It's too long.

Clinician: What are some potential solutions?

Charlie: Well, I'd just fire her.

Joseph: She's free, she can't fire her. Plus, it's free help!

Clinician: Remember, everyone, let's get all the ideas out before we select the best option.

JENNIFER: You could try to discuss the problem with her.

GRACE: I have told her how tired I get.

LIZ: Maybe you could tell her the window of time that you have available.

MARIA: Maybe you could be direct with her and say that it's not helpful to you to work more than two hours.

JENNIFER: Isn't that kind of the rule anyway?

CHARLIE: Does she know the rules?

GRACE: I gave her a copy of the Instructions for Coaches, but we didn't discuss it much.

JENNIFER: Maybe you could do that. Or maybe the group leader could talk to your coach.

CLINICIAN: Good suggestions! So far, you have suggested: firing her, discussing the problem with her, scheduling a specific time block, telling her that a two-hour limit is best, and discussing the Instructions for Coaches. Grace, which of these solutions would you like to try out? Which ones seem most feasible and comfortable for you?

GRACE: Discussing the Instructions for Coaches might be okay. I could also say that we discussed in group that two-hour blocks are typically best.

CLINICIAN: Which would you like to try out first?

GRACE: Maybe I can give her another copy of the Instructions for Coaches at our next session on Monday.

CLINICIAN: That sounds reasonable. Could you also go through it with her?

GRACE: Yes, I can do that.

MARIA: I would be interested to hear how that works out.

GRACE: I'll let you all know next week.

Objective 4: Preparations and Exercise for Non-Acquisition Trip in Session 15

In preparation for the next session, you will need to identify and inform group members where the group non-acquisition trip will be located. Choose a meeting spot that is accessible for everyone in the group (e.g., consider public transportation, and whether the setting is accessible for any group members with physical disabilities). Ideally, the location will be as private as possible; in some bookstores you can request a private room; otherwise you may meet at a coffee shop or a nearby park. The site should have sufficient variability in items (e.g., food, clothing, office supplies, books, newspapers) so that all group members can identify those that would be of moderate difficulty (Subjective Units of Distress Scale (SUDS) = 4 or 5) on their hierarchies. Good options are local department stores, large pharmacies, or malls with multiple small stores.

At the end of this session, allow enough time for each client to review their Acquiring Form (*Workbook* Chapter 3, p. 38) and select the types of items for the non-acquisition exposure exercise. Some group members might benefit from practice visualizations, Need versus Want, or other exercises before the "in vivo" non-acquisition exposure exercise. These can be assigned as home commitments.

Video Exercise

We recommend showing a video demonstrating a behavioral experiment during a non-shopping trip by Dr. Randy Frost, posted on the International Obsessive Compulsive Disorder Foundation (IOCDF) website (www.ocfoundation.org/hoarding/videos.aspx). After viewing it, discuss group members' reactions and any remaining questions about the upcoming non-acquisition trip.

Objective 6: Home Commitment

1. Identify one or two people who could be a potential coach and why they might be a good coach. If no one comes to mind, then determine a plan on finding a coach.
2. Review Instructions for Coaches with the coach.
3. Practice visualizing the target item for the non-acquisition practice (e.g., visualize seeing it in the store, handling it, and departing without it) and rate your distress levels.
4. Review Rules for Acquiring and practice other exercises that seem helpful in preparation for the non-acquisition trip.

Objective 7: Complete Clinician Forms

- Clinician directs the clients to write their home commitment on the Group Session Form (see Appendix 12) and completes the Clinician's Group Progress Notes (see Appendix 15).

Chapter 18 *Session 15: Non-Acquisition Practice*

(Portions of this session correspond to Chapter 5 of the Workbook)

Materials Needed

- Acquiring Form (*Workbook* Chapter 3, p. 38, Appendix 25)
- Non-Acquiring Help Card (Appendix 31)
- Acquiring Questions Form (*Workbook* Chapter 5, p. 51)
- Rules for Acquiring Form (*Workbook* Chapter 5, p. 52)
- Practice Form (*Workbook* Chapter 4, p. 47, Appendix 32)
- Advantages-Disadvantages Worksheet for Acquiring (*Workbook* Chapter 5, p. 53)
- Need versus Want Scales (*Workbook* Chapter 8, p. 94)
- Instructions for Coaches (Appendix 24)
- Behavioral Experiment Form (*Workbook* Chapter 7, p. 83, Appendix 28)

Session Agenda

- Conduct a group non-acquisition exposure exercise.

Preparation for the Non-Acquiring Group Exercise

During Session 6 and in the previous session (Session 14), you will have decided on the meeting place and setting for the non-acquisition trip for this session. As recommended previously, the location should be accessible, relatively private, and have many different types of items so all group members can find target items of moderate difficulty (distress rating of a 4 or 5). In the last session, each client should have identified target items from their Acquiring Form that will be the focus of this exposure exercise. At the meeting spot, divide members into two subgroups, each led by one of the group leaders. As noted in Session 14, assign members according to types of items, interpersonal dynamics, and stage of change of the group members.

Objective 1: Check-in

Meet the group at the planned meeting place and conduct a brief check-in prior to the non-acquisition exposure.

- Distribute and review the Group Session Form.
- Verify that each group member has identified one or more target items and one helpful coping skill to use during the group practice session.

Objective 2: Non-Acquisition Exposure Exercise

Review with group members the non-acquisition plan and establish their commitment not to acquire, as this is an exposure exercise. Provide clients with copies of the Non-Acquiring Help Card (see Appendix 31) that reiterate their non-acquiring goals, personal rules for acquiring, and questions to ask themselves based on earlier sessions. Assess everyone's level of distress (0–10) before, during, and after the non-acquisition exercise, and facilitate a brief discussion about coping skills that the group members can utilize.

Divide into the two subgroups as planned and ask that each subgroup stay together as they walk through the store and handle the target items (chosen in advance). As the leader, you will want to be sure that all group members get an opportunity to identify items they want and to practice skills in resisting the urge to acquire. Plan which areas of the store or shops to visit and in what order; sale and clearance areas are often helpful locations as these contain "bargains" group members may find appealing. Check in about members' distress ratings as the subgroup sets out. Remind group members to utilize coping and decision-making skills (e.g., Questions about Acquiring and Rules for Acquiring—see the Non-Acquiring Help Card, Advantages and Disadvantages, Need versus Want) as well as the Instructions for Coaches to assist their fellow group members during the non-acquisition exposure. Help clients become aware of their thinking patterns during acquiring practice by asking about their thoughts and identifying problematic thinking styles. Once the error or style is identified, discuss alternative thoughts by asking, "What's another way of thinking about this?" If clients have trouble coming up with a replacement thought, suggest one (e.g., "Even if I feel uncomfortable about not acquiring this, I might get used to it") and discuss.

During the non-acquiring exposures, ask the group members to record their discomfort level using a scale of 0 to 10 about every 10 minutes, or whenever they notice a change in their discomfort. This can be done on a small card carried in their hand or using the Practice Form (*Workbook* Chapter 4, p. 47, Appendix 32). They may be surprised by how quickly the intensity of the urge and the associated discomfort diminish, as suggested in *Workbook* Chapter 5.

Wrap-up of Non-Acquisition Exercise

Prior to reconvening as a larger group, check in about the items that individuals are holding or have handled and returned to the shelves. Help clients return all items to the shelves before the small groups reconvene for the check-out exercise.

If possible, reconvene in the same location as check-in. Ask group members to elaborate on their distress ratings. They may have varying levels of distress by this point, as some levels will have already decreased while others remain elevated. Be aware that sometimes group members' ratings are low because the item that they have identified is less expensive elsewhere or they plan to buy it another time. Ask clients to commit to not buying the item after the exercise is finished so they don't return to the store after the group leaders and members have left, or buy the item elsewhere. Utilize the behavior experiment exercise and encourage clients to rate their current level of distress, how long they believe it will last, and their thoughts about leaving the store without the item. Indicate that at the check-in for the next session (Session 16), everyone can compare their anticipated ratings to their actual experience with the post–non-acquisition exercise.

The non-acquisition exposure activity often creates opportunities for socializing and mutual aid as group members explore the store and items in small groups. Encourage them to identify and apply techniques when making their own decisions and to support and coach each other in this process. Occasionally, some group members may undermine others' motivation and make it more difficult for clients to leave the store without acquiring items, requiring your intervention to address the problem. The case vignettes below demonstrate both mutual aid and potential undermining, as well as the group leaders' responses.

Case Vignette

This subgroup includes Liz, Jennifer, Carl, and Grace.

CLINICIAN: Liz, it's your turn.

LIZ: Well, actually what caught my eye when we entered this store was the stack of coupon books in the entryway. You know the ones that are free for anyone to take?

[*Group walks to the entryway and stands in front of the stack*]

JENNIFER: I have to work really hard not to pick up the free flyers. It's been a real problem for me. Especially the ones printed on shiny paper.

LIZ: *[holding a coupon book]:* I want to pick up a small stack. I can give them to others. There is even a coupon for a coffee, and I could use it right now.

CARL: Coffee does sound good.

CLINICIAN: What is your distress rating at this moment?

LIZ: Honestly, it's very high. I want these coupon books and can use them now. So my rating is about a 9.

CARL: They are useful, and I would like a cup of coffee. I'm at a 5.

CLINICIAN: Grace and Jennifer, how about you?

GRACE: I am doing okay.

JENNIFER: I don't like coffee.

CLINICIAN: Carl and Liz, let's consider which questions about acquiring you have identified as most helpful. Please look at your Non-acquiring Help Card.

LIZ: One of the questions on my list is whether I could use it. And the answer is yes. I don't have much money, and the savings from the coupons make a big difference for me.

CLINICIAN: Okay, is one of your goals to only spend money on necessities.

LIZ: Yes.

CLINICIAN: How about we examine this idea that the coupons always save you money?

LIZ: Okay.

CLINICIAN: Did you plan to buy coffee prior to seeing the coupon?

LIZ: Well, I always like coffee, but it wasn't on my list of things to buy today. And I know we are technically not supposed to buy anything here. But does the coffee shop count?

Jennifer: The rule is that we don't buy anything, so I think coffee is included.

Clinician: So Liz, you did not plan to buy coffee, which means that you would spend no money on coffee. How much does a coffee cost?

Liz: $2.00.

Clinician: What is the coupon discount?

Liz: It's 50 cents off plus a free chocolate chip cookie.

Carl: Um. That sounds good. You are making me hungry.

Clinician: So you planned to spend nothing; how much would you spend if you used the coupon?

Liz: Well, I guess $1.50 plus tax.

Clinician: So how does that fit with your original goal, and does using the coupon save you money?

Liz: Hmmm, I guess the coupon is making me spend $1.50 more than I planned. I never really thought about coupon books costing me money. I can make coffee at home for a lot less.

Clinician: What is your distress rating now about not acquiring the coupon book?

Liz: I am at a 6–7 now, though I still think there are coupons that I could use for things I need.

Jennifer: How about the question, "Does acquiring this coupon book help you with your hoarding problem right now?"

Liz: I guess not. I could live without them. But I know I will keep thinking about them.

Carl: You're strong! We probably don't need any more coffee.

Clinician: Nice work Liz. Okay, so should we move on to the next person's item?

Carl: I'm next… [*Group walks to the books section.*]

Note that Carl's responses were not helpful to Liz in this context, whereas Jennifer tried to help Liz stick to the rules established for the group exercise. In such cases, the wisest course is often to not respond to Carl's comments and move on with strategies such as evaluating the costs and benefits, as this leader did.

In-Office or Alternative Non-Acquisition Exercise

For some groups it will not be feasible to arrange an offsite non-acquisition trip. One alternative is to create a non-acquisition activity in the room where the group meets. Prepare group members at the end of the previous session for this in-office experience by telling them that you will be bringing in items that are intended to be moderately difficult for each of them not to acquire. Prepare for this activity by making a list of the items that the group members find moderately difficult to resist acquiring (about a 5 on their hierarchy), based on the intake assessments and the sessions covering exposure hierarchies (Sessions 7 and 8). Items could include newspapers, clothing, purses, books, plastic bags, sugar packets, etc. Distribute or set up these items around the room where the group meets with signs nearby that say "Free Stuff." This in-office exposure activity will follow similar directions as described for the store visit. Divide members into two subgroups, each led by one of the group leaders.

Case Vignette

[*Walking into the group room*]

MARIA: Oh, look at those Christmas ornaments! Aren't they beautiful!

CHARLIE: Well, I don't really care about them, but I could really use that printer for the parts.

SALLY: Is it true? Are these really free?

CHARLIE: No, it's part of the activity, don't you remember? Today, we are supposed to just window-shop!

CLINICIAN: That's right, Charlie. Today is the non-acquisition activity. Please take a look around, but for now we are just looking, okay?

[*Group members nod*]

CLINICIAN: Let's review the homework first. Who wants to share what they wrote on the Acquisition Form?

CHARLIE: Well I did it, and now I'm looking at an item right in front of me that registers a 5 on this (0–10).

JOSEPH: What is it?

CHARLIE: *[looking annoyed]:* The printer, of course

CLINICIAN: Okay, what does a rating of 5 feel like?

CHARLIE: Like I want to take it and put it in my car. But I know I can't.

JENNIFER: Do you have room for it? Is that a good question to ask?

CLINICIAN: Good, Jennifer. Charlie, why can't you take it?

CHARLIE: It's against our rules for today, right?

CLINICIAN: Yes! You are right, today we are going to choose an item that is between a 3 and 5 on our hierarchy and we are going to plan to leave it and investigate our thoughts and feelings.

JOSEPH: Well, there's nothing here that I care about, so my investigation is done. I don't need anything here.

CLINICIAN: Okay. Well, what rules did you come up with on your Non-Acquiring Form, Joseph?

JOSEPH: No more trade magazines, and no more bringing home any papers about work. None.

LIZ: How is that for you? I mean, can you really not pick them up when you see them?

JOSEPH: Yep, I have no room for them and no money, none. I guess I'm over the acquiring issue and now I just can't get rid of what I already have.

MARIA: That's great that you don't bring more stuff in the house!

JOSEPH: Thanks.

CLINICIAN: Back to the homework review. Anyone else want to share?

[*Group members shake heads no*]

LIZ: I just want to get on with this activity. I can't stop looking at that hat. Look at that hat, isn't it beautiful? Now that hat is calling my name!

JENNIFER [SMILING]: Uh oh, is it going to be hard to leave it here?

LIZ: I know I can't take it home, so maybe I'll just stare at it.

JOSEPH: We'll be watching you as you walk out today. [*smiling*]

LIZ: Don't you worry about me, I can do this.

SALLY: I'm glad you can, but I'm telling you, that red purse has my name all over it. [*To clinician*]: Are you sure you don't want to sell that purse?

CLINICIAN: What do you think? [*Smiling*]. Okay, since we seem to have already gotten started, let's talk about what thoughts and feelings arise when you look at the items that you like? Okay?

SALLY: I feel my heart beating and my hands sweaty. I really like that purse. I mean it goes with my style!

CLINICIAN: Let's also talk about the strategies that you have learned to help you make the decision to not acquire.

JOSEPH: How many red purses do you already have?

SALLY: Oh, I don't know, maybe 6 or 7...

JENNIFER: Does anyone have those questions? Can I borrow the questions?

SALLY: I know, I know. How many do I need? How many would be enough? I guess I don't need another red purse. I already have several that are a similar color.

MARIA: Have you already made a decision?

SALLY: I can leave it, I mean, it's yours [*referring to clinician*], so I can't really take it anyway, right?

CHARLIE: No, that's the point of the exercise.

CLINICIAN: What is your level of distress when you remind yourself that you cannot keep this?

SALLY: I guess right now it's a 5, but I think 10 minutes ago it was an 8 or 9! Asking myself the questions and knowing that it's not really available helps get my ratings down to a 5.

JOSEPH: But you [*referring to the clinician*] aren't there when I buy things. I don't see how this helps.

CLINICIAN: That is a good point. The purpose here is to observe that one's rating may change with the context and over time.

JENNIFER: Plus, that's a big drop!

CLINICIAN: So when you are faced with the decision of whether to acquire an item, you can engage in a behavioral experiment whereby you compare your predicted level of distress to your actual experience.

Note the group members' demonstration of mutual aid as they push each other to work, appropriate for this phase of group development. The leader also reached for engagement from all members who assisted Sally with her decision.

Objective 3: Home Commitment

- Complete the non-acquisition behavior experiment with regard to ratings associated with not acquiring the item at the group session.
- Complete another non-acquiring practice for a similar type of item.
- Identify a sorting goal (e.g., target items or areas) for the week.
- Bring items for sorting to the next group session.

Objective 4: Clinician Forms

- Clinician directs the clients to write their home commitment on the Group Session Form (see Appendix 12) and completes the Clinician's Group Progress Notes (see Appendix 15).

Chapter 19 *Session 16: Barriers to Progress*

Materials Needed

- Client's General Conceptual Hoarding Model (*Workbook* Chapter 3, p. 33, Appendix 17)
- Personal Worksheet for Managing Barriers (Appendix 33)
- Task List (*Workbook* Chapter 6, p. 65)
- Family Response to Hoarding Scale (FRHS) (Appendix 34)

Session Agenda

- Discuss strategies for managing barriers.
- Complete Personal Worksheet for Managing Barriers.
- Apply problem-solving skills to address barriers.
- Discuss strategies for managing attention and creating structure.

Objective 1: Check-in

- Distribute and review the Group Session Form.
- Each client identifies a potential coach, their plan for finding a coach, and/or discusses their experience of reviewing the Instructions for Coaches with their coach.

- Review Behavior Experiment from non-acquisition trip and subsequent non-acquiring practice for a similar type of item.
- Identify one or more things that members of their subgroup did that was helpful during the non-acquisition exposure.
- Each client notes whether they reached their sorting goal for the week, identifying barriers that interfered or that they overcame.

Objective 2: Troubleshooting Barriers to Progress

Emphasize that managing barriers is part of the process of addressing hoarding problems. Even the most highly motivated people experience barriers to their progress. A number of factors can make dealing with hoarding especially difficult. Note some of the barriers that group members have shared during the development of their models and during their home commitments, as well as a couple of successes overcoming such barriers. Distinguish between personal barriers (e.g., depression, attention-focusing problems, OCD symptoms, health problems, feeling overwhelmed) and external barriers (e.g., lack of social support, pressure from family members or authorities, lack of time because of a busy lifestyle). Comment on the barriers that seem most relevant to the members of your group.

Explore these barriers using a strengths' perspective (see the Case Vignette in this chapter) and problem-solving methods from Session 9. Remind group members to consider their strengths and how those strengths can help them address the barriers to progress. In our experience, solutions are often possible. Various strategies for addressing potential barriers are described in Table 19.1. This table is intended for group leader reference only, as distributing it to group members will be too overwhelming. Instead, use the table to identify potential solutions to problems that group members raise.

Exercise: Personal Worksheet for Managing Barriers

The Personal Worksheet for Managing Barriers provided in the Appendix 33 of this guide can help clients identify personal barriers, strengths, and

Table 19.1 Managing Barriers

Barriers	Description of how they interfere with progress on hoarding	Strategies
Personal Barriers		
Depression	Affects ~50% of those with HD *Examples*: poor appetite, sleeping problems, low energy, suicidal ideation (less common)	Psychiatric evaluation Antidepressant medications or CBT Exercise and social activities
Anxiety and worry	GAD affects ~30% of those with HD Worries about many life concerns and bad consequences if desired items are not acquired or are discarded	Standard CBT methods
Social anxiety and autism spectrum disorders (ASD)	Social anxiety affects ~25% of people with HD Lower marriage rate; limited social support network Difficult time with allowing coaches, other professionals, and family members to assist them at home	Encourage client to allow carefully chosen and well trained in-home assistants
OCD symptoms	Contamination fears and washing or cleaning rituals Fears of making mistakes and compulsive checking Avoidance of decision-making Seeking reassurance from clinician, friends, or others	When mild, ask clients to minimize OCD rituals and avoidance and gradually eliminate OCD symptoms Use Questions about Possessions, behavioral experiments; establish formal rules Determine automatic thoughts and interpretations Minimize or eliminate requests for reassurance Practice with feared situations or items Obtain additional exposure or cognitive therapy for OCD symptoms
Attention deficits	Distractibility or difficulty staying focused on any task, not just de-cluttering Managing time	Measure and increase attention span Use calendars for scheduling tasks Set and track priorities Establish routines and assess usefulness (see Objective 3)

Table 19.1 (Continued)

Barriers	Description of how they interfere with progress on hoarding	Strategies
Stealing	~ 10% of HD cases	Help clients analyze behaviors and thoughts that lead to stealing Develop a strategy to interrupt sequence When stealing is impulsive, visualize consequences (police arrive, handcuffs, going to jail, calling relatives from jail)
PTSD and trauma history	More trauma histories among HD clients; PTSD rate is not higher than for other mental health problems	Assess trauma history and connection to hoarding beliefs Use cognitive strategies
Cognitive disabilities	People with developmental disabilities may have hoarding symptoms	Train basic skills for problem-solving, organizing, decision-making Reinforce non-hoarding behaviors Develop rules for acquiring Practice non-shopping, sorting, organizing and discarding at home Omit cognitive therapy methods
Sensitivity to criticism	Jump to conclusions easily about others' views of them Report a lifelong history of criticism for their hoarding and are highly sensitive about this	If problem is suspected but not stated by client, ask for feedback: *Clinician*: "Sometimes people get angry or hurt by things I say. It is very important to tell me whenever this happens so I can fix the problem." Examine actual evidence for perceived criticism to correct faulty thinking
Anger	Defensive reaction by clients who are sensitive to criticism could indicate suspicion and paranoid thinking for clients with these personality features	Ask about client's feelings and whether they think the perceived attack was intentional or mean-spirited Reflect and summarize client's statements and ask if that is accurate Admit mistakes and apologize briefly Do not blame clients, interpret feelings, or imply they are inappropriate Explore cause of anger or frustration, including cognitive biases (e.g., "Criticism about a mistake means I'm a total failure.") Formulate and test hypotheses in a behavioral experiment

Table 19.1 (Continued)

Barriers	Description of how they interfere with progress on hoarding	Strategies
Feeling overwhelmed	Problem seems so huge that it's difficult to know how or where to start or whether progress is even possible Procrastination/avoidance of homework assignments	Structure tasks in a simple and stepwise manner Ask clients to report immediately if an assignment seems too hard and/or they experience negative feelings
Lack of social support	Unable to make progress when working alone at home Family members are critical or controlling	Identify potential coaches Review instructions for coaches Ask coach to observe clinician working with the client Avoid encouraging coaching from family members who are critical or controlling
Avoidance of feelings	Prematurely draw conclusions about the meaning of possessions without processing thoughts and feelings Save most items without considering their true value	Encourage processing time by asking client to verbalize thoughts and feelings about objects to understand their meaning and habituate to uncomfortable feelings prior to decision making
Unusual beliefs	*Examples*: A fear of death—removal of clutter means it's time to die Fear of losing interest in everything, including life, if possessions are removed	Use cognitive strategies for faulty thinking Ask clients to clarify what they believe and how they came to this conclusion Evaluate belief with Socratic questioning
Health and medical concerns	Obesity, diabetes, arthritis and joint problems, high blood pressure, asthma, autoimmune disorders Presence of hazardous material (e.g., mold, insects, spoiled food, pathogens) Lack of electricity, heat, or plumbing	Assess health complications and home sanitation Communicate with health officer to learn how to correct the problem (requires client consent)
External Barriers		
Impending deadlines to remove clutter	Deadlines from law enforcement or community agencies Ultimatums from family members who threaten to leave or are planning forced clutter removal	Intensive sorting and hauling sessions with help from coaches/others Hire professional organizer or cleaning company with experience with hoarding (required when clutter poses health risk)

Table 19.1 (Continued)

Barriers	Description of how they interfere with progress on hoarding	Strategies
Family behaviors	Family members experienced current or childhood burden Family member expresses hostility and rejection of HD client Family members also report hoarding behavior	Assess family reaction and cause Use the Family Response to Hoarding Scale (FRHS; Steketee, Ayers, Umbach, Tolin & Frost, 2013; see Appendix 34) Plan a family meeting to discuss treatment expectations and the need for HD client to make independent decisions Determine how to address family members' hoarding in planning homework and other treatment strategies
Financial problems	Non-payment of bills; collection agencies Problems with paying taxes, insurance, credit cards, assets Legal consequences	Developing paper-organizing systems Identify sources of financial education and assistance from local task force or other agencies
Housing problems	Conflict with landlords Threat of eviction	If client is mandated to treatment, find internal motivation to set goals Communicate with landlord to delay eviction and/or find alternative housing (may raise confidentiality concerns)
Unsafe home	Significant risk of physical injury or fire due to clutter and/or home conditions	Assess with Safety Questions Evaluate needs of elderly or disabled clients Remove flammable materials near sources of heat Open blocked exits, windows, and pathways
Endangerment of children and elders	Most states mandate that mental health clinicians must report home conditions that threaten the health or safety of children or elders	Review your state's laws for mandated reporting to ensure compliance Notify client of laws and requirements Consult with authorities to assess level of threat and possible need to remove elders or children Work with case manager in oversight agency to increase the chances of a positive outcome

Table 19.1 (Continued)

Barriers	Description of how they interfere with progress on hoarding	Strategies
Problems with animal care	Animals not provided with adequate food, shelter, health care	Assess animal care Consider temporary placement of animals outside the home Devise plan for adequate care of pets remaining in the home

CBT = cognitive and behavioral treatment; GAD = generalized anxiety disorder; HD = hoarding disorder; OCD = obsessive-compulsive disorder

strategies they'd like to try for managing the barriers. An example of a completed form is given in Table 19.2. Photocopy the blank forms from the Appendix 33 and distribute to group members during the session. Draw the table on the board and complete a couple of rows based on the group members' responses; this will serve as a model to the group as they fill in their own worksheets.

Table 19.2 Example of Personal Worksheet for Managing Barriers

Barrier	Personal Strengths	Troubleshooting Strategies (brainstorm potential solutions; problem-solve)
Depression—feeling down and don't want to do anything	Sense of humor	Watch a comedy Contact my friend Rhonda who laughs at my jokes
Inattention—unable to focus for more than a few minutes during sorting session	Good at knitting Enjoy listening to music	Set a timer Knit before sorting exercise to get myself grounded Knit after sorting exercise to reward myself
Procrastination—Putting off home commitment until right before group session	Following through with commitments Caring enough about myself to try to do the home commitment	Schedule specific times and reminders to do the home commitment Break down the home commitment into more manageable steps

Case Vignette

SALLY:	I am so depressed sometimes I can't even get out of bed to brush my teeth.
MARIA:	Me, too! Then my kids get on me and call and tell me to get up and take care of myself. They get so mad. They just don't understand, and all those calls just make me want to crawl back to bed.
CHARLIE:	I don't have depression. I don't know what I have. I don't really think there is much wrong with me. I just like to be prepared to fix anything.
JOSEPH:	Well, I do have depression: I'm depressed because I lost everything. Why would I want to throw away those things in my life that represent the happier times? I'll probably never be happy like before.
LIZ:	Oh, that's sad.
JENNIFER:	How do you know you won't be happy again? Maybe you will. Maybe you will find work. Sounds like you are using one of those problematic thinking styles! What is it called? Fortune-telling?
CLINICIAN:	Yes, Jennifer, that does sound like fortune-telling. So the question is how do we deal with these barriers?
JENNIFER:	Use coping skills—I learned a lot about coping skills when I was in the hospital.
CLINICIAN:	Yes, coping skills are very important, and so are the personal strengths that many of you have already recognized in yourselves. Let's work on identifying the problems and finding possible solutions on the Personal Worksheet for Managing Barriers.

Objective 3: Managing Attention and Creating Structure

It is likely that clients will identify difficulties with attention as a barrier, given how common this problem is for clients with hoarding disorder. Creating structure can help with those challenges. Teaching strategies that help focus their attention and limit the scope and duration of tasks may help group members who are unable to sustain attention on repetitive chores like organizing and sorting (Hartl, Duffany, Allen, Steketee & Frost, 2005). Many clients are unsure of where to keep items and doubt being able to find things if they were put away. Instead, they rely heavily on keeping objects in view to remember them, resulting in piles of things that cover the furniture and floors. The short-term relief provided by setting items within sight is outweighed by the long-term costs of losing items in the clutter. As noted in Session 10, hoarding clients tend to create too many categories while sorting their own things (Wincze et al., 2007) and have trouble conceptualizing how and where to store items. Reiterate to group members that learning to categorize, file, and store items out of sight is essential to clearing space for more comfortable living and to using the spaces as they'd like. Publications by professional organizers and manuals for addressing attention-deficit problems can provide additional strategies (see the Readings and Resources list in the Appendix).

Introduce a variety of strategies that are useful for managing attention and focus during organizing:

- Measuring current attention span and working to increase it over time
- Using calendars to schedule practice
- Setting and keeping track of priorities for practice
- Establishing routines and assessing their usefulness

You may not have sufficient time to cover all of these strategies during this session. Using calendars and establishing routines may also be incorporated into the next session (Session 17), which will partly focus on routines and systems.

Attention Span

To measure clients' attention span, ask clients to time how long they are able to sort their possessions at home until they become distracted or confused; timing this can be part of their home commitment. The time may vary depending on the types of items being sorted, as clients are often more distractible when the task is difficult. After determining the usual attention span (which may be only a few minutes), suggest that clients set a timer for this time period and practice (sorting or organizing) until the timer goes off. That is, if their usual attention span is 10 minutes, they would start by setting the timer for only 10 minutes. Once they can sort successfully for 10 minutes several times in a row, suggest that clients increase the time by a few minutes—perhaps 3 to 5 minutes. Ideally, a coach or in-home support person would help the client continue this procedure until they can work without distraction for long enough to feel some accomplishment (for example, 30 minutes if the original time to distraction was 10 minutes). This procedure also exposes clients to the discomfort of making hard decisions about saving, discarding, and organizing. Longer practice will help habituate them to this discomfort. Encourage them to make a home commitment of expanding their sorting time when they are working alone at home, and making it even longer when assisted by their coach.

Use of Calendars

Emphasize that creating structure in their lives will also help clients reduce their attention problems. For example, using a calendar (electronic or written, per the client's preference) to establish a routine improves their functioning and helps them feel more in control of their lives. Ask group members whether they are currently using a calendar this way, and troubleshoot any barriers. For example, recommend that their calendar should list *all* of their planned activities, including their home commitments. Ask them to update their calendars as often as new time commitments arise, so they are always up-to-date. Help clients schedule appointments for organizing and sorting sessions to fit times that work best for them (e.g., mornings or afternoons, before a regular favorite activity that provides a reward for their work).

Setting Priorities

Emphasize to group members that setting priorities and keeping track of them in the *Workbook* are keys to managing distractibility for those who find that their priorities often shift depending on their mood and other life events. Encourage clients to use the Task List (*Workbook* Chapter 6, p. 65) with columns for task description, priority ranking, the date it was put on the list, and when it was completed. Safren et al. (2005) recommend using three priority rankings:

- Priority "A" for tasks to be done within a day or two,
- Priority "B" for tasks that can take longer,
- Priority "C" for less important tasks that might be attractive and fun, but are not essential.

Establishing Routines

Ask clients to follow a consistent routine during times scheduled to work on their hoarding (several times a week, or daily if time permits), and to reduce any distractions (e.g., by turning off the TV, radio, telephone, computer, etc.). However, some clients find background music or noise helpful in calming an anxious mood or lifting a depressed one. Next, ask clients to review their priority list and select an appropriate goal for the upcoming week. Help them break down the goal into small and manageable steps that are clearly defined and easily implemented. They might need to self-monitor what distracts them in order to improve their attention focus. Common distractions are telling stories about possessions or having to find something else before deciding about the possession at hand. Setting up categories and locations for possessions, as described in Session 10, may speed the process along.

Help clients establish these routines and check on their usefulness at group sessions until clients are able to use them automatically. Use problem-solving strategies described in Session 9 to deal with difficulties that arise. For example, clients who find their eyes wandering to other items in the room might limit this distraction by using sheets to cover areas next to the section they are working on. Clients who find that their thinking jumps forward in time to upcoming tasks might solve this problem by breaking the current task into brief segments they can execute quickly so they have the feeling of moving forward in their work. They might also write down distracting thoughts for later review in order to stay on task (this is similar to the "parking lot" rule in group sessions). In addition, repeated practice and use of cognitive strategies (Session 12) usually help clients develop more adaptive ways of approaching tasks, and in turn, help minimize distractions caused by negative emotions.

Assembling a Team

As shown in Table 19.1, the barriers that impede progress with hoarding are complex and involve personal and external factors. In general, when hoarding is severe and other comorbidities are present, we encourage you to engage appropriate other human service professionals in your client's treatment. As mentioned in Chapter 2, professionals involved in hoarding task forces are often very knowledgeable about hoarding and about community resources that can be especially helpful. You may need advice or assistance from public health officers, fire and safety officers, housing inspectors, or other professionals who understand the relevant codes. A variety of social service professionals can also be helpful with regard to housing and other services, including social workers and case managers working with the department on aging, disabilities, protective services, or other special needs areas. When mental health comorbidity is significant and threatens to derail the focus on hoarding, we strongly recommend helping your client engage another therapist who can address the non-hoarding diagnoses and related functioning problems. This will free you to focus mainly on hoarding, which is often the problem of greatest immediate concern because of its social, economic, employment, and functional costs.

Objective 4: Home Commitment

- Clients time how long they can sort their possessions at home until they become distracted or confused, and work to increase this time gradually.
- Each client identifies and tests a strategy to address one barrier (e.g., call a friend to improve low mood).
- Clients work toward the goal from the priority list that they identified for the week by using specific strategies (e.g., breaking down the goal into more manageable steps, using a calendar, establishing routines).

Objective 5: Complete Clinician Forms

- Clinician directs the clients to write their home commitment on the Group Session Form (see Appendix 12) and completes the Clinician's Group Progress Notes (see Appendix 15).

Chapter 20 *Session 17: Maintaining Systems and Gains*

(Corresponds to Chapter 9 of the Workbook)

Materials Needed

- Weekly Schedule Worksheet (Appendix 35)
- My Pleasurable Alternative Activities form (*Workbook* Chapter 5, p. 57)
- List of Treatment Techniques (*Workbook* Chapter 9, p. 114, Appendix 36)

Session Agenda

- Plan for maintaining gains and routines.
- Discuss coping with empty space.
- Plan alternative sources of enjoyment and coping.
- Begin discussion of termination.
- Sorting exercise.

Objective 1: Check-in

- Distribute and review Group Session Form.
- Report on progress with one strategy to address one barrier.
- Report on the use of calendars, routines, etc.

Objective 2: Maintaining Systems and Gains

Extending the discussion about routines from Session 16, emphasize to group members that continuing to use decision-making skills (e.g., rules, categories, file systems) and establishing daily routines to replace old habits will not only address existing clutter but prevent new disorganized clutter from accumulating. To continue to improve and maintain these gains, the following alternative behaviors may be useful:

- Pick a time to sort new mail and papers every day.
- Incorporate recreational time after sorting to boost your spirits and reinforce the work.
- Empty the trash twice weekly (more often if required).
- Take trash out for pickup (or deliver to sanitation facilities) at the same time every week.
- Do dishes daily in order to wake up to a clean sink and counter.
- Do laundry every week (more often if required).
- Establish times and a system for paying bills to meet due dates.
- Put all new purchases away upon their arrival or within the same day.
- Put away any used items as soon as the task is done.

Ask group members what routines they have in place (e.g., laundry, emptying trash) and how frequently they engage in these behaviors. Ask them what days trash and recycling are picked up in their neighborhood, typical due dates for bills, etc. Ask the clients to schedule some of these tasks (e.g., taking out the trash, paying bills, doing laundry) in their calendars. For those who are not using calendars yet, consider handing out Weekly Schedule Worksheet forms (see Appendix 35) and asking clients to schedule these activities.

Additionally, a few succinct general organizing rules such as the following (courtesy of Anne Goodwin; personal communication) can be posted on clients' refrigerator doors or in another prominent location.

- If you take it out, put it back
- If you open it, close it

- If you throw it down, pick it up
- If you take it off, hang it up
- If you use it, clean it up

Objective 3: Coping with Empty Space

For some group members, progress that is visible because some spaces are now empty reinforces their de-cluttering and non-acquisition work. But for others, the empty space may trigger fears of danger or vulnerability and lead them to re-clutter the area to reduce their anxiety. If any group members' reactions seem unusually strong, they may be associated with past traumas that make it difficult for them to address their hoarding. In such cases, consider making a referral for individual treatment of the trauma history (see Table 19.1 of barriers to progress in Session 16). To clarify their experiences, ask whether clients feel the urge to fill up any spaces created by de-cluttering. If so, discuss strategies for coping with these urges, such as enjoying having the room to move around, developing an uncluttered aesthetic, filling the space with a single item like a large plant, and developing a new use for the space (e.g., displaying artwork, using workspace).

Objective 4: Alternative Sources of Enjoyment and Coping

Remind group members that in Session 6 of the group they brainstormed pleasurable alternative activities to acquiring that were feasible, enjoyable, and consistent with their personal goals and interests (see My Pleasurable Alternative Activities form from the client *Workbook*, Chapter 5, p. 57). Ask clients about their progress on engaging in helpful replacement and coping activities. For example, ask about the frequency with which they engage in non-acquisition and coping activities, as well as their levels of enjoyment and relief from stress (0 = "none" to 10 = "maximum"). Ask clients how well they have integrated these pleasurable activities and coping strategies into their lives—are they part of their daily or weekly routine? Ask group members what effect, if any, they think the alternative activities have had on their mood and on their acquiring and saving behaviors. Encourage group members to work together to problem-solve identified barriers and brainstorm solutions.

Objective 4: Discuss the End of the Group Treatment

Invite group members to voice their thoughts and fears about the end of treatment. Some clients may be concerned about their progress and the prospect of ending regular contact with the clinician and the group. If these concerns seem irrational, use Socratic questioning strategies to help evaluate faulty thinking. Ask about the advantages of ending treatment (e.g., less dependence on group leaders, a chance to practice their skills and feel self-confident, more time for other activities, less expense). Reassure clients that they are not alone in their struggle, and it is very common for people with hoarding to need to continue their work for some months to come. Remind clients of the discussion during their first session that addressing their hoarding problems is an ongoing process, and recovery requires continuing practice after the group meetings have ended. Also, remind clients that the group will review the strategies that seemed to work best in the next session (Session 18) and assess their progress on their goals in the session after that (Session 19) in order to develop a plan for continuing the work based on their needs. Direct group members to the List of Treatment Techniques in the client *Workbook*, Chapter 9, p. 114. For their home commitment, ask clients to review the list and identify the techniques that are the most helpful. Please note that some of the techniques in the list were not covered in group treatment (see Appendix 36).

Prior to the final session, each individual group member will need a plan for continued support and additional treatment if they would like it. If you have incorporated home visits into the protocol, then the last home visit can be used for the final assessment and the termination plan. We recommend scheduling these home visits just before the final group session. If home visits are not a regular part of treatment, other possibilities for termination plans may include: (1) designating some time during the final three group sessions for individual contact with clients, or (2) scheduling separate individual sessions with each client. It is helpful to have a prepared list of resources that group members might want (e.g., individual therapists, prescribing providers, support groups, elder services) based on the local area where each client resides.

Case Vignette

CLINICIAN:	Today, we are going to discuss how to maintain the gains that you have made so far.
JENNIFER:	Gains? I don't feel like I have made any progress. I can't believe that this group will be ending in just three sessions. I thought that I would have had my whole house organized by this point.
SALLY:	I'm with you, Jennifer! I have made some progress, but I have a long way to go!
MARIA:	Well, I've made a little progress and I'm proud of it; and so have you two. Jennifer, didn't I hear you say in check-in that you were able to donate a whole box of cards to the church near your house?
JENNIFER:	Yes, but I still have a long way to go.
CLINICIAN:	As we discussed in the beginning of the group, you are all learning skills to change your thoughts and behaviors, and that takes time, as it does for any skill. You have all been coming to this group and learning these skills so you can achieve your goals. As we have discussed, working on hoarding problems is not easy.
GRACE:	Even though my house isn't completely empty of clutter, I feel like I have made a lot of changes in the way that I think about my stuff.
CLINICIAN:	Could you share some of these changes with the group?
GRACE:	Well, for example, before I buy something, I really do ask myself the questions.

JOSEPH: I have started using a scheduler, you know, a calendar, for the first time in my life. It's actually helped me remember my appointments. It's been a couple of months since I missed one.

JENNIFER: This just feels like it's going to take the rest of my life to de-clutter my home.

CLINICIAN: Maybe it will help to think of this work as like other aspects of healthy living—for example, exercise. The first few months that people work out, they set goals, learn specific exercises and skills, and even see some gains in strength and weight loss if they stick to their regimen. It becomes part of the daily activities of their life, but they still have to work on it for many months, if not years.

LIZ: This reminds me of losing weight. I have struggled with eating my whole life. And I still have to work at it. But at some point, I did learn how to eat more healthily and build that into my life. Like hoarding, I had to make better daily choices about me. It's actually pretty similar. And there are times when I don't do as well with it, but then I go to the nutrition meeting, remind myself of what I need to do, and try to maintain it.

CLINICIAN: That is such an excellent example, Liz. Working on hoarding is about daily living and using the skills to work on reducing clutter, preventing an increase in clutter, and taking care of ourselves.

JENNIFER: This is making me feel a little better. I am worried about not having you guys to support me. No one understands this problem like you all do.

CLINICIAN: It sounds like this group has really meant a lot to you. Many of you may be wondering about next steps, which we will continue to talk about over the next few sessions as we wrap up the group.
[*Charlie walks in 20 minutes late. Group members wave, say "Hi," and "You made it!"*]

CHARLIE: Sorry I'm late.

CLINICIAN: Well, I'm glad you made it! What held you up?

CHARLIE: Nothing in particular, it just seems harder to get here on time the closer we get to the end.

CLINICIAN: How do you feel about the end of the group?

JENNIFER: I feel panicked!

SALLY: I feel sad. What do you feel, Charlie?

CHARLIE: I guess I'm going to miss you all: I didn't want to be here, now we're talking about ending, and in some ways I feel like I need it to just end.

MARIA: All this time, you really did like us! [*smiling*]

CLINICIAN: I know this is hard for you. It's not unusual for group members, especially groups like yours where people have really worked hard together, to have mixed emotions about ending. Sometimes to avoid those endings, group members will start coming late or not show up. Let's try to make this the best ending as a group that we can, okay?

JENNIFER: That means we are all coming to the last three groups, right?
[*Group members nod, affirming commitment to attend the last groups.*]

Note the mutual aid Maria showed in supporting Jennifer and Sally and pointing out their success. Charlie arrives quite late for group, most likely a reaction to the group's ending as he had been on time for nearly every session. The group leader directly asks how group members feel about the end of group and provides them with information about common responses to endings. In a very helpful gesture, Jennifer gets the group to contract about their attendance for the last three groups.

Objective 6: In-Session Sorting

As time allows, ask group members to divide into pairs to sort items that they have brought in to the group.

Objective 7: Home Commitment

- Develop a plan for using cleared spaces and keeping them clear of new clutter.
- Review the List of Treatment Techniques and highlight the methods that were the most helpful (client *Workbook,* Chapter 9, p. 114).
- Try out an alternative strategy or pleasurable activity for managing urges, available time, and/or open space.
- Schedule a specific day and time for continued sorting.

Objective 8: Clinician Forms

- Clinician directs the clients to write their home commitment on the Group Session Form (see Appendix 12) and completes the Clinician's Group Progress Notes (see Appendix 15).

Chapter 21 *Session 18: Review of Treatment Methods*

(Corresponds to Chapter 9 of the Workbook)

Materials Needed

- Client's General Conceptual Hoarding Model (*Workbook* Chapter 3, p. 33, Appendix 17)
- Client's Personal Goals form (*Workbook* Chapter 4, p. 42)
- List of Treatment Techniques (*Workbook* Chapter 9, p. 114, Appendix 36)

Session Agenda

- Review the List of Treatment Techniques.
- Identify the treatment methods that worked best for each client.

Objective 1: Check-in

- Distribute and review the Group Session Form.
- Clients identify a pleasant activity and/or a use for uncluttered spaces.
- Clients identify one treatment strategy that was particularly helpful.

Objective 2: Review Treatment Techniques

Explain to the group members that reviewing the therapy process may enable them to recall what they did and what worked particularly well, and help guide their efforts to continue to improve and to prevent relapse. Begin by reviewing the Hoarding and Acquiring Models developed early in treatment (see *Workbook*, Chapter 3, p. 33; and Session 2 of this *Guide*). Ask clients whether they think they need to make any further modifications to the models, and if so, ask them to do so. Ask the group members what the models imply about what they need to do after treatment ends. Help them recall the general principles on which they have been working during treatment and formulate these in a way that emphasizes their own skills and personal goals. Examples are:

1. Begin with easier items and work toward harder ones.
2. Be patient; change takes time.
3. Notice small gains.
4. Ask for help when you aren't strong enough to do it alone.
5. Be firm with yourself, but not perfectionistic.

Next, remind clients of their original treatment goals by examining the Personal Goals form they completed in Session 4 (*Workbook*, Chapter 4, p. 42). During Session 19, the group will review their progress toward these goals. For now, focus on reminding them of the specific treatment methods and strategies that are relevant for them to achieve their personal goals.

Review the techniques learned during therapy by going over the Group Session forms and material in their client *Workbook*. Instruct clients to review the List of Treatment Techniques in the *Workbook* (p. 114) and in Table 21.1, to pick out strategies for use in the future. Use the metaphor of a toolbox, describing each technique as a tool. Help clients identify the methods that worked best for them and in which contexts (acquiring, sorting and organizing, discarding). If you do not have sufficient time to complete this review, incorporate it into the home commitment.

Table 21.1 List of Treatment Techniques

- Review the client's General Conceptual Hoarding Model and consider possible updates to the following (Session 2; *Workbook* Chapter 3, p. 33):
    - Personal and family vulnerabilities
    - Information-processing problems
    - Thoughts and reasons for saving
    - Positive and negative emotions
    - Acquiring, saving, and avoidance behaviors
- Review the Brief Thought Record (Session 2; *Workbook* Chapter 3, p. 37)
- Repeat the clutter, unclutter, and ideal home visualizations to determine client reactions (Session 3; *Workbook* Chapter 4)
- Review Personal Goals (Session 4; *Workbook* Chapter 4, p. 42)
- Review the functional analysis of acquiring episodes (Session 6; *Workbook* Chapter 3, p. 39)
- Acquiring—Examine and review the following (Sessions 5–7; *Workbook* Chapter 5):
    - Acquiring Form, to see progress and determine whether unwanted items continue to come into the home (Session 5, *Workbook* Chapter 3, p. 38)
    - Advantages-Disadvantages (Session 5, *Workbook* Chapter 5, p. 53)
    - Acquiring Questions Form (Session 5, *Workbook* Chapter 5, p. 51)
    - Client's Rules for Acquiring (Session 5, *Workbook* Chapter 5, p. 52)
    - Hierarchy of acquiring situations to determine additional work needed (Session 5, *Workbook* Chapter 5, p. 55)
    - Progress on alternative sources of enjoyment (Session 5, *Workbook* Chapter 5, p. 57)
    - Faulty thinking about acquiring (Session 5, *Workbook* Chapter 5, p. 56, 58–59)
    - Cognitive strategies—Downward Arrow, estimating probability, Need versus Want (Session 12; *Workbook* Chapter 5)
- Consider the presence of any problematic avoidance behaviors related to acquiring, sorting, and discarding (Sessions 2, 5, and 7; *Workbook* Chapters 3, 5, and 7)
- Review Questions about Possessions and/or rules for saving that facilitate decision-making (Session 8; *Workbook* Chapter 7, p. 80–82)
- Review Thought Listing exercise (Session 8; *Workbook* Chapter 7, p. 78)
- Review Behavioral Experiment Form (Session 9; *Workbook* Chapter 7, p. 83)
- Review *in vivo* exposures to discarding and loss of possessions and information (Sessions 8 and 9; *Workbook* Chapter 7)

(continued)

Table 21.1 (Continued)

- Review Problem-Solving steps (Session 9; *Workbook* Chapter 6, p. 64)
- Review Personal Organizing Plan and Filing Paper Form (Sessions 10 and 11; *Workbook* Chapter 6, p. 68, p. 72):
  - Keep discarding decisions simple: trash, recycle, sell, donate
  - Keep supplies on hand for organizing
  - Review progress on the Only Handle it Once (O.H.I.O.) rule
  - Implement decisions as soon as possible
  - Review rules for how long to save paper
  - Schedule times to organize and file
  - Keep surfaces clear to prevent re-cluttering
- Review the following cognitive strategies for parting with possessions (Sessions 8, 12, and 13; *Workbook* Chapters 7 and 8):
  - Thinking Styles list (Session 12; *Workbook* Chapter 8, pp. 86–89)
  - Questions about Possessions (Session 8; *Workbook* Chapter 7, p. 80)
  - Advantages-Disadvantages (Sessions 13; *Workbook* Chapter 8, p. 90)
  - Downward Arrow (Session 12; *Workbook* Chapter 8, p. 92)
  - Need versus Want (Session 13; *Workbook* Chapter 8, p. 94)
  - Examine the evidence for keeping or discarding items (Session 12)
  - Take another perspective—review questions (Not covered in group treatment)
  - Thought Record Form (Session 12; *Workbook* Chapter 8, p. 93)
  - Perfection Continuum Scale (Not covered in group treatment; *Workbook* Chapter 8, p. 96)
  - Metaphors and Stories (Not covered in group treatment)
  - Valuing Time (Not covered in group treatment; *Workbook* Chapter 8, p. 96)
  - Finding alternatives to problematic core beliefs (Session 12; *Workbook* Chapter 8)
- Review strategies for managing attention (Session 16; *Workbook* Chapter 5)
- Review progress on any barriers to working on hoarding (Session 16; *Workbook* Chapter 9)
- Plan social activities outside your home (Session 17; *Workbook* Chapter 5)
- Invite others to visit you at home (Session 17)
- Schedule practice sessions (Session 19)

As a group, identify and describe each treatment technique. Consider having each group member take turns reading each technique aloud, followed by the other members' recalling the technique aloud. Many of the treatment techniques apply not only to letting go of possessions, but also to resisting acquiring and to organizing. In addition to reviewing the techniques, ask group members to identify the methods below that worked best for them.

Remind clients that when they experience discomfort when practicing non-acquiring and sorting, it is usually a sign they have used the method correctly and need to keep going. It is often easier to change behaviors first, and then observe whether changes in attitudes and emotions follow. Remind clients that when formal treatment ends, many people experience an increase in general discomfort, but that this is likely to subside as they continue to persevere in their commitment to continuing their work on the problem.

Some beliefs and behaviors may not have changed as much as desired for certain group members. In such cases, leaders may choose to reassess the worst fears using the Downward Arrow method, as sometimes the worst fears are missed because they are buried beneath more obvious fears and only emerge when these are resolved. If the Downward Arrow turns up concerns that were not previously identified, encourage clients to use skills they have already gained to address those problems as well. Problem-solving skills may also enable clients to gain control over problem areas not yet resolved. Toward this end, remind clients of the steps in the problem-solving process to consider whether they could be useful after therapy ends. Examples might be when certain expected stressors occur, when someone offers to give them items they do not want to keep, or when a plan goes awry and they are disappointed.

Case Vignette

CLINICIAN: During check-in, we talked about some methods that seemed particularly helpful. Before we continue, let's review our personal General Conceptual Hoarding Models. As you may recall, in Session 4, we discussed each of your treatment goals and how they were related to the General Conceptual Hoarding Model. [*Shows a model on the board.*] The strategies that you learned over the course of the group were outlined for each aspect of the model. Today, we are going to review each of your personal models and summarize the specific strategies [*pointing to the list in the book*] that you have learned to address your vulnerabilities, information-processing problems, problematic beliefs, excessive acquiring, difficulty discarding, and clutter [*pointing to the General Conceptual Hoarding Model on the board*].

CARL: I didn't realize we learned so many skills.

LIZ: I am still trying to figure out what those problematic thinking styles have to do with my hoarding.

SALLY: Well, I have an example. I use that "all or nothing thinking" all the time. I think that if I don't catch those good deals, I'll never find the items at such a good price again. I have those thoughts a lot, but I learned that it's not necessarily true. So I say, "Thanks anyway, Brain, but I am not buying it."

JENNIFER: Or like last session, when I was upset and thinking that de-cluttering my home would never happen or would take the rest of my life. That was "fortune-telling" and "catastrophic thinking."

CLINICIAN: Those are great examples. So, Liz, is that helpful?

LIZ: I guess I do a lot of "fortune-telling."

CLINICIAN: The problematic thinking styles are most relevant to which aspects of the model?

GRACE: You are talking about thinking, so it must be relevant to the "beliefs" box.

CLINICIAN: Right. So there were a number of cognitive strategies that we covered during group that address unhelpful thinking. These methods help you understand and deal with thoughts that lead to difficulties with acquiring and discarding.

Carl: So, looking at this list, the Downward Arrow still confuses me.

Clinician: [pointing to the "core vulnerabilities" box in the model]: So, the purpose of the Downward Arrow is to uncover the thoughts and core beliefs that contribute to the hoarding problem.

Joseph: The Downward Arrow helped me to realize that I hold onto my trade magazines because I'm afraid I am going to miss out on important information for my job, and then I'd be a failure.

Clinician: Thanks, Joseph, you helped us see that one reason for holding onto stuff is related to identity and can be linked to core beliefs and fears around failure, a common core belief.

Carl: I remember now.

Maria: Joseph's example really helped me understand the purpose of the Downward Arrow and how I need to put my thoughts "on trial" and examine evidence. So for me, I need to have everything out so I can see it because I don't trust my memory.

Clinician: Good, let's move on to "information processing."

Charlie: Categorizing my electronics was good, because when I looked in the box I realized how many computer wires I already own and many of them were the same, like to connect the computer and monitor. And phone cords, too.

Sally: When I did the categorizing and put all my purses into a big box, it actually made me really anxious, because I realized that I was going to have to make some really hard decisions about which ones to keep. I wasn't sure if I could do it.

Clinician: So your emotion was anxiety.

SALLY: Yes, I just wanted to avoid it. I would do anything not to have to make those decisions.

CLINICIAN: Right, because your purses were much higher on your hierarchy.

SALLY: Oh, right, we built those hierarchies.

GRACE: Those were really helpful to me to figure out where to start.

JENNIFER: We did those behavior experiments and that helped me see that getting rid of certain items wasn't as bad as I thought it would be. I mean it was really hard, but I didn't fall apart like I predicted.

LIZ: And I learned that I could live without coffee when we went to the store!

CLINICIAN: Yes, the non-acquisition trip included a behavior experiment for not acquiring. So not acquiring and discarding are linked to a range of emotions, right? And some of our avoidances are rewarded with feelings of relief.

SALLY: Buying clothing used to feel so good, and now the guilt or regret happens a lot sooner. It's just not as enjoyable as it once was. Plus, I have started walking, not in malls of course, and I am feeling better, generally.

JOSEPH: I have been feeling a little better, too.

MARIA: We really did do a lot.

CLINICIAN: Looking through the list, what are other skills that would be helpful to review?

Your tasks as group leaders during the ending phase of the group include reviewing and reminiscing about the group progress, including the skills learned by the members and the strength of group members' connection to each other (as pointed out when Maria states, "We really did do a lot"). The vignette above illustrates how leaders can facilitate group members' ability to recognize and identify what they have learned during the course of their work together.

Objective 3: Home Commitment

- List anticipated stressors and potential coping strategies.
- Continue reviewing the List of Treatment Techniques (*Workbook*, Chapter 9, p. 114), identifying the methods that worked best and in which contexts (acquiring, sorting and organizing, discarding).

Objective 4: Complete Clinician Forms

- Clinician directs the clients to write their home commitment on the Group Session Form (see Appendix 12) and completes the Clinician's Group Progress Notes (see Appendix 15).

Chapter 22 *Session 19: Assessment and Review of Progress*

(Portions of this session correspond to Chapter 9 of the Workbook)

Materials Needed

- Client's Personal Goals form (*Workbook* Chapter 4, p. 42)
- Client's General Conceptual Hoarding Model (*Workbook* Chapter 3, p. 33, Appendix 17)
- Saving Inventory—Revised (SI-R) (*Workbook* Chapter 9, pp. 101–102, Appendix 3)
- Clutter Image Rating (CIR) (*Workbook* Chapter 9, pp. 103–106, Appendix 4)
- Hoarding Rating Scale (HRS) (*Workbook* Chapter 9, p. 100, Appendix 2)

Session Agenda

- Clients complete final assessments.
- Review each client's progress during the course of the group.
- Discuss strategies for dealing with setbacks.
- Help members develop strategies for continuing work and support.
- Ask clients for feedback and reflections on their group experience.

Objective 1: Check-in

- Distribute and review the Group Session Form.
- Each client identifies a potential coping strategy for managing ongoing stressors.

Objective 2: Re-administer Hoarding Assessments

We strongly recommend re-administering the assessment forms given at the outset of treatment, including the Saving Inventory–Revised, Clutter Image Rating, and Hoarding Rating Scale, as well as the questions about safety and structural problems. Ask clients to complete the forms during the session and submit them to you. Following this, facilitate a discussion about what group members believe they have learned about themselves, and how much progress they have made in acquiring, organizing, and sorting and discarding clutter.

After group, we suggest that group leaders score the forms (e.g., SI-R) and compare them to those from the same measures taken at the start of group. The scores provide helpful information for assessing each client's progress through treatment and may inform the group leaders' post-group recommendations and referrals.

Objective 3: Reviewing Progress

Remind clients of their original treatment goals by examining the Personal Goals Form from their *Workbook* (Chapter 4, p. 42), which they completed in Session 4. Ask group members what they have actually accomplished with regard to their goals. Take special note of improvement in reduced acquiring, clutter, and improving their ability to get rid of things, as well as skills of problem-solving, managing attention, organizing, and decision-making. Emphasize what clients have accomplished in order to foster their confidence in maintaining and improving gains. This must be an honest appraisal that also considers clients' weaknesses and how to overcome them. Compliment clients on their progress so far and their use of particular tools from the therapy. Ask clients what they think their future course is likely to be with regard to hoarding symptoms. Most group members will have made very good progress, but will not be completely free from hoarding problems yet. They will need to work on remaining clutter and periodic strong urges to acquire and difficulty discarding for some months to come. Remind clients that it is not unusual for people with hoarding to require more than a year to see very substantial progress in their homes. Encourage those who have made very limited progress to seek individual treatment.

If you are meeting with group members individually, whether in the office or at a home visit, we suggest reviewing the original photos of the home and comparing those to new photos of the home as it looks currently. A photo record of progress is important for future reference as well. Recommend that clients examine their photo record again in six months to see what they have been able to accomplish after the group ends.

Objective 4: Dealing with Setbacks

Ask clients to identify potential indicators that they are falling prey to avoidance behavior, not practicing skills, and so forth. For example, ask them to notice if they skipped a couple of days of opening their mail, didn't put away dirty dishes or items that they were using, acquired some things they did not need and hadn't planned to get. Ask them to decide what the next step should be, how to implement it, and how to reinforce it. Ask them who might assist them in solving these problems when they arise (see Session 14).

Ask whether clients feel prepared for ups and downs and have a plan for what to do if they hit a low point in their progress. In addition, discuss the difference between a lapse and a relapse:

> *A* lapse *is a temporary period during which some of the behaviors return. This doesn't necessarily indicate a* relapse. *Just because some clutter accumulates or you buy more than you planned does not mean you have failed, but it is a warning sign. A temporary return of*

symptoms is usually a sign that something stressful is going on in your life. What would you do if this happened?

Discuss various strategies in the group for managing such setbacks (e.g., call the clinician, seek help from a friend, review treatment notes). Make it clear that low points are normal, and these usually get shorter and less severe as time passes. Encourage group members to identify potentially stressful situations that might exacerbate residual hoarding symptoms. What stressors do they expect over the coming year? How would they handle them? Examples might be stressful interpersonal situations or expectations, extra responsibilities, media information that is disturbing, or a serious loss. Consider posing an unexpected stressor, such as the following:

- Suppose [*a family member*] died unexpectedly and left you her things. What would you do?
- Suppose you have a major expense you hadn't planned on. How would you handle that?

Ask group members to describe what they anticipate their initial reactions might be to such circumstances. Identify possible thinking styles or mistaken interpretations and inquire about alternative ways of thinking about the situation. Identify bad habit patterns that might return, and discuss how some of the strategies they have learned might apply. Encourage them to use strategies from the list to deal with setbacks. For example, they might conduct experiments to test predictions (e.g., about needing information) in response to these stressors or use problem-solving methods to come up with creative solutions.

Objective 5: Continuing Practice and Maintaining Contact after the Group Ends

Scheduling Personal Sessions

Help members think about a self-treatment plan they can implement after the group treatment ends. We suggest that clients schedule personal sessions on the same day and time slot when the group usually met. For example, if sessions usually occurred on Mondays at 4:00 p.m., suggest that members consider setting aside this time for their own work on hoarding. Encourage clients to take out their calendars and schedule at least a month of weekly personal sessions in advance. They can taper these weekly sessions gradually as they make progress—to twice a month, once a month, and so on.

Ask clients to write down the advantages and disadvantages and any fears about scheduling their own personal sessions. For example, an advantage might be to make it easier for clients to remember to use techniques when they need them; disadvantages might be that sessions seem to take too much time, or aren't needed. Encourage clients to evaluate the pros and cons of these viewpoints.

Reactions and Future Contact

The ending of the group will inevitably trigger a variety of reactions among group members. These reactions are influenced by previous personal experiences (for example, with loss), and by the level of cohesion achieved by the group. Personal and group factors result in varying emotions and behaviors that include denial, sadness, anger, isolation, and fears of relapse. Explore and validate these feelings within the group by facilitating a discussion about the advantages of staying connected to each other (e.g., motivation, support, social connection, accountability), as well as the disadvantages (e.g., responsibility, time commitment, emotional energy). Share some of your own observations of therapeutic factors you noticed within the group (e.g., cohesion, socializing, imitating each other, encouraging hope) and point out examples of mutual aid (e.g., supportive comments, expecting each other to work hard, help with problem-solving ideas). Explain that these therapeutic factors and mutual aid may be vital to achieving their personal goals. This means that some members may want to attend booster sessions or to join a maintenance group or support group (described below) in order to maintain social contact and find support while they use skills and techniques covered during the treatment group.

Case Vignette

SALLY: [Reading white board session number]: Session 19! Only two more groups.

JENNIFER: I can't believe our group is ending. Can we keep meeting?

CLINICIAN: How are you all feeling about the group ending?

JENNIFER: Well, it makes me sad. I have gotten used to coming here on Friday mornings. It's the only place where I feel like people understand what I'm going through.

JOSEPH: I know. Me, too.

CLINICIAN: I will miss you all, too.

LIZ: Can't we keep meeting? Can we keep in touch with each other?

CLINICIAN: That is up to each of you. You can share information with each other as you choose. Some people decide to become clutter buddies or even to start a support group.

SALLY: It would be good to continue to meet in some way. You all keep me accountable.

CLINICIAN: I will leave this to you all to discuss among yourselves either before or after the last group, or between this session and the next.

Booster Sessions

We recommend that leaders and group members plan two to three group booster sessions, scheduled once per month after the group ends. This eases the transition, and booster sessions can help clients feel connected and motivated to continue their work. Sessions can focus on any aspects of hoarding that remain problematic, or on related concerns that arise once hoarding is under control (e.g., comorbid problems; current life problems such as old debts). Some group members may benefit from monthly phone or electronic check-ins with each other, if this helps them maintain motivation to work on the problem.

Maintenance Groups

If possible, we recommend that you form a maintenance group open to any participant who completed the 20-week hoarding groups. Ideally, such maintenance groups would meet monthly (an extension of booster sessions) to provide group support with clinician or non-clinician facilitators. The purpose of the maintenance group is to continue using the previously learned strategies such as cognitive restructuring, motivational methods, and skills training that may require more time to apply effectively. The maintenance group also provides a safe space for group members to reduce their isolation, increase social skills, and enjoy opportunities for behavioral rehearsal. The structure of maintenance groups will vary based on agency requirements and the leader's assessment of the needs of the group members. Thus, groups might be:

1. Open-ended open groups (anyone who has completed the 20-week group can come)
2. Open-ended closed group (once the group begins, no new members can join)
3. Open-ended, partially closed group (new members are permitted when a space becomes available)
4. Close-ended group (a specific number of sessions—e.g., 10—are scheduled for a selected group of people).

We recommend that maintenance groups meet monthly or every other month for 1.5 to 2 hours per session and can have a single leader or co-leaders. The session structure is usually similar to that of the 20-week treatment group:

- Check-in
- Homework review
- Review a skill or technique
- Agree on homework

If structured as an open group (you may not be sure who will be attending each week), consider setting a standard home commitment (e.g., regular sorting sessions, bringing items in to sort, or reporting on techniques utilized). You can then incorporate these commitments into the group guidelines.

Flexibility is important in the maintenance group. A particular theme may emerge in the check-in that would be helpful for all group members to explore more deeply. For example, three of the five group members might mention problems with focus during check-in that calls for a general discussion. While leaders can prepare specific materials to cover, it is most helpful to allow agenda-setting based on the expressed needs of the group.

Support Groups

Clients might also join or organize a *Buried In Treasures* (BIT) workshop. BIT workshops are peer-led support groups of 6 to 9 people who meet for 15 sessions over approximately 20 weeks. The meetings are highly structured and action-oriented for working on hoarding. Evidence from several studies indicates that these groups are effective in reducing hoarding symptoms and keeping people active in battling clutter. Suggest that such groups can provide a great way for clients to continue making progress on conquering their hoarding disorder. Inform clients that detailed instructions for setting up and running a BIT workshop can be found on the International Obsessive Compulsive Disorder Foundation website, at www.ocfoundation.org/hoarding. Provide clients with written information about other local or online support groups, if available. Other support strategies include joining organizations such as the International Obsessive Compulsive Disorder Foundation (www.ocfoundation.org) and reading self-help books such as Tolin, Steketee & Frost's (2013) *Buried in Treasures*. The resources section at the end of this book provides reading and resources on hoarding.

Treating hoarding is a process, and recovery will require further practice beyond the group. The 20-week hoarding group is often just the beginning of that change. The booster sessions, maintenance group, and support groups offer the opportunity for ongoing support to build on the gains made in group treatment.

Objective 6: Feedback and Reflections

Ask clients to reflect on the entire course of their treatment to describe what they have learned about themselves and what they believe they need to do next. Specifically ask for feedback from group members about their reactions to the group process, the therapy methods, and ways to improve future groups. Reach for honest evaluations that include positive and negative aspects of the group, thus staving off a "farewell-party syndrome" where negative feedback and powerful emotions are avoided during the ending process (Schwartz, 1961; Shulman, 2011, p. 190).

Objective 7: Home Commitment

- List and locate potential sources of support for continuing non-acquiring and clutter removal efforts.

Objective 8: Complete Clinician Forms

- Clinician directs the clients to write their home commitment on the Group Session Form (Appendix 12) and completes the Clinician's Group Progress Notes (see Appendix 15).

Chapter 23 *Session 20: Graduation and Next Steps*

Materials Needed

- General Resource List (Appendix)
- Index cards
- Certificates of Completion (Appendix 37)
- Refreshments (optional)

Session Agenda

- Affirmation card exercise or some other ending exercise
- Presentation of certificates
- Group celebration

Consider bringing refreshments to celebrate the final session. You may wish to invite group members to bring something to share if they would like to do so, but be sure they understand that this is not an expectation or obligation.

Objective 1: Check-in

- Distribute and review the Group Session Form.

- Ask clients to describe one emotion reflecting how they are feeling about the ending of the group.
- Ask each client to identify one resource for ongoing support.

Objective 2: Resource List

If you have not already done so, consider handing out a list of general resources during the final session, as well as a list of local resources that these group members might find helpful. Refer to the Reading and Resources list (see Appendix) when developing resource lists for your group members.

Objective 3: Affirmation Card Activity

Describe the purpose of the affirmation card activity: to create an opportunity for the group members to appreciate each other and themselves and what they have brought to the group. The activity proceeds as follows:

1. Hand out one small index card to each client to represent each group member, including the leaders. If there are 8 group members and 2 leaders, each person will get 10 cards.
2. Direct the group members to write the name of each group member (including the group leaders and their own name) on one side of each card.
3. Ask them to write one positive word or statement about each person on the other side of the card with that person's name on it.
4. Collect all the cards, organize them by person, then put each group member's cards in an envelope, and write the name of the group member on the outside of the envelope.
5. Hand out the envelopes to each group member.
6. Each person receives the envelope, takes out the cards that they received, and, if they would like to, reads them aloud to the group.

Here's an example of Sally's cards: *Committed, thoughtful, honest, open, caring, compassionate, kind, hardworking, dedicated.*

Follow this exchange with a brief conversation about what group members are taking away from their experience in this group.

Objective 4: Certificates of Completion

Present each group member with a Completion Certificate to signify the end of the group and to acknowledge the successes of the group members. A sample certificate is provided in the Appendix 37.

Comment especially on progress and clients' hard work, and on the knowledge and skills they've gained during treatment. Finally, express honest feedback to each client: "It was great working with you," "I'll miss working with you," I'm so glad our work together helped," "I have a lot of confidence in you," "I know it was a struggle and I'm really glad you hung in there."

Objective 5: Group Celebration

Following the presentation of the certificates, allow time for group members to enjoy the refreshments, reminisce, and discuss future plans. This is unstructured time.

Objective 6: Complete Clinician Forms

- Complete the Clinician's Group Progress Notes (see Appendix 15).

Appendices

1. Hoarding Interview
2. Hoarding Rating Scale (HRS) (*Workbook* Chapter 2, pp. 12–13; Chapter 9, p. 100)
3. Saving Inventory—Revised (SI-R) (*Workbook* Chapter 2, p. 14–16; Chapter 9, pp.101–102)
4. Clutter Image Rating (CIR) (*Workbook* Chapter 2, pp. 17–21; Chapter 9, pp. 103–106)
5. Saving Cognitions Inventory (SCI) (*Workbook* Chapter 2, p. 22–23; Chapter 9, pp. 107–108)
6. Activities of Daily Living for Hoarding (ADL-H) (*Workbook* Chapter 2, pp. 24–25, Chapter 9, p. 108)
7. Safety Questions (*Workbook* Chapter 2, p. 26; Chapter 9, p. 109)
8. Home Environment Index (HEI) (*Workbook* Chapter 2, pp. 27–28, Chapter 9, pp. 110–111)
9. Binder Information Sheet
10. Session Schedule
11. Example of Completed Group Session Form
12. Group Session Form
13. Confidentiality Contract
14. Hoarding Disorder DSM-5 Criteria
15. Clinician's Group Progress Notes
16. Example of Clinician's Group Progress Note
17. General Conceptual Model of Hoarding (*Workbook* Chapter 3, p. 33)
18. Brief Thought Record (*Workbook* Chapter 3, p. 37)
19. Clutter Visualization Form (*Workbook* Chapter 4, p. 44)
20. Unclutter Visualization Form (*Workbook* Chapter 4, p. 45)
21. Signals of Ambivalence and Strategies
22. Motivational Enhancement Strategies
23. Advantages and Disadvantages of Change Worksheet
24. Instructions to Coaches (*Workbook* Appendices, pp. 138–140)
25. Acquiring Form (*Workbook* Chapter 3, p. 38)

All forms and worksheets in the Appendix are available for download and printing at www.oup.com/us/ttw

26. Acquiring Visualization Form (*Workbook* Chapter 4, p. 46)
27. Thought Listing Exercise Form
28. Behavioral Experiment Form (*Workbook* Chapter 7, p. 83)
29. Problematic Thinking Styles (Session 12; *Workbook* Chapter 5, pp. 56, 58–59; *Workbook* Chapter 8, pp. 86–89)
30. Thought Record (*Workbook* Chapter 8, p. 93)
31. Non-Acquiring Help Card
32. Practice Form (*Workbook* Chapter 4, p. 47)
33. Personal Worksheet for Managing Barriers
34. Family Response to Hoarding Scale (FRHS)
35. Weekly Schedule Worksheet
36. List of Treatment Techniques
37. Certificate of Completion

Hoarding Interview

Client initials: ______________ Date: ______________

1. What kind of home do you live in? Who else lives there with you?

   ____

   ____

   ____

2. Let's talk about the rooms in your home. [*Use the Clutter Image Rating pictures to determine the extent of clutter in each room and also in other living spaces like the attic, basement, garage, car, etc.*] How much does the clutter interfere with how you'd like to use each room, and which rooms bother you most?

   Living room: ____

   Dining room: ____

   Kitchen: ____

   Bedrooms: ____

   Bathrooms: ____

   Hallways: ____

   Basement: ____

   Attic: ____

   Porch: ____

   Garage: ____

   Yard: ____

   Car: ____

   Work or office space: ____

   Other: ____

continued

3. Do you keep any items in other places outside your home, like a storage space, another person's home, etc.? How much stuff is there and what kinds of items?

____

____

____

4. What kinds of things do you save? For example, what would I mainly see in these rooms?

____

____

____

5. Tell me about your emotions when you look at or think about the clutter (e.g., anxiety, guilt, sadness, pleasure, etc.).

____

____

____

6. How much discomfort would you feel if you had to get rid of some of your ______ (ask about each category of items identified earlier, such as books, junk mail, kitchen trash, bottle caps).

____

____

____

7. Which rooms would you like to work on first? Why? Which one will be easiest and which one the most difficult? Why? [*Discuss where the pros and cons with regard to the usefulness of space if clutter is cleared, the quickest visual improvement in the space, the most pressing need to locate important items, the most reduction of distress, and so forth.*]

____

____

____

8. Are your possessions organized in some way? How do you decide what goes where? How well does this plan work for you?

____

____

____

9. How do you acquire new things? Tell me about the most recent things you got—how did you get them? (e.g., shopping, store sales, yard or tag sales, trash picking, free things).

10. Let's talk about the sequence of thoughts, emotions, and behaviors when you acquire new items. For example, the [*most recent items acquired*], how did you feel when you first got it, and what were you thinking? What did you do with it once you got it home?

11. What happens if you try to avoid getting something?

12. Tell me about why you save these items. [*If clients do not mention the reasons below, ask about each.*]

    a. Sentimental: Do you save things because they seem sentimental or emotionally significant to you? That is, are you so emotionally attached to items that you do not want to part with them? Can you give an example?

    b. Instrumental/useful: Are you afraid of losing important information you might need someday when you try to throw something out? Are you concerned about being wasteful because the object may eventually be put to good use? Can you give an example?

continued

c. Intrinsic/beauty: Do you save things just because you like them or think they are pretty? Do you think they will be valuable someday? Can you give an example?

____

____

____

13. Do your family members or friends help you get items or store them for you?

____

____

____

Do some people help you organize things you can't deal with?

____

What about helping you get rid of things?

____

Does anyone get upset by your collecting and clutter, or do they mostly tolerate it?

____

Do you prevent others from touching your things?

____

Are your family members or significant others supportive of treatment? If so, would any of them be interested in coming with you to a treatment session?

____

14. Does the clutter present a health or safety problem for you or your family? [*If yes*]: What kinds of problems? (e.g., falling, fire hazard, hygiene, medical problems, nutrition, insect infestation). [*If no*]: Do other people think the clutter presents a problem for you or for your health or safety?

____

____

____

15. Has your buying or acquiring things caused any problems? (e.g., family arguments, financial burden or debt, negative mood such as guilt, depression, anxiety). [*If yes*]: What kinds of problems? [*If no*]: Do family or friends think buying or acquiring items is causing any problems?

____

____

____

16. Has your social life been affected by the clutter? (avoid having visitors; avoid going to others' home because you can't reciprocate). Are you interested in having some people come over once the clutter is less of a problem? Who, for example?

____

____

____

17. Do you have any problems with washing, checking, putting things in order, repeating actions, or other mental compulsions? Do these thoughts and behaviors affect the hoarding problem? (e.g., contamination fears make it difficult to put things away, "checking" lengthens the time it takes to put away or discard items)

____

____

____

18. Do other family members have hoarding problems? Who? Tell me about the saving and clutter.

____

____

____

19. When you were young, did you spend a lot of time in any other household (e.g., grandparents', other family members', friends') that was cluttered?

____

____

____

20. Did anyone in the household you grew up in acquire things excessively? Who? What types of things?

____

____

____

continued

Hoarding Interview *continued*

21. When you were a child, did you experience any kind of deprivation (e.g., not enough to eat, not enough clothes, too few toys, no spending money) or serious losses (e.g., death, major move)? How old were you when this occurred? Do you think it has any relationship to your hoarding problem?

____

____

____

22. When was the first time you noticed that you had trouble acquiring too many things, throwing things away, or had a lot of clutter in your home? How old were you? Was anything special going on in your life at that time? (e.g., traumatic experience, moving, loss of a family member, etc.).

____

____

____

23. Have you had any previous therapy (medication, behavior therapy, psychotherapy, family efforts to help) for hoarding problems? What about for other types of problems? How long did the treatment last? Did it help? Why or why not? [*Later on, you will need to give a rationale for the hoarding treatment that addresses concerns the client may have because of previous treatment experiences.*]

____

____

____

24. Have other people tried to intervene in the hoarding problem? Have you ever been contacted by landlords, health department officials, or other officials about problems related to your hoarding. What happened? What was your reaction?

____

____

____

25. Are there other aspects of hoarding you haven't mentioned, like legal or financial problems, problems with collecting animals, any special embarrassments?

____

____

____

Hoarding Rating Scale (HRS)

Date: ___________

1. Because of the clutter or number of possessions, how difficult is it for you to use the rooms in your home?

0 ---------- 1 ---------- 2 ---------- 3 ---------- 4 ---------- 5 ---------- 6 ---------- 7 ---------- 8

0	2	4	6	8
Not at all Difficult	Mild	Moderate	Severe	Extremely Difficult

2. To what extent do you have difficulty discarding (or recycling, selling, giving away) ordinary things that other people would get rid of?

0 ---------- 1 ---------- 2 ---------- 3 ---------- 4 ---------- 5 ---------- 6 ---------- 7 ---------- 8

0	2	4	6	8
Not at all difficult	Mild	Moderate	Severe	Extremely difficult

3. To what extent do you currently have a problem with collecting free things or buying more things than you need or can use or can afford? [Use the scale below]

0 ---------- 1 ---------- 2 ---------- 3 ---------- 4 ---------- 5 ---------- 6 ---------- 7 ---------- 8

0	2	4	6	8
No problem	Mild, occasionally (less than weekly) acquires items not needed, or acquires a few unneeded items	Moderate, regularly (once or twice weekly) acquires items not needed, or acquires some unneeded items	Severe, frequently (several times per week) acquires items not needed, or acquires many unneeded items	Extreme, very often (daily) acquires items not needed, or acquires large numbers of unneeded items

4. To what extent do you experience emotional distress because of clutter, difficulty discarding, or problems with buying or acquiring things?

0 ---------- 1 ---------- 2 ---------- 3 ---------- 4 ---------- 5 ---------- 6 ---------- 7 ---------- 8

0	2	4	6	8
None/not at all	Mild	Moderate	Severe	Extreme

5. To what extent do you experience impairment in your life (daily routine, job / school, social activities, family activities, financial difficulties) because of clutter, difficulty discarding, or problems with buying or acquiring things?

0 ---------- 1 ---------- 2 ---------- 3 ---------- 4 ---------- 5 ---------- 6 ---------- 7 ---------- 8

0	2	4	6	8
None/not at all	Mild	Moderate	Severe	Extreme

continued

Hoarding Rating Scale (HRS) *continued*

To calculate the total score on the HRS, sum all five items.

Cutoff Scores and Typical HRS Scores in Hoarding and Non-Hoarding Samples

	Cutoff scores (scores at or above this indicate hoarding)	Average scores for people with HD (standard deviation)	Average scores for people without HD (standard deviation)
Total HRS	14	24.22 (5.7)	3.34 (5.0)
#1 Clutter	3	5.18 (1.4)	0.64 (1.1)
#2 Difficulty Discarding	4	5.10 (1.4)	0.82 (1.4)
#3 Acquisition	2	4.08 (1.9)	0.75 (1.3)
#4 Distress	3	4.83 (1.3)	0.73 (10)
#5 Interference	3	5.03 (1.4)	0.42(1.0)

(Tolin, Frost & Steketee, 2010; Tolin, Frost, Steketee, Gray & Fitch, 2008; Tolin, Meunier, Frost & Steketee, 2010)

Saving Inventory—Revised (SI-R)

Date: ___________

For each question below, circle the number that corresponds most closely to your experience DURING THE PAST WEEK.

0	1	2	3	4
None	A little	A moderate amount	Most/Much	Almost all/ Completely

1. How much of the living area in your home is cluttered with possessions? (Consider the amount of clutter in your kitchen, living room, dining room, hallways, bedrooms, bathrooms, or other rooms).	0	1	2	3	4
2. How much control do you have over your urges to acquire possessions?	0	1	2	3	4
3. How much of your home does clutter prevent you from using?	0	1	2	3	4
4. How much control do you have over your urges to save possessions?	0	1	2	3	4
5. How much of your home is difficult to walk through because of clutter?	0	1	2	3	4

For each question below, circle the number that corresponds most closely to your experience DURING THE PAST WEEK.

0	1	2	3	4
Not at all	Mild	Moderate	Considerable/ Severe	Extreme

6. To what extent do you have difficulty throwing things away?	0	1	2	3	4
7. How distressing do you find the task of throwing things away?	0	1	2	3	4
8. To what extent do you have so many things that your room(s) are cluttered?	0	1	2	3	4
9. How distressed or uncomfortable would you feel if you could not acquire something you wanted?	0	1	2	3	4
10. How much does clutter in your home interfere with your social, work or everyday functioning? Think about things that you don't do because of clutter.	0	1	2	3	4
11. How strong is your urge to buy or acquire free things for which you have no immediate use?	0	1	2	3	4

continued

Saving Inventory—Revised (SI-R) *continued*

DURING THE PAST WEEK:

0 ---------------------- 1 --------------------- 2 --------------------- 3 ---------------------4

Not at all	Mild	Moderate	Considerable/ Severe	Extreme

12. To what extent does clutter in your home cause you distress?	0	1	2	3	4
13. How strong is your urge to save something you know you may never use?	0	1	2	3	4
14. How upset or distressed do you feel about your acquiring habits?	0	1	2	3	4
15. To what extent do you feel unable to control the clutter in your home?	0	1	2	3	4
16. To what extent has your saving or compulsive buying resulted in financial difficulties for you?	0	1	2	3	4

For each question below, circle the number that corresponds most closely to your experience DURING THE PAST WEEK.

0 ---------------------- 1 --------------------- 2 --------------------- 3 ---------------------4

Never	Rarely	Sometimes/Occasionally	Frequently/ Often	Very Often

17. How often do you avoid trying to discard possessions because it is too stressful or time consuming?	0	1	2	3	4
18. How often do you feel compelled to acquire something you see? e.g., when shopping or offered free things?	0	1	2	3	4
19. How often do you decide to keep things you do not need and have little space for?	0	1	2	3	4
20. How frequently does clutter in your home prevent you from inviting people to visit?	0	1	2	3	4
21. How often do you actually buy (or acquire for free) things for which you have no immediate use or need?	0	1	2	3	4
22. To what extent does the clutter in your home prevent you from using parts of your home for their intended purpose? For example, cooking, using furniture, washing dishes, cleaning, etc.	0	1	2	3	4
23. How often are you unable to discard a possession you would like to get rid of?	0	1	2	3	4

Scoring the SI-R: For the SI-R total, reverse score items 2 and 4 and sum with the remaining 21 items. For the Clutter scale, sum items 1, 3, 5, 8, 10, 12, 15, 20, and 22. For the Difficulty Discarding scale, reverse score item 4 and add items 6, 7, 13, 17, 19, and 23. For the Excessive Acquisition scale, reverse score item 2 and add items 9, 11, 14, 16, 18, and 21.

Cutoff Scores and Typical Saving Inventory—Revised (SI-R) Scores in Hoarding and Non-Hoarding Samples

	Cutoff scores (scores at or above this indicate hoarding)	Average scores for people with HD (standard deviation)	Average scores for people without HD (standard deviation)
Total SI-R	41	62.0 (12.7)	23.7 (13.2)
Clutter	17	26.9 (6.6)	8.2 (7.1)
Difficulty Discarding	14	19.8 (5.0)	9.2 (5.0)
Excessive Acquisition	9	15.2 (5.4)	6.4 (3.6)

(Frost, Steketee & Grisham, 2004; Tolin, Meunier, Frost & Steketee, 2011)

Clutter Image Rating (CIR)

Date:________

Using the three series of pictures (CIR: Living Room, CIR: Kitchen, and CIR: Bedroom), please select the picture that best represents the amount of clutter for each of the rooms of your home. Put the number on the line below.

Please pick the picture that is closest to being accurate, even if it is not exactly right.
If your home does not have one of the rooms listed, just put NA for "not applicable" on that line.
Also, please rate other rooms in your house that are affected by clutter on the lines below.

Room	Number of closest corresponding picture (1–9)
Living Room	_______
Kitchen	_______
Bedroom #1	_______
Bedroom #2	_______

Use the *CIR: Living Room* pictures to make these ratings.
Scores in the 3 to 4 range in any room are cause for concern.

Dining room	_______	
Hallway	_______	
Garage	_______	
Basement	_______	
Attic	_______	
Car	_______	
Other	_______	Please specify: ____________________________

Clutter Image Rating: Living Room

Please select the photo below that most accurately reflects the amount of clutter in your room.

1

2

3

4

5

6

7

8

9

continued

Clutter Image Rating Scale: Kitchen

Please select the photo below that most accurately reflects the amount of clutter in your room.

1

2

3

4

5

6

7

8

9

Clutter Image Rating: Bedroom

Please select the photo below that most accurately reflects the amount of clutter in your room.

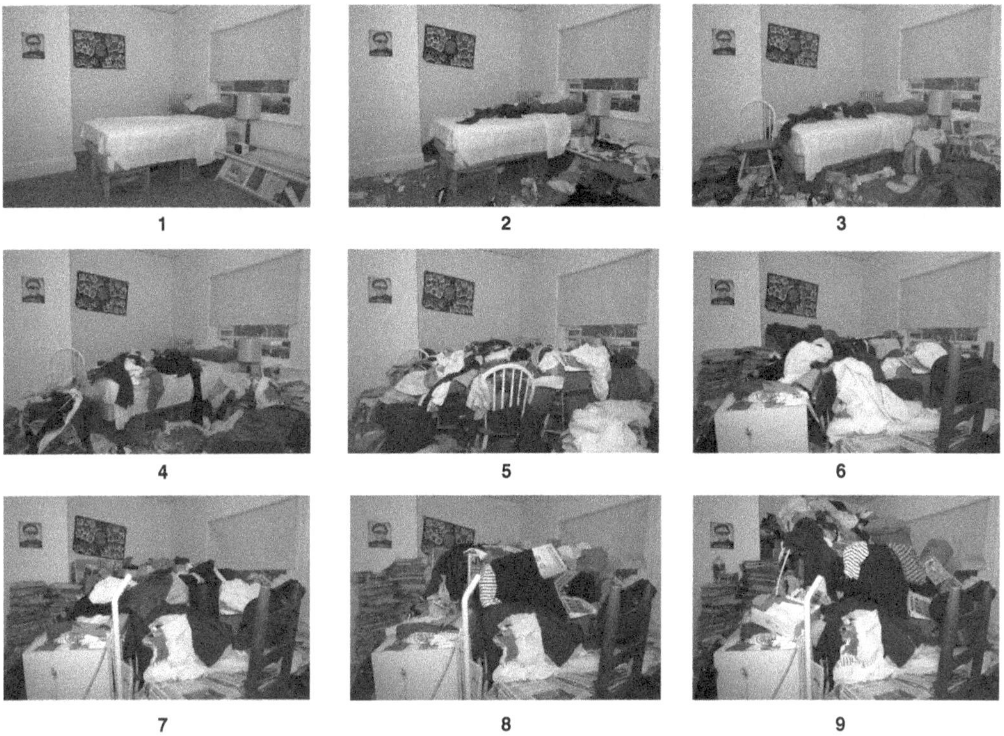

Typical Clutter Image Rating Scores in Hoarding and Non-Hoarding Samples

	Average scores for people with HD (standard deviation)	Average scores for people without HD (standard deviation)
Living Room	3.7 (2.0)	1.3 (1.0)
Kitchen	3.4 (1.6)	1.2 (0.6)
Bedroom	4.1 (1.6)	1.3 (0.8)

(Frost, Steketee, Tolin & Renaud, 2006)

Saving Cognitions Inventory (SCI)

Date: ___________

Use the following scale to indicate the extent to which you had each thought when you were deciding whether to throw something away DURING THE PAST WEEK. (If you did not try to discard anything in the past week, indicate how you would have felt if you had tried to discard.)

1	2	3	4	5	6	7
not at all			sometimes			very much

1.	I could not tolerate it if I were to get rid of this.	1 2 3 4 5 6 7
2.	Throwing this away means wasting a valuable opportunity.	1 2 3 4 5 6 7
3.	Throwing away this possession is like throwing away a part of me.	1 2 3 4 5 6 7
4.	Saving this means I don't have to rely on my memory.	1 2 3 4 5 6 7
5.	It upsets me when someone throws something of mine away without my permission.	1 2 3 4 5 6 7
6.	Losing this possession is like losing a friend.	1 2 3 4 5 6 7
7.	If someone touches or uses this, I will lose it or lose track of it.	1 2 3 4 5 6 7
8.	Throwing some things away would feel like abandoning a loved one.	1 2 3 4 5 6 7
9.	Throwing this away means losing a part of my life.	1 2 3 4 5 6 7
10.	I see my belongings as extensions of myself; they are part of who I am.	1 2 3 4 5 6 7
11.	I am responsible for the well-being of this possession.	1 2 3 4 5 6 7
12.	If this possession may be of use to someone else, I am responsible for saving it for them.	1 2 3 4 5 6 7
13.	This possession is equivalent to the feelings I associate with it.	1 2 3 4 5 6 7
14.	My memory is so bad I must leave this in sight or I'll forget about it.	1 2 3 4 5 6 7
15.	I am responsible for finding a use for this possession.	1 2 3 4 5 6 7
16.	Throwing some things away would feel like part of me is dying.	1 2 3 4 5 6 7
17.	If I put this into a filing system, I'll forget about it completely.	1 2 3 4 5 6 7
18	I like to maintain sole control over my things.	1 2 3 4 5 6 7
19.	I'm ashamed when I don't have something like this when I need it.	1 2 3 4 5 6 7
20.	I must remember something about this, and I can't if I throw this away.	1 2 3 4 5 6 7

21.	If I discard this without extracting all the important information from it, I will lose something.	1 2 3 4 5 6 7
22.	This possession provides me with emotional comfort.	1 2 3 4 5 6 7
23.	I love some of my belongings the way I love some people.	1 2 3 4 5 6 7
24.	No one has the right to touch my possessions.	1 2 3 4 5 6 7

Scoring the SCI:
For the SCI total, sum all items.
For the Emotional Attachment subscale, sum items 1, 3, 6, 8, 9, 10, 13, 16, 22, and 23.
For the Control subscale, sum items 5, 18, and 24.
For the Responsibility subscale, sum items 2, 7, 11, 12, 15, and 19.
For the Memory subscale, sum items 4, 14, 17, 20, and 21.

Typical Saving Cognitions Inventory (SCI) Scores in Hoarding and Non-Hoarding Samples

	Average scores for people with HD (standard deviation)	Average scores for people without HD (standard deviation)
Total SCI	95.9 (31.0)	42.2 (20.9)
Emotional Attachment	37.7 (16.0)	14.8 (8.7)
Control	15.8 (4.2)	8.4 (5.1)
Responsibility	22.3 (8.2)	10.4 (6.0)
Memory	20.3 (8.1)	8.8 (4.8)

(Steketee, Frost & Kyrios, 2003)

Activities of Daily Living for Hoarding (ADL-H)

Date: ____________

Sometimes clutter in the home can prevent you from doing ordinary activities. For each of the following activities, please circle the number that best represents the degree of difficulty you experience in doing this activity because of the clutter or hoarding problem. If you have difficulty with the activity for other reasons (for example, unable to bend or move quickly due to physical problems), do not include this in your rating. Instead, rate only how much difficulty you would have due to hoarding. If the activity is not relevant to your situation (for example, you don't have laundry facilities or animals), select Not Applicable (NA).

Activities affected by clutter or hoarding problem	Can do it easily	Can do it with a little difficulty	Can do it with moderate difficulty	Can do it with great difficulty	Unable to do	Not Applicable
1. Prepare food	1	2	3	4	5	NA
2. Use refrigerator	1	2	3	4	5	NA
3. Use stove	1	2	3	4	5	NA
4. Use kitchen sink	1	2	3	4	5	NA
5. Eat at table	1	2	3	4	5	NA
6. Move around inside the house	1	2	3	4	5	NA
7. Exit home quickly	1	2	3	4	5	NA
8. Use toilet	1	2	3	4	5	NA
9. Use bath/shower	1	2	3	4	5	NA
10. Use bathroom sink	1	2	3	4	5	NA
11. Answer door quickly	1	2	3	4	5	NA
12. Sit in sofa/chair	1	2	3	4	5	NA
13. Sleep in bed	1	2	3	4	5	NA
14. Do laundry	1	2	3	4	5	NA
15. Find important things (such as bills, tax forms, etc.)	1	2	3	4	5	NA

Typical ADL-H Scores in Hoarding and Non-Hoarding Samples

	Average scores for people with HD	Average scores for people without HD Controls
Total ADL-H	2.20 (.74)	1.15 (.75)

We recommend classifying the scores as:

1.0–1.4: None to minimal
1.5–2.0: Mild
2.1–3.0: Moderate
3.1–4.0: Severe
4.1–5.0: Extreme

(Frost, Hristova, Steketee & Tolin, 2013)

Safety Questions

Date: ___________

Sometimes the clutter in your home can cause safety problems. Please circle the number below that best indicates how much of a problem you have with the following conditions in your home:

Safety problems in the home	None	A little	Somewhat/ moderate	Substantial	Severe
1. Structural damage to the floors, walls, roof, or other parts of the home	1	2	3	4	5
2. Water not working	1	2	3	4	5
3. Heat not working	1	2	3	4	5
4. Does any part of your house pose a fire hazard? (stove covered with paper, flammable objects near the furnace, etc.)	1	2	3	4	5
5. Would medical emergency personnel have difficulty moving equipment through your home?	1	2	3	4	5
6. Are exits from your home blocked?	1	2	3	4	5
7. Is it unsafe to move up or down the stairs or along other walkways?	1	2	3	4	5

For the Safety Questions, a score of 2 or above on any question is meaningful and needs attention.

Home Environment Index (HEI)

Date: ___________

Clutter and hoarding problems can sometimes lead to sanitation problems. Please circle the answer that best fits the current situation in the home.

To what extent are the following situations present in the home?

1. Fire hazard
   0 = No fire hazard
   1 = Some risk of fire (for example, lots of flammable material)
   2 = Moderate risk of fire (for example, flammable materials near heat source)
   3 = High risk of fire (for example, flammable materials near heat source; electrical hazards, etc.)

2. Moldy or rotten food
   0 = None
   1 = A few pieces of moldy or rotten food in kitchen
   2 = Some moldy or rotten food throughout kitchen
   3 = Large quantity of moldy or rotten food in kitchen and elsewhere

3. Dirty or clogged sink
   0 = Sink empty and clean
   1 = A few dirty dishes with water in sink
   2 = Sink full of water, possibly clogged
   3 = Sink clogged, with evidence that it has overflowed onto counters, etc.

4. Standing water (in sink, tub, other container, basement, etc.)
   0 = No standing water
   1 = Some water in sink/tub
   2 = Water in several places, especially if dirty
   3 = Water in numerous places, especially if dirty

5. Human/animal waste/vomit
   0 = No human waste, animal waste, or vomit visible
   1 = No human waste or vomit; no animal waste or vomit outside cage or box
   2 = Some animal or human waste or vomit visible (for example, in unflushed toilet)
   3 = Animal or human waste or vomit on floors or other surfaces

6. Mildew or mold
   0 = No mildew or mold detectable
   1 = Small amount of mildew or mold in limited amounts and expected places (for example, on edge of shower curtain or refrigerator seal)
   2 = Considerable, noticeable mildew or mold
   3 = Widespread mildew or mold on most surfaces

continued

7. Dirty food containers
   0 = All dishes washed and put away
   1 = A few unwashed dishes
   2 = Many unwashed dishes
   3 = Almost all dishes are unwashed

8. Dirty surfaces (floors, walls, furniture, etc.)
   0 = Surfaces completely clean
   1 = A few spills, some dirt or grime
   2 = More than a few spills, may be a thin covering of dirt or grime in living areas
   3 = No surface is clean; dirt or grime covers everything

9. Piles of dirty or contaminated objects (bathroom tissue, hair, toilet paper, sanitary products, etc.)
   0 = No dirty or contaminated objects on floors, surfaces, etc.
   1 = Some dirty or contaminated objects present around trash cans or toilets
   2 = Many dirty or contaminated objects fill bathroom or area around trash cans
   3 = Dirty or contaminated objects cover the floors and surfaces in most rooms

10. Insects
    0 = No insects are visible
    1 = A few insects visible; cobwebs and/or insect droppings present
    2 = Many insects and droppings are visible; cobwebs in corners
    3 = Swarms of insects; high volume of droppings; many cobwebs on household items

11. Dirty clothes
    0 = Dirty clothes placed in hamper; none are lying around
    1 = Hamper is full; a few dirty clothes lying around
    2 = Hamper is overflowing; many dirty clothes lying around
    3 = Clothes cover the floor and many other surfaces (bed, chairs, etc.)

12. Dirty bed sheets/linens
    0 = Bed coverings very clean
    1 = Bed coverings relatively clean
    2 = Bed coverings dirty and in need of washing
    3 = Bed coverings very dirty and soiled

13. Odor of house
    0 = No odor
    1 = Slight odor
    2 = Moderate odor; may be strong in some parts of house
    3 = Strong odor throughout house

During the last month, how often did you (or someone in your home) do each of the following activities?

14. Do the dishes
    0 = Daily or every 2 days; 15 to 30 times per month
    1 = 1 or 2 times a week; 4 to 10 times per month
    2 = Every other week; 2 to 3 times per month
    3 = Rarely; 0 times per month

15. Clean the bathroom
    0 = Daily or every 2 days; more than 10 times per month
    1 = 1 or 2 times a week; 4 to 10 times per month
    2 = Every other week; 2 to 3 times per month
    3 = Never; 0 times per month

To score the HEI, sum the responses for all 15 items. The average score for a large Internet sample of people with hoarding was 12.7 (standard deviation = 6.9; range = 0–43). A score of 2 or above on any question warrants attention.

Rasmussen, J. L., Steketee, G., Frost, R. O., & Tolin, D. F. (2013, under review). *Assessing Squalor in Compulsive Hoarding: The Home Environment Index.*

Binder Information Sheet

Group Leader(s) Name(s)

Phone Number

Email Address

Address

Group Meeting Time (ex. Mondays, 5:30–7:00)

Where to put my binder? ______________________________ (location).

Session Schedule

Session Number	Date	Topic
1	____________	Introduction and Education
2	____________	Model Building
3	____________	Motivation
4	____________	Goals and Treatment Planning
5	____________	Reducing Acquiring
6	____________	More on Acquisition
7	____________	Exposure Practice for Non-Acquisition
8	____________	Decisions about Saving and Discarding
9	____________	More on Decisions about Saving and Discarding
10	____________	Skills Training for Organizing
11	____________	Organizing Paper
12	____________	Cognitive Strategies
13	____________	Cognitive Therapy Skills for Letting Go
14	____________	Coaching and Letting Go
15	____________	Non-Acquisition Practice
16	____________	Barriers to Progress
17	____________	Maintaining Systems and Gains
18	____________	Review of Treatment Methods
19	____________	Assessment and Review of Progress
20	____________	Graduation and Next Steps

Example of Completed Group Session Form

Session #: 1 Date:________________

Agenda

- ☐ Welcome and introduction
- ☐ Discussion of format and development of group rules
- ☐ Review of definition of hoarding disorder
- ☐ Discussion of home commitments
- ☐ Complete brief assessment

Main Points/Methods

- ☐ Confidentiality contract
- ☐ DSM-5 criteria for hoarding disorder
- ☐ Hoarding Rating Scale
- ☐ ____

To Discuss Next Time (in Session 2):

New home commitment

- ☐ Read Chapter 1 of the *Workbook* to learn more about hoarding behaviors
- ☐ Assemble the binder and put it in the agreed upon location

Example of Completed Group Session Form

Session #: 2 Date:____________

Agenda

- ☐ Work with each client to develop a model of hoarding
- ☐ Guide clients to complete a Brief Thought Record

Main Points/Methods

- ☐ "What Is Hoarding" reading
- ☐ General Conceptual Hoarding Model
- ☐ Brief Thought Record

To Discuss Next Time (in Session 3):

New Home Commitment

- ☐ Monitor thoughts and feelings using the Brief Thought Record form (*Workbook*, Chapter 3, p. 37) while sorting at home or when acquiring.
- ☐ Review the model (Figure 3.1 in the *Workbook*, Chapter 3, p. 33) at home to identify additional components that contribute to saving or acquiring.

Example of Completed Group Session Form

Session #: 3 Date:________________

Agenda

- ☐ Rate motivation for and confidence in change
- ☐ Complete visualization and practice exercises
- ☐ Examine ambivalence
- ☐ Use motivational strategies to address problems with home commitment
- ☐ Deal with undermining among group members

Main Points/Methods

- ☐ Brief Thought Record
- ☐ General Conceptual Hoarding Model
- ☐ Clutter Visualization Form
- ☐ Unclutter Visualization Form
- ☐ Motivational Enhancement Strategies
- ☐ Signals of Ambivalence and Strategies
- ☐ Advantages and Disadvantages of Change Worksheet

To Discuss Next Time (in Session 4):

New Home Commitment

- ☐ Make a list of the advantages and disadvantages (pros and cons) of addressing hoarding, using the Advantages and Disadvantages of Change Worksheet in the Appendix 23.

Group Session Form

Session #:____ Date:__________

Agenda

Main Points/Methods

To Discuss Next Time (Session __):

New Home Commitment

Confidentiality Contract

1. This document is a contract for confidentiality among members of this group, whose purpose is the reduction of hoarding among its members.
2. Each member of the group acknowledges the need to keep personal information shared in the group private.
3. For the purpose of this group, any information shared by a group member about himself or herself should be considered personal and private information.
4. In order to become a group member and maintain membership in the group, each person must agree to protect this private information. Information gathered about other group members cannot be shared with anyone else. That information shall remain with the group members and not be transmitted or communicated to any other person.
5. If you agree to abide by these restrictions, please acknowledge your agreement by signing the space below.

Date: ____________________

Signatures of group members (Please sign your first name and last initial only.)

____________________	____________________
____________________	____________________
____________________	____________________
____________________	____________________
____________________	____________________
Clinician	Clinician

Hoarding Disorder DSM-5 Criteria

Obsessive-Compulsive and Related Disorders:

Hoarding Disorder 300.3 (F42)

A. Persistent difficulty discarding or parting with possessions, regardless of their actual value.

B. This difficulty is due to a perceived need to save the items, and distress associated with discarding them.

C. The difficulty discarding possessions results in the accumulation of possessions that congest and clutter active living areas and substantially compromises their intended use. If living areas are uncluttered, it is only because of the interventions of third parties (e.g., family members, cleaners, authorities).

D. The hoarding causes clinically significant distress or impairment in social, occupational, or other important areas of functioning (including maintaining a safe environment for self and others).

E. The hoarding is not attributable to another medical condition (e.g., brain injury, cerebrovascular disease, Prader-Willi syndrome).

F. The hoarding symptom is not better accounted for by the symptoms of another DSM-5 disorder (e.g., obsessions in obsessive-compulsive disorder, decreased energy in major depressive disorder, delusions in schizophrenia or another psychotic disorder, cognitive deficits in major neurocognitive disorder, restricted interests in autism spectrum disorder).

Specify if:

With excessive acquisition: If difficulty discarding possessions is accompanied by excessive acquisition of items that are not needed or for which there is no available space.

Specify if:

Good or fair insight: The individual recognizes that hoarding-related beliefs and behaviors (pertaining to difficulty discarding items, clutter, or excessive acquisition) are problematic.

Poor insight: The individual is mostly convinced that hoarding-related beliefs and behaviors (pertaining to difficulty discarding items, clutter, or excessive acquisition) are not problematic despite evidence to the contrary.

Absent insight (*i.e., delusional beliefs about hoarding*): The individual is completely convinced that hoarding-related beliefs and behaviors (pertaining to difficulty discarding items, clutter, or excessive acquisition) are not problematic despite evidence to the contrary.

Clinician's Group Progress Notes

Session #: ___________ Date: ________________

Home Commitment:

____

(1 = did not attempt; 2 = attempted but did not complete; 3 = did about 25%; 4 = did about 50%; 5 = did about 75%; 6 = did all homework)

Client Name	Degree of homework compliance (1 to 6)	Comments
____________________	____________________	____________________
____________________	____________________	____________________
____________________	____________________	____________________
____________________	____________________	____________________
____________________	____________________	____________________
____________________	____________________	____________________
____________________	____________________	____________________
____________________	____________________	____________________

Comments on Group Process:

____

____

____

____

____

____

____

Example of a Clinician's Group Progress Note

Session 5 Date: ______________

Home commitment:

- Finish the Acquiring Form (*Workbook* Chapter 3, p. 38) and indicate degree of discomfort if the item is not acquired.
- Complete the Advantages and Disadvantages for Acquiring Worksheet (*Workbook* Chapter 5, p. 53)

(1 = did not attempt; 2 = attempted but did not complete; 3 = did about 25%; 4 = did about 50%; 5 = did about 75%; 6 = did all homework)

Client Name	**Degree of homework compliance (1 to 6)**	**Comments**
Sally	5	Completed most of both the Form and Worksheet.
Charlie	1	Did not attempt. Reported that he forgot.
Liz	1	Stated couldn't find workbook.
Joseph	3	Finished part of the Acquiring Form.
Maria	5	Completed the Acquiring Form and half of the Advantages and Disadvantages
Jennifer	6	Completed all homework
Grace	3	Started the Acquiring Form
Carl	4	Completed Advantages and Disadvantages

Comments on Group Process:

Charlie seemed annoyed and distracted during group. When Sally asked him if he was okay, Charlie reported that he had better things to do than to come to the group, pointing out that "I don't really have a problem with acquiring." Liz chimed in and stated she was missing an event at the library. Jennifer empathized with them and stated that she was missing yoga but didn't feel as bad when she thought about how the group might help her with the hoarding problem.

General Conceptual Model of Hoarding

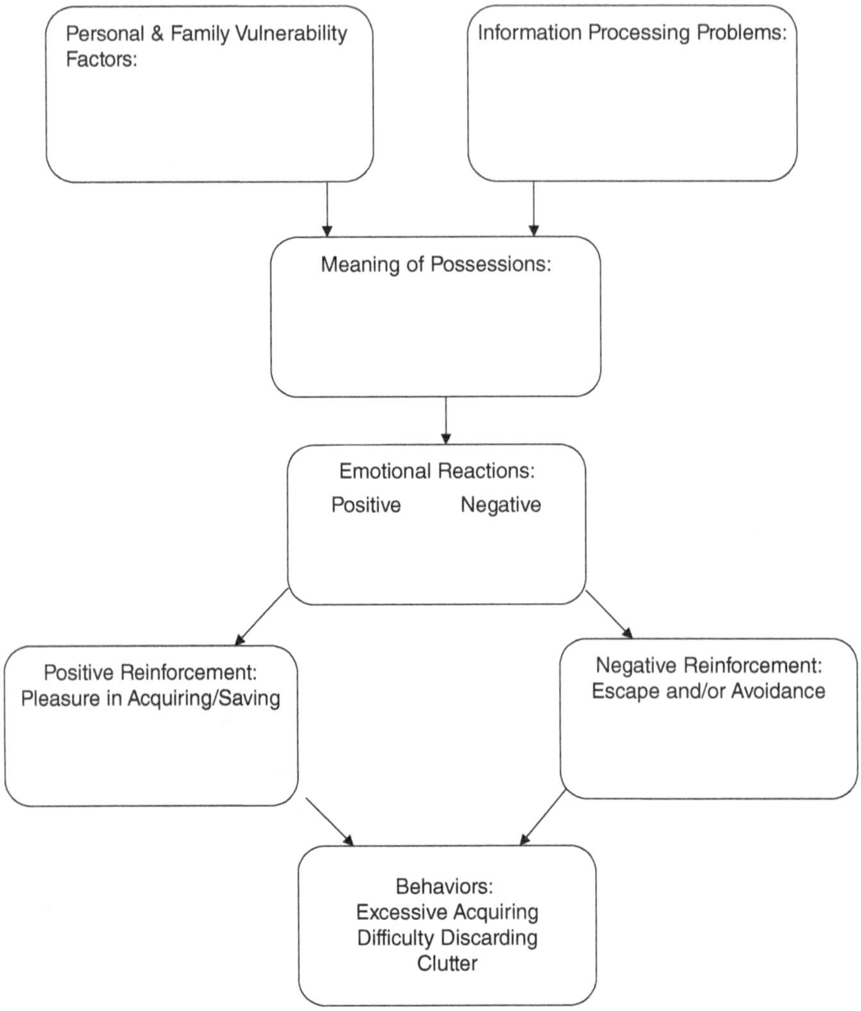

Brief Thought Record

Initials: ____________ Date: ________________

Trigger Situation	Thought or Belief	Emotions	Actions/Behaviors

Clutter Visualization Form

Room:

A. Visualize this room with all of its present clutter. Imagine standing in the middle of the room, slowly turning to see all of the clutter.

B. How uncomfortable did you feel while imagining this room with all the clutter? Use a scale from 0 to 100, where 0 = no discomfort and 100 = the most discomfort you have ever felt.

Initial Discomfort Rating: _______

C. What feelings were you having while visualizing this room?

1. ____________________

____

____

2. ____________________

____

____

3. ____________________

____

____

D. What thoughts (beliefs, attitudes) were you having while visualizing this room?

1. ____________________

____

____

2. ____________________

____

____

3. ____________________

____

____

Unclutter Visualization Form

Room:

A. Visualize this room with the clutter gone. Imagine that all the items are in a place where you can find them, and picture cleared surfaces and floors, tabletops without piles, and uncluttered floors with only rugs and furniture.

B. How uncomfortable did you feel while imagining this room without all the clutter? Use a scale from 0 to 100, where 0 = no discomfort and 100 = the most discomfort you have ever felt.

Initial Discomfort Rating: _____

C. What thoughts and feelings were you having while visualizing this room?

1. ______________________________

____

____

2. ______________________________

____

____

3. ______________________________

____

____

D. Imagine what you can do in this room now that it is not cluttered. Describe your thoughts and feelings.

1. ______________________________

____

____

2. ______________________________

____

____

3. ______________________________

____

____

E. How uncomfortable did you feel while imagining the room this way? (0 = no discomfort and 100 = the most discomfort you have ever felt)

Final Discomfort Rating: ______

Signals of Ambivalence and Strategies

Verbal and Motor Behaviors That Signal Ambivalence:	Examples:	Strategies:
Relentless complaining and diverting discussion to other topics	"I don't see why I can't just live like this; I'm really not bothering anybody." "The City has no right to do this." Repeated questions: "Why do I have this problem?"	Assess interest in working on the hoarding problem. Determine whether treatment for hoarding was appropriate at this time. Use broken-leg analogy: Repairing the leg is the first priority, and then clients can determine why it happened, to prevent a recurrence. Treat repeated "why" questions as diversions from the central goal.
Arguing	"That doesn't really make sense: how am I going to remember what I want to get if I don't get it right then?"	Re-establish collaborative spirit. Reminder that they will make all decisions about possessions.
Non-verbal signals of ambivalence	Sighing, not paying attention, and turning sideways	Stop and inquire what the sigh [or other action] meant or offer the hypothesis that the client was unhappy with the exchange.
Arriving late, canceling and "forgetting" appointments	Arriving late, canceling and "forgetting" appointments Other more pressing problems interfere with clients' energy and time to devote to work on hoarding Discomfort with the therapy or the clinician	Help clients articulate their ambivalence before strengthening their commitment and confidence in their ability to change. Problem-solving strategy: Reschedule therapy for a later date to avoid irregular sessions, wasted efforts, and unsteady progress. Routinely request feedback.
Not doing homework	"I haven't had time to go to any stores to practice." "I have a hard time finding time to sort. I have things I need to do to get ready for the next day." "I don't want to get depressed or anxious so I keep busy with friends; I really don't have time to sort."	Motivational methods and problem-solving strategies before trying to move forward in treatment
Discouraged despite progress	Discounting progress (especially when depressed) Holding perfectionistic standards Have so much clutter that small improvements are difficult to see	Use updated photographs for comparison to recognize even small changes. Emphasize importance of focusing work in one area, so progress is more evident.

Motivational Enhancement Strategies

Strategies	Description of Strategy	Example of Strategy
Developing discrepancy	Heighten the clients' awareness of discrepancies between their current circumstance and their personal goals and values.	"How does this fit your goal of having your granddaughter visit you?"
Rolling with resistance	Resistance reflects clients' beliefs and best attempts to cope with their circumstances; it signals the need for a different response. Examples are arguing, interrupting, denying, and ignoring.	Invite new perspectives and consider your client the primary resource in identifying solutions.
Open-ended questions	"What," "why," "how" questions encourage clients to provide information about themselves.	"What led you to decide to come for treatment?" "Why do you think the clutter got out of hand?"
Affirming and supporting self-efficacy	Make general statements about clients' strengths and resources, as well as specific ones about strengths and positive steps toward goals. Supportive and appreciative statements convey respect for clients' feelings, struggles, and accomplishments.	"You understand peoples' needs and are very thoughtful." "You are pretty organized and a good problem solver at work. I suspect you will learn to do this at home, too."
Reflective listening statements	Indicates you heard the client or noticed his or her reactions; helps clients feel understood. "Reflections" include repeating, rephrasing, and paraphrasing, especially feelings and thoughts. Include educated guesses about clients' thoughts and feelings and direct comments about ambivalence.	"You didn't like that." "These things are important to you." "You don't want your daughter to interfere." "On one hand you feel ____, on the other hand you. . . . "
Summarizing	Briefly recap what clients have said over the past few minutes to help them hear themselves with a little more perspective. Summaries can reinforce some points more than others. Avoid qualifiers or unnecessary modifiers. Usually finished with an open-ended question.	"You are very angry with your landlord for making the complaint and think he exaggerates your problem. You have worked hard to clean up the hallway and living room, but this has taken more time than you expected or he allowed. You'd like him and your family to get off your back, and you are sure you can solve the clutter problem by yourself." "What do you think of all this?" [*open-ended question*]

continued

Motivational Enhancement Strategies *continued*

Strategies	Description of Strategy	Example of Strategy
Informing and advising	Provide simple information or advice when clients ask for it, or ask permission before offering it. Indicate your respect for their right to make their own decisions by acknowledging that they may not agree with or heed the advice.	"Accountants recommend keeping tax information for seven years." "Many people use a one-week rule for keeping newspapers." "You might consider keeping all of the art supplies in the same cupboard in the room where you like to work."
Evocative questions	Go beyond open-ended questions by directing clients to discuss the effects of their hoarding. Provoke statements of recognition or concern about the problem, or denote an intention and optimism about making changes.	"How has this affected your husband?" "How does the clutter fit with the things you value in life?" "What are the successes you've had that make you think you could do this?"
Taking the negative side	Playing devil's advocate helps disarm someone who is used to defending their hoarding. Tentative motivational statements can be strengthened by asking what seem like paradoxical questions.	"Why would you want to change this? You really enjoy having [*buying*] all these things." "Why would you want to change this, especially when it would feel like giving up part of yourself?"
Exploring pros and cons	Elucidates both the positive and negative elements of the problem.	"What do you like about tag sales?" "Are there things you don't like about them?" "What do you enjoy most about having these things?" "What are your least favorite parts of owning all these things?" "You mentioned that you spent more money than you wanted to. Is that a disadvantage? Maybe you don't really overspend." "I got the idea from your comments that a downside to the hoarding is your self-esteem has suffered. Is that true? How big a deal is that for you?"
Asking for elaboration	Encourages clients to expand on the negative consequences of problematic behaviors. Requests for elaboration of statements about changing hoarding behavior are especially useful to enhance commitment to change.	"You mentioned that sometimes you waste time looking for things. Has this happened recently?" When clients report complaints by others that seem to avoid the main issue, consider asking: "Was that her main concern?"

Strategies	Description of Strategy	Example of Strategy
Using extreme contrasts	Can help amplify reluctance to change hoarding behavior, as well as the benefits of working on the problem.	"What's the worst thing that can happen if you go along as you have been?" "If you were to decide to work on this problem seriously with me, what do you think would happen?" "What are the best things that could happen?"
Looking forward and looking back	Help amplify concerns by asking clients to project themselves into the future or into the past. Can be especially useful for clients who tend to blame others for their problem. Looking back will only be useful for clients whose history contains a period in which hoarding was not a significant problem.	"If you think ahead five years, what would you like your life to be like?" "Suppose you were planning to commit time to working on this problem, what would that mean for your marriage?" "Contrast now with how you felt before these problems began. What was your life like then?
Reframing	Intended to clarify ambivalence and help clients' alter their interpretation of events by emphasizing the positive aspects of the situation.	"You think that behind your wife's nagging about your collecting things is a real concern for you, although you still find it annoying."
Change talk	Refers to clients' statements about their desire, ability, reasons, need, and commitment to change. Strengthen their commitment and confidence by asking simple questions after clients have made tentative statements about making changes.	"What would you like to do next?" "What might be your first goal?"
Rating importance and confidence in change	To enhance change talk, ask clients to indicate how important it is to change their hoarding problem, on a scale from 0 = "not at all" to 10 = "extremely important." Follow with questions about why and the next steps to take. Ask how confident they feel about being able to change their hoarding problem, on a scale from 0 = "not at all" to 10 = "extremely confident." Follow with questions.	"Why did you choose that number?" For a high number: "Why is it important?" For a low number (3 or 4): "Why didn't you pick a lower number? What would need to happen for you to move from a 4 to an 8 on the scale?" Summarize the clients' statements: "Where does that leave you now?" "What are you thinking about your hoarding at this point?" "What's the next step?" "Where does hoarding fit into your future?"

Advantages and Disadvantages of Change Worksheet

Addressing my clutter problem	
Advantages	Disadvantages

Instructions for Coaches

Overcoming compulsive hoarding is often very difficult. Many people find it extremely helpful to have a support person or "coach" who can assist them with the process. As a coach, you will work with the clinician and the person with the hoarding problem as a team. This guide outlines some ways to make your involvement most helpful.

Compulsive hoarding is not a single, simple problem, but consists of several interconnected problems. These usually include:

- *Excessive clutter*: This is the most easily recognized symptom of hoarding. Often, the clutter becomes so overwhelming that the person has a hard time knowing where to start.
- *Problems organizing and making decisions*: A person with a hoarding problem may have difficulty thinking clearly about their clutter or what to do about it. They may have a hard time recognizing the difference between items that are useful vs. non-useful, valuable vs. non-valuable, or sentimental vs. non-sentimental. Therefore, to be on the safe side, they may treat all items as if they are useful, valuable, or sentimental. This leads to difficulty in deciding when it is time to throw something out.
- *Difficulty letting go of possessions*: One of the most striking problems is difficulty letting go of and removing things—discarding, recycling, selling, and giving away items. This occurs even with items that seem to have little or no value. The amount of distress associated with removing clutter is often enormous.
- *A tendency to avoid or procrastinate*: People with hoarding problems often feel very overwhelmed by the sheer volume of clutter and the difficult task of decision-making. They may also feel depressed or nervous, which can add to a sense of fatigue and a tendency to avoid taking action. As a result, the person with hoarding is often tempted to decide, "This is too big to tackle today. I'll do it tomorrow."
- *Difficulty resisting urges to acquire objects*: For many people with hoarding problems, the urge to acquire things can be very strong, almost irresistible. Some people may feel a need to buy things; others may feel a need to pick up free things.

Not everyone who hoards has all of these problems. Every person and every hoarding problem is a little bit different, but all involve strong emotional reactions to possessions, thoughts, and beliefs about saving things that may not always seem rational to you, and behaviors that enable the problem to persist. As part of the treatment program, the clinician will carefully review these aspects of hoarding with the person you are assisting and determine which problems are particularly troublesome. This is important, because the particular kinds of problems the person is facing will guide the team in deciding what interventions to use.

continued

We recommend that coaches do the following:

- *Meet as a team* with the clinician and the person with the hoarding problem. Three people working together is a recipe for success, whereas three people working in different directions is unlikely to work.
- *Help the person remain focused* on the task in front of them. People with hoarding problems often find themselves easily distracted, especially when they are trying to reduce clutter, make decisions about possessions, or resist the urge to acquire things. Often, the coach can be very helpful by politely reminding the person what they are supposed to be doing right now.
- *Provide emotional support.* Because people who hoard have often been criticized by others, it is very important not to act like a taskmaster, as this just makes people feel nervous or angry and interferes with their ability to learn new approaches. Use a gentle touch, and when it feels right to you, express sympathy with statements such as, "I can see how hard this is for you," or "I understand that you have mixed feelings about whether to tackle this clutter." The person with the hoarding problem is going through some major stress, and often needs a sympathetic ear or even a shoulder to cry on.
- *Help the person make decisions, but DO NOT make decisions for them.* During treatment, the person with the hoarding problem is learning to develop new rules for deciding what to keep and what to remove. The coach can remind the person of these rules by asking questions, but not by telling them what to do. Ask them to simply talk out loud about their decision-making process for saving and discarding an item. Your task is not to convince them to get rid of things, but just to support them while they work through the process of making a decision. It may seem tedious, but often your mere presence will speed them along.
- *Be a cheerleader.* Sometimes we all need an extra boost when things get difficult. Calling the person to remind them of their homework assignment, telling them you believe they can do it, and noticing when they are doing a good job are all good cheerleading strategies. But at the same time, don't do too much of this or the encouragement will seem burdensome and the praise hollow.
- *Help with hauling.* Many people who hoard have accumulated so much clutter that it would take them a year or more to discard it all by themselves. This makes it easy to get discouraged because progress is slow. Coaches are very helpful when they roll up their sleeves and help remove items from the home, as long as the person with hoarding makes all the decisions and remains fully in charge of the process.
- *Accompany the person on non-acquiring trips.* For people who acquire too many things, treatment often requires going to tempting stores or yard sales and not buying anything. It can be extremely helpful to have someone go with them to help them resist temptation and make the trip a success.

We have also found that even the most well-meaning coaches can make themselves less helpful by using the wrong strategies. Here are some DON'Ts:

- *Don't argue* with the person about what to get rid of and what to acquire. Long debates about the usefulness of an item or the need to get rid of it will only produce negative emotional reactions that don't facilitate progress. Instead, whenever you feel in conflict, take a break, relax a bit, and remind yourself how difficult this is for the person.
- *Don't take over decisions.* It would certainly be easier and quicker if coaches simply took charge, decided what should stay and what should go, and hauled the clutter out themselves. But this method doesn't teach people how to manage their problem. The clutter will just build up again. Instead, be sure the person with hoarding is in charge at all times and makes all decisions, with the coach's support and guidance.
- *Don't touch or move anything without permission.* Imagine how you would feel if a well-meaning person came into your home and handled your things without permission. Doing this can damage the trust between you and make it impossible for the person to proceed.
- *Don't tell the person how they should feel.* It can be very hard to understand why someone feels so sentimental about keeping what looks like trash to you or fearful about getting rid of something that is clearly useless. But these feelings developed for reasons even the client may not yet understand. Be as patient as you can. We know that coaching can be frustrating.
- *Don't work beyond your own tolerance level.* To be a good coach, you have to take care of yourself first, and then help your friend or family member. So feel free to set limits on how long and how much work you can do on any given occasion. Pat yourself on the back for your own efforts; helping someone who hoards is very hard work.

We hope these guidelines are helpful in working with someone who has a hoarding problem.

Acquiring Form

List the types of items you typically bring home and how you acquire them. Include items you acquired last week and those you acquire during the coming week. Do not include groceries or other perishable goods.

Rate how uncomfortable you would feel if you had not acquired this item when you saw it.

Item and location where you found it:	**Discomfort if not acquired (0 to 100)**

Acquiring Visualization Form

Visualize a typical situation in which you have a strong urge to acquire something. In your image, don't actually pick up the item, just look at it. Please describe the location and item you imagined.

____

____

Rate how strong was your urge to acquire the item (0 = "no urge to acquire," 100 = "irresistible urge").

Acquiring Urge ________

What thoughts did you have while you imagined this scene?

1. ____

____

____

2. ____

____

____

3. ____

____

____

Visualize this scene again, but this time, imagine leaving without the item. How much discomfort did you experience while imagining (0 to 100)?

Discomfort Rating ________

Please list any thoughts you think would help you not acquire an object.

1. ____

____

____

2. ____

____

____

3. ____

____

____

Now rate how uncomfortable you feel about leaving without the item(s), from 0 to 100.

Discomfort Rating ________

Thought Listing Exercise Form

Initials ____________________ Date __________________

Selected item: ____

Anticipated distress rating (from 0 = "none" to 10 = "maximum"): ________________

Predicted duration of distress: ________________

Thoughts about discarding:

____

____

____

____

____

Discarding Decision (circle): *Discard* or *Keep*

Distress rating after decision: ________________

Distress rating after 10–15 minutes: ________________

Distress rating after 30 minutes: ________________

Notes from exercise:

____

____

____

____

Behavioral Experiment Form

Initials: ___________ Date: ___________

1. Behavioral experiment to be completed:

____

____

____

____

2. What do you predict (are afraid) will happen?

____

____

____

____

3. How strongly do you believe this will happen (0%–100%)

____

____

4. Initial discomfort (0–10)

____

5. What actually happened?

____

____

____

____

____

____

____

Behavioral Experiment Form *continued*

6. Final discomfort (0–10)

   ____

7. Did your predictions come true?

   ____

8. What conclusions do you draw from this experiment?

   ____

   ____

   ____

   ____

   ____

   ____

Problematic Thinking Styles

Problematic Thinking Styles	Definition	Acquiring Examples	Discarding Examples
All-or-nothing thinking:	Black-and-white thinking exemplified by extreme words like "most," "everything," or "nothing" often reflect perfectionistic standards.	"This is the *most* beautiful teapot I have ever seen"; "I won't remember *anything* about this if I can't bring home this reminder."	"It seems like *everything* in this box is just so important."
Over-generalization:	Generalization from a single event to all situations, using words like "always" or "never."	"I always regret not buying things like this"; "I'll never have another opportunity if I don't get this now."	"I will *never* find this if I move it"; and "If I don't keep this, I'll *always* regret it."
Jumping to conclusions:	Predicting negative outcomes without supporting facts; akin to catastrophizing	"I'll need something just as soon as I walk away without it."	"You know I'll need this just as soon as I decide to get rid of it."
Catastrophizing:	Exaggerating the severity of possible outcomes.	"If I don't buy it now, I'll regret it forever."	"If I throw it away, I'll go crazy thinking about it."
Discounting the positive:	Positive experiences are not counted.	"Yeah, I suppose I resisted the urge and saved some money, but what if I can't stop thinking about it?"	"Creating a filing system isn't really progress because there is so much more to do."
Emotional reasoning:	Emotions are used instead of logic, so feelings substitute for facts.	"I feel uncomfortable walking away without this, so I should just get it."	"If I feel uncomfortable about throwing this away, it means I should keep it."
Moral reasoning:	"Should" statements ("must," "ought," " have to") accompanied by guilt and frustration; often driven by perfectionist standards.	"I must get this magazine or I won't know all the facts."	"I have to keep this health information in case something happens to John."

continued

Problematic Thinking Styles *continued*

Problematic Thinking Styles	Definition	Acquiring Examples	Discarding Examples
Labeling:	Attaching a negative label to oneself or others.	"I'd be an idiot not to take advantage of this great sale."	I can't find my electric bill. I'm such an idiot"; and "She's just greedy and wants all my stuff."
Under- and over-estimating:	Under-estimating the time to accomplish a task or one's ability to cope or, conversely, over-estimating one's ability to complete a task or the emotional costs of doing so.	"I know I have a lot of magazines, but I'll be able to read them all eventually"; "If I don't get this, I won't be able to handle it."	"I'll be able to read those newspapers eventually."

Thought Record

Initials: ______________ Date: ______________

Trigger situation	Thoughts	Emotions	Rational alternative	Outcome

Non-Acquiring Help Card

My goals for reducing acquiring are:

1. ______________________________

2. ______________________________

3. ______________________________

My rules for acquiring:

- I plan to use it within the next month.
- I have enough money (not credit) right now to pay for it.
- I have a place to put it so it doesn't add to the clutter.
- I have a true NEED, not just a wish, for this item.
- I am confident I will not return the item.
- Acquiring this item is consistent with my goals and values for my life.
- Other:______________________________

Questions to ask myself:

- Does this fit with my own personal values and needs?
- Do I already own something similar?
- Am I only buying this because I feel bad (angry, depressed, etc.) right now?
- Later on, will I regret getting this?
- Could I manage without it?
- Will I actually use this item in the near future?
- Do I have a specific place to put this?
- Is this truly valuable or useful or does it just seem so because I'm looking at it now?
- Is it good quality (accurate, reliable, attractive)?
- Will *not* getting this help me solve my hoarding problem?
- ______________________________
- ______________________________

Practice Form

What item did you choose? ______________________________

Initial discomfort (0 = "none" to 10 = "maximum") _____

What did you decide to do (not acquire, trash, recycle, give away, other)?

____

____

Discomfort rating (0 to 10) after:		
	10 minutes	______________
	20 minutes	______________
	30 minutes	______________
	40 minutes	______________
	50 minutes	______________
	1 hour	______________
	2 hours	______________
	3 hours	______________
	6 hours	______________
	Next day	______________
	Second day	______________

Conclusions:

____

____

____

____

Personal Worksheet for Managing Barriers

Barrier	Personal strengths	Troubleshooting strategy

Family Response to Hoarding Scale (FRHS)

INSTRUCTIONS: The purpose of these questions is to learn about the ways you may be modifying your behavior or routines because of a loved one (for example, family member, friend, significant other) with hoarding problems.
Please note that *hoarding* is defined by:

- Persistent difficulty discarding or parting with possessions, regardless of their actual value.
- Strong urges to save items and/or distress associated with discarding.
- Clutter in the living areas of the home so these spaces cannot be used as intended.
- Significant distress or impairment in social, occupational, or other important areas of functioning.

For each question below, in part "a.," please indicate whether the behavior occurred ***during the past month.*** If you answer YES to part "a.," please indicate in part "b." how often that behavior occurred. If you answer NO to part "a." please leave part "b." blank.

During the past month, did you:

	1	**2**	**3**	**4**
1. a. Did you help your family member decide whether to acquire, save, or discard items because he/she was having difficulty making a decision?	Yes	No		
b. [if yes] How often did you help him/her decide on discarding or saving?	1–2 times	3–4 times	5–9 times	10 or more times

continued

2. a. Did you wait for your family member because of hoarding-related behaviors, interfering with plans you had made? (For example, did it prolong the time you would normally spend shopping in a store, or take longer to leave the house because of difficulty finding items?)	Yes	No		
b. [if yes] How often, during the past month, did you wait for your family member because of his/her hoarding?	1–2 times	3–4 times	5–9 times	10 or more times
3. a. Did you keep items longer than you normally would because of your family member's hoarding? (For example, did you keep old newspapers or trash because he/she had not reviewed them?)	Yes	No		
b. [if yes] How often, during the past month, did you not discard items you normally would throw out?	1–2 times	3–4 times	5–9 times	10 or more times
4. a. Did you discard, recycle or remove items without telling your family member?	Yes	No		
b. [if yes] How often, during the past month, did you discard items secretly without telling your family member?	1–2 times	3–4 times	5–9 times	10 or more times
5. a. Did you help your family member acquire items that may have contributed to their hoarding? (For example: providing money to buy items, telling them about a sale, buying something likely to be hoarded, bringing home extra copies, providing storage space.)	Yes	No		
b. [if yes] How often during the past month, did you help your family member undertake or complete compulsive acquiring behaviors?	1–2 times	3–4 times	5–9 times	10 or more times
6. a. Did you engage in odd or senseless behaviors at your family member's request, or because you thought he/she would want you to do these things? (For example: checking items to make sure he/she didn't lose or miss something important.)	Yes	No		

	1	2	3	4
b. [if yes] How often, during the past month, did you engage in these behaviors?	1–2 times	3–4 times	5–9 times	10 or more times
7. a. Did you take over duties that would be your family member's responsibility if s/he did not have a hoarding problem? (For example: paying bills, doing taxes, taking out trash.)	Yes	No		
b. [if yes] How much/often do you do these things?	I occasionally handle one of my family member's responsibilities, but there has been no substantial change in my role.	I have assumed my family member's responsibilities in one area of life.	I have assumed my family member's responsibilities in more than one area of life.	I have assumed most or all of my family member's responsibilities.
8. a. Did you modify your personal, leisure, or family activities because of your family member's hoarding? (For example: are you unable to watch TV, engage in hobbies, or cook because of hoarding?)	Yes	No		
b. [if yes] How much are you modifying these activities?	I have modified these activities slightly but my overall functioning has not been affected.	I have definitely modified my activities in one area of life.	I have definitely modified my activities in more than one area of life.	I am unable to attend to leisure, work, or family responsibilities.
9. a. Did you modify your social activities because of your family member's hoarding? (For example: not inviting friends or relatives to the home.)	Yes	No		

continued

b. [if yes] How much are you modifying these activities?	I have modified these activities slightly but my overall functioning has not been affected.	I have definitely modified my activities in one area of life.	I have definitely modified my activities in more than one area of life.	I am unable to engage in social activities.
10. a. Have you modified your work activities because of your family member's hoarding problems? (For example: changing work schedule to attend to clutter; unable to work at home because of clutter.)	Yes	No		
b. [if yes] How much are you modifying these activities?	I have modified my work slightly but my overall functioning has not been affected.	I have definitely modified some aspect of my work.	I have definitely modified my work routine in more than one area of work.	My work is extremely disrupted.
11. a. Did you spend money you would not normally spend because of your family member's hoarding? (For example: storage expenses, purchasing extra items, rebuying items lost in clutter, billing or tax penalties, or compulsive buying using funds intended for other things.)	Yes	No		
b. [if yes] How much are you spending?	I have slight extra expenses but there is no overall effect on my budget.	I have definite extra expenses, but there is only a minor effect on my budget.	I have many extra expenses, and this prevents me from buying things I need.	I have so many extra expenses that I am unable to afford basic household items.

	1	2	3	4
12. a. Have you experienced health problems because of your family member's hoarding? (For example: asthma exacerbated by dirty home, dermatitis due to bathing difficulties, home infested with insects or rodents due to hoarding, injury from fall due to hoarding.)	Yes	No		
b. [if yes] How bad are your health problems due to hoarding?	I have slight health problems due to hoarding.	I have moderate health problems due to hoarding.	I have serious health problems due to hoarding.	I have extreme health problems due to hoarding.
13. a. Have you experienced problems with hygiene or cleanliness because of your family member's hoarding? (For example: unable to use the bath or shower, unable to clean the home, or other unsanitary conditions because of hoarding.)	Yes	No		
b. [if yes] How severe are the hygiene or cleanliness problems?	I/we have slight hygiene or cleanliness problems due to hoarding.	I/we have moderate hygiene or cleanliness problems due to hoarding.	I/we have serious hygiene or cleanliness problems due to hoarding.	I/we have extreme hygiene or cleanliness problems due to hoarding.
14. a. Did you experience emotional distress because of your family member's hoarding? (For example: anxiety, guilt, frustration, embarrassment, depression, sleeplessness due to hoarding.)	Yes	No		

continued

b. [if yes] How severe is the emotional distress?	I/we have mild emotional distress due to hoarding.	I/we have moderate emotional distress due to hoarding.	I/we have serious emotional distress due to hoarding.	I/we have extreme emotional distress due to hoarding.
15. a. Have you experienced difficulty in your relationships because of your family member's hoarding? (For example, disagreements or arguing about hoarding.)	Yes	No		
b. [if yes] How severe are the relationship problems?	We have mild relationship problems or minor arguments due to hoarding.	We have moderate relationship problems or occasional disagreements due to hoarding.	We have serious relationship problems or frequent disagreements due to hoarding.	We have extreme relationship problems, open hostility, or refuse to communicate due to hoarding.
16. a. Have you experienced difficulty planning for the future due to your family member's hoarding? (For example: unable to sell home, unable to move to desired dwelling, unable to complete plans for event or goal.)	Yes	No		
b. [if yes] How severe is the difficulty in planning for the future?	I have mild problems planning for the future due to hoarding but it is minimally disruptive.	I have moderate problems planning for the future in 1 or 2 areas of life due to hoarding.	I have serious problems planning for the future in several areas of life due to hoarding.	I have extreme problems planning for the future due to hoarding and an unable to plan or make important changes.

Scores on the total scale and for the two subscales are given in the table below:

Family Response to Hoarding Scale(FRHS) for 400 family members	**Meanscore**	**Standard deviation**	**Range**
Total score	15.0	10.4	0–53
Behavior Change	6.0	5.9	0–27
Consequences	6.9	4.2	0–20

(FRHS; Steketee, G., Ayers, C., Umbach, A., Tolin, D. F., & Frost, R. O. (2013). Family response to hoarding: Assessment and features in an internet sample. Unpublished manuscript.

Weekly Schedule Worksheet

	Sunday	Monday	Tuesday	Wednesday	Thursday	Friday	Saturday
6:00							
7:00							
8:00							
9:00							
10:00							
11:00							
12:00							
1:00							
2:00							
3:00							
4:00							
5:00							
6:00							
7:00							
8:00							
9:00							
10:00							
11:00							

List of Treatment Techniques

- Review the client's General Conceptual Hoarding Model (Session 2; *Workbook* Chapter 3) and consider possible updates to:
  - Personal and family vulnerabilities
  - Information-processing problems
  - Thoughts and reasons for saving
  - Positive and negative emotions
  - Acquiring, saving, and avoidance behaviors
- Review the Brief Thought Record (Session 2; *Workbook* Chapter 3)
- Repeat the clutter, unclutter, and ideal home visualizations to determine client reactions (Session 3; *Workbook* Chapter 4)
- Review Personal Goals (Session 4; *Workbook* Chapter 4)
- Review the functional analysis of acquiring episodes (Session 6; *Workbook* Chapter 3)
- Acquiring—examine and review the following (Sessions 5–7; *Workbook* Chapter 5):
  - Acquiring Form to see progress and determine whether unwanted items continue to come into the home (Session 5)
  - Advantages-Disadvantages (Session 5)
  - Acquiring Questions Form (Session 6)
  - Client's Rules for Acquiring (Session 6)
  - Hierarchy of acquiring situations to determine additional work needed (Session 7)
  - Progress on alternative sources of enjoyment (Session 6)
  - Faulty thinking about acquiring (Session 12)
  - Cognitive strategies—Downward Arrow, estimating probability, need versus want (Session 12; *Workbook* Chapter 8)
- Consider the presence of any problematic avoidance behaviors related to acquiring, sorting, and discarding (Sessions 2, 5, and 7; *Workbook* Chapters 3, 5, and 7)
- Review Questions about Possessions and/or Rules for Saving that facilitate decision-making (Session 8; *Workbook* Chapter 7)

List of Treatment Techniques *continued*

- Review Thought Listing Exercise (Session 8; *Workbook* Chapter 7)
- Review Behavioral Experiment Form (Session 9; *Workbook* Chapter 7)
- Review *in vivo* exposures to discarding and loss of possessions and information (Sessions 8 and 9; *Workbook* Chapter 7)
- Review Problem-Solving steps (Session 9; *Workbook* Chapter 6)
- Review Personal Organizing Plan and Filing Paper Form (Sessions 10 and 11; *Workbook* Chapter 6):
  - Keep discarding decisions simple: Trash, recycle, sell, or donate
  - Keep supplies on hand for organizing
  - Review progress on OHIO rule
  - Implement decisions as soon as possible
  - Review rules for how long to save paper
  - Schedule times to organize and file
  - Keep surfaces clear to prevent re-cluttering
- Review the following cognitive strategies for parting with possessions (Sessions 8, 12, and 13; *Workbook* Chapters 7 and 8):
  - Thinking Styles list (Session 12; *Workbook* Chapter 8)
  - Questions about Possessions (Session 8; *Workbook* Chapter 7)
  - Advantages-Disadvantages (Session 13; *Workbook* Chapter 8)
  - Downward Arrow (Session 12; *Workbook* Chapter 8)
  - Need versus Want (Session 13; *Workbook* Chapter 8)
  - Examine the evidence for keeping or discarding items (Session 12)
  - Take another perspective—review questions (Not covered in group treatment)
  - Thought Record Form (Session 12; *Workbook* Chapter 8)
  - Perfection Continuum Scale (Not covered in group treatment; *Workbook* Chapter 8)
  - Metaphors and Stories (Not covered in group treatment)
  - Valuing Time (Not covered in group treatment; *Workbook* Chapter 8)
  - Finding alternatives to problematic core beliefs (Session 12; *Workbook* Chapter 8)

- Review strategies for managing attention (Session 16; *Workbook* Chapter 5)
- Review progress on any barriers to working on hoarding (Session 16; *Workbook* Chapter 9)
- Plan social activities outside your home (Session 17; *Workbook* Chapter 5)
- Invite others to visit you at home (Session 17)
- Schedule practice sessions (Session 19)

AGENCY NAME

IS PLEASED TO PRESENT

CLIENT NAME

With this

CERTIFICATE OF COMPLETION

for the 20-week hoarding group

Given this ___ day of __________, 20__

PERSONAL NOTE: You were a committed group member who was a role model for open, honest communication. We appreciated your thoughtful comments and caring nature

____________________	____________________
Group Leader	Group Leader

References

Abramowitz, J. S., Franklin, M. E., Schwartz, S. A., & Furr, J. M. (2003). Symptom presentation and outcome of cognitive behavior therapy for obsessive compulsive disorder. *Journal of Consulting and Clinical Psychology*, *71*, 1049–1057.

American Psychiatric Association (2013). *Diagnostic and Statistical Manual of Mental Disorders* (5th ed.). Washington, D.C.: APA.

Beck, A. T., Steer, R. A., & Brown, G. K. (1996). *Manual for Beck Depression Inventory–II*. San Antonio, TX: Psychological Corporation.

Berman-Rossi, T. (1993). The tasks and skills of the social worker across stages of group development. *Social Work with Groups*, *16*(1/2), 69–81.

Bieling, P. J., McCabe, R. E., & Antony, M. M. (2006). *Cognitive-Behavioral Therapy in Groups*. New York: Guilford.

Black, D. W., Monahan, P., Gable, J., Blum, N., Clancy, G., & Baker, P. (1998). Hoarding and treatment response in 38 nondepressed subjects with obsessive-compulsive disorder. *Journal of Clinical Psychiatry*, *59*, 420–425.

Bratiotis, B., Sorrentino Schmalisch, C., & Steketee, G. (2011). *The Hoarding handbook: A Guide for Human Service Professionals*. New York: Oxford.

Brown, N. W. (2003). Conceptualizing process. *International Journal of Group Psychotherapy*, *53*(2), 225–244.

Bulli, F., Melli, G., Sara, M., Carraresi, C., Stopani, E., Pertusa, A., & Frost, R. O. (2013). Hoarding behaviour in an Italian non-clinical sample. *Behavioural and Cognitive Psychotherapy*, *41*, 1–15.

Burns, D. (1990). *Feeling Good Handbook*. New York: Morrow.

Davidow, J., & Muroff, J. (2011, July). Coaching and hoarding: What's the right approach? Poster presented at the Annual Conference of the International OCD Foundation. San Diego, CA: July 29–31, 2011.

Frost, R., & Hartl, T. (1996). A cognitive-behavioral model of compulsive hoarding. *Behaviour Research and Therapy*, *34*, 341–350.

Frost, R. O., & Mueller, A. (2013). Acquisition of possessions in hoarding disorder. In R. O. Frost & G. Steketee (Eds.), *Oxford Handbook of Hoarding and Acquiring*. New York: Oxford.

Frost, R. O., Hristova, V., Steketee, G., & Tolin, D. F. (2013). Activities of daily living in hoarding disorder. *Journal of Obsessive Compulsive and Related Disorders*, *2*, 85–90.

Frost, R. O., Pekarava-Kochergina, A., & Maxner, S. (2011a). The effectiveness of a biblio-based support group for hoarding disorder. *Behaviour Research and Therapy*, *49*, 628–634.

Frost, R. O., Ruby, D., & Shuer, L. (2012). The Buried in Treasures Workshop: Wait list control trial of facilitated self-help for hoarding disorder. *Behaviour Research and Therapy*, *50*, 661–667.

Frost, R. O., & Steketee, G. (Eds.) (2013). *Oxford Handbook of Hoarding and Acquiring*. New York: Oxford.

Frost, R. O., Steketee, G., & Grisham, J. (2004). Measurement of compulsive hoarding: Saving Inventory–Revised. *Behaviour Research and Therapy*, *42*, 1163–1182.

Frost, R. O., Steketee, G., & Tolin, D. F. (2011b). Comorbidity in hoarding disorder. *Depression and Anxiety*, *28*, 876–884.

Frost, R. O., Steketee, G., Tolin, D. F., & Renaud, S. (2008). Development and validation of the Clutter Image Rating. *Journal of Psychopathology and Behavioral Assessment*, *30*, 180–192.

Frost, R. O., Tolin, D. F., & Maltby, N. (2010). Insight-related challenges in the treatment of hoarding. *Cognitive and Behavioral Practice*, *17*, 404–413.

Garland, J. A., Jones, H. E., & Kolodny, R. L. (1965). A model for stages of development in social work groups. In S. Bernstein (Ed.), *Explorations in Group Work* (pp. 17–71). Boston: Boston University School of Social Work.

Gazda, G. M., Ginter, E. J., & Horne, A. M. (2001). *Group Counseling and Group Psychotherapy*. Boston: Allyn & Bacon.

Gilliam, C. M., Norberg, M. M., Villavicencio, A., Morrison, S., Hannan, S. E., & Tolin, D. F. (2011). Group cognitive-behavioral therapy for hoarding disorder: An open trial. *Behaviour Research and Therapy*, *49*(11), 802–807.

Gitterman, A., & Shulman, L. (2005). *Mutual Aid Groups, Vulnerable and Resilient Populations, and the Life Cycle*. New York: Columbia University Press.

Grisham, J., Frost, R. O., Steketee, G., Kim, H-J., & Hood, S. (2006). Age of onset of compulsive hoarding. *Journal of Anxiety Disorders, 20*, 675–686.

Hartl, T. L., Duffany, S. R., Allen, G. J., Steketee, G., & Frost, R. O. (2005). Relationships among compulsive hoarding, trauma, and attention deficit hyperactivity disorder. *Behaviour Research and Therapy, 43*, 269–276.

Hartl, T. L., & Frost, R. O. (1999). Cognitive-behavioral treatment of compulsive hoarding: A multiple baseline experimental case study. *Behaviour Research and Therapy, 37*, 451–461.

Hepworth, D., Rooney, R., Rooney, G., & Strom-Gottfried, K. (2013). *Direct Social Work Practice: Theory and Skills*. (9th ed.). Pacific Grove, CA: Brooks/Cole.

Hirschtritt, M. E., & Mathews, C. A. (2013). Genetics and family models of hoarding disorder. In R. O. Frost & G. Steketee (Eds.), *Oxford Handbook of Hoarding and Acquiring*. New York: Oxford.

Iervolino, A. C., Perroud, N., Fullana, M. A., et al. (2009). Prevalence and heritability of compulsive hoarding: A twin study. *American Journal of Psychiatry, 166*, 1156–1161.

Kim, H-J., Steketee, G., & Frost, R. O. (2001). Hoarding by elderly people. *Health & Social Work, 26*, 176–184.

Linehan, M. (1993). *Cognitive-Behavioral Treatment of Borderline Personality Disorder*. New York: The Guilford Press.

Mataix-Cols, D., Frost, R. O., Pertusa, A., Clark, L. A., Leckman, J. E., Saxena, S. . . . & Wilhelm, S. (2010). Compulsive hoarding: A new disorder for DSM-V? *Depression and Anxiety, 27*, 556–572.

Mataix-Cols, D., Rauch, S. L., Manzo, P. A., Jenike, M. A., & Baer, L. (1999). Use of factor-analyzed symptom dimensions to predict outcome with serotonin reuptake inhibitors and placebo in the treatment of obsessive-compulsive disorder. *American Journal of Psychiatry, 156*, 1409–1416.

Miller, W. R., & Rollnick, S. (2013). *Motivational Interviewing: Helping People Change* (3rd ed.). New York: Guilford.

Muroff, J., Steketee, G., Bratiotis, C., & Ross, A. (2012). Group cognitive and behavioral therapy and bibliotherapy for hoarding: A pilot trial. *Depression and Anxiety, 29*(7), 597–604.

Muroff, J., Steketee, G., Frost, R. O., & Tolin, D. F. (2013, under review). Cognitive behavior therapy for hoarding disorder: Follow-up findings and predictors of outcome.

Muroff, J., Steketee, G., Rasmussen, J., Gibson, A., Bratiotis, C., & Sorrentino, C. (2009). Group cognitive and behavioral treatment for compulsive hoarding: A preliminary trial. *Depression and Anxiety, 26*(7), 634–640.

Norberg, M., & Snowdon, J. (2013). Severe domestic squalor. In R. O. Frost & G. Steketee (Eds.), *Oxford Handbook of Hoarding and Acquiring*. New York: Oxford.

Nosko A. (2002). Adventures in co-leadership in social group work practice. *Social Work with Groups, 25*, 175–183.

Pollard, C. A. (2012, April). Assessment of treatment-interfering behavior: A collaborative approach. Presentation at annual conference of Anxiety Disorders Association of America, Washington, D.C.

Pertusa, A., Frost, R. O., & Mataix-Cols, D. (2010). When hoarding is a symptom of OCD: A case series and implications for DSM-V. *Behaviour Research and Therapy, 48*, 1012–1020.

Rasmussen, J. L., Steketee, G., Frost, R. O., & Tolin, D. F. (2013, under review). *Assessing Squalor in Compulsive Hoarding: The Home Environment Index*. Safren, S. A., Perlman, C. A., Sprich, S., & Otto, M. W. (2005). *Mastering Your Adult ADHD: A Cognitive-Behavioral Treatment Program*. New York: Oxford.

Samuels, J. F., Bienvenu, O. J., Grados, M. A., Cullen, B., Riddle, M. A., Liang, K. Y.... & Nestadt, G. (2008). Prevalence and correlates of hoarding behavior in a community-based sample. *Behaviour Research and Therapy, 46*, 836–844.

Samuels, J., Bienvenu III, O. J., Riddle, M. A., Cullen, B., Grados, M. A., Liang, K. Y.,... & Nestadt, G. (2002). Hoarding in obsessive compulsive disorder: Results from a case-control study. *Behaviour Research and Therapy, 40*, 517–528.

Saxena, S. (2014). Pharmacotherapy of compulsive hoarding. In R. O. Frost & G. Steketee (Eds.), *Oxford handbook of hoarding and acquiring*. New York: Oxford.

Saxena, S., Ayers, C. R., Maidment, K. M., Vapnik, T., Wetherell, J. L., & Bystritsky, A. (2011). Quality of life and functional impairment in compulsive hoarding. *Journal of Psychiatric Research, 45*, 475–480.

Saxena, S., Brody, A. L., Maidment, K. M., & Baxter, L. R. (2007). Paroxetine treatment of compulsive hoarding. *Journal of Psychiatric Research, 41*(6), 481–487.

Saxena, S., Maidment, K. M., Vapnik, T., Golden, G., Rishwain, T., Rosen, R.,... & Bystritsky, A. (2002). Obsessive-compulsive hoarding: Symptom severity and response to multimodal treatment. *Journal of Clinical Psychiatry, 63*, 21–27.

Schwartz, W. (1961). The social worker in the group. In: *New Perspectives on Services to Groups: Theory, Organization, and Practice*, 7–34.

Shulman, L. (2011). *The Skills of Helping Individuals, Families, Groups, and Communities*. Pacific Grove, CA: Brooks/Cole.

Sorrentino Schmalisch, C., Bratiotis, C., & Muroff, J. (2010). Processes in group cognitive and behavioral treatments for hoarding. *Cognitive and Behavioral Practice, 17*(4), 414–425.

Steinberg, D. M. (2010). Mutual aid: A contribution to best-practice social work. *Social Work with Groups, 33*(1), 53–68.

Steketee, G., Ayers, C., Umbach, A., Tolin, D. F., & Frost, R. O. (2013). Family response to hoarding: Assessment and features in an internet sample. Unpublished manuscript.

Steketee, G., & Frost, R. (2013). *Compulsive Hoarding and Acquiring: Therapist Guide* (2nd ed.). New York: Oxford University Press.

Steketee, G., & Frost, R. (2013). *Compulsive Hoarding and Acquiring: Client Workbook* (2nd ed.). New York: Oxford University Press.

Steketee, G., & Frost, R. O. (2013). Phenomenology of hoarding. In R. O. Frost & G. Steketee (Eds.), *Oxford Handbook of Hoarding and Acquiring*. New York: Oxford.

Steketee, G., Frost, R. O., & Kyrios, M. (2003). Beliefs about possessions among compulsive hoarders. *Cognitive Therapy & Research, 27*, 463–479.

Steketee, G., Frost, R. O., Tolin, D. F., Rasmussen, J., & Brown, T. A. (2010). Waitlist-controlled trial of cognitive behavior therapy for hoarding disorder. *Depression and Anxiety, 27*, 476–484.

Steketee, G., Frost, R. O., Wincze, J., Greene, K., & Douglass, H. (2000). Group and individual treatment of compulsive hoarding: A pilot study. *Behavioural and Cognitive Psychotherapy, 28*, 259–268.

Tolin, D. F., Frost, R., & Steketee, G. (2010b). A brief interview for assessing compulsive hoarding: The Hoarding Rating Scale–Interview. *Psychiatry Research, 178*, 147–152.

Tolin, D. F., Frost, R. O., Steketee, G., & Fitch, K. E. (2008b). Family burden of compulsive hoarding: Results of an Internet survey. *Behaviour Research and Therapy, 46*(3), 334–344.

Tolin, D. F., & Villavicencio, A. (2011). Inattention, but not OCD, predicts the core features of hoarding disorder. *Behaviour Research and Therapy, 49*(2), 120–125.

Tolin, D. F., Fitch, K. E., Frost, R. O., & Steketee, G. (2010a). Family informants' perceptions of insight in compulsive hoarding. *Cognitive Therapy and Research, 34*, 69–81.

Tolin, D. F., Frost, R. O., & Steketee, G. (2007). An open trial of cognitive-behavioral therapy for compulsive hoarding. *Behaviour Research and Therapy, 45*, 1461–1470.

Tolin, D. F., Frost, R. O., & Steketee, G. (2013). *Buried in Treasures: Help for Compulsive Acquiring, Saving, and Hoarding*. New York: Oxford University Press.

Tolin, D. F., Frost, R. O., Steketee, G., Gray, K. D., & Fitch, K. E. (2008a). The economic and social burden of compulsive hoarding. *Psychiatry Research, 160*, 200–21.

Tolin, D. F., Meunier, S. A., Frost, R. O., & Steketee, G. (2010b). The course of compulsive hoarding and its relationship to life events. *Depression & Anxiety, 27*, 829–838.

Turner, K., Steketee, G., & Nauth, L. (2010). Treating elders with compulsive hoarding: A pilot program. *Cognitive and Behavioral Practice, 17*, 449–457.

VanDyke, M. M., & Pollard, C. (2005). Treatment of refractory obsessive-compulsive disorder: The St. Louis Model. *Cognitive And Behavioral Practice, 12*(1), 30–39.

Wagner, C. C., & Ingersoll, K. S. (2013). *Motivational Interviewing in Groups*. New York: The Guilford Press.

Walters, S. T., Ogle, R., & Martin, J. (2002). Perils and possibilities of group-based motivational interviewing. In W. R. Miller & S. Rollnick (Eds.), *Motivational Interviewing: Preparing People for Change* (2nd ed., Vol. 2, pp. 377–390). New York: Guilford Press.

Wilhelm, S., & Steketee, G. (2006). *Treating OCD with Cognitive Therapy*. Oakland, CA: New Harbinger.

Winsberg, M. E., Cassic, K. S., & Korran, L. M. (1999). Hoarding in obsessive-compulsive disorder: A report of 20 cases. *Journal of Clinical Psychiatry, 60*, 591–597.

Wincze, J. P., Steketee, G., & Frost, R.O (2007). Categorization in compulsive hoarding. *Behaviour Research and Therapy, 45*, 63–72.

Yalom, I. D. (2005). *The Theory and Practice of Group Psychotherapy* (5th ed.). New York: Basic Books.

Readings and Resources

Books on Hoarding

Bratiotis, C., Schmalisch, & Steketee, G. (2011). *The hoarding handbook: A guide for human service professionals.* New York: Oxford.

Frost, R. O., & Steketee, G. (2010). *Stuff: Compulsive hoarding and the meaning of things.* New York: Houghton Mifflin/Harcourt.

Frost, R. O., & Steketee, G. (Eds.) (2013). *Oxford handbook of hoarding and acquiring.* New York: Oxford.

Neziroglu, F., Bubrick, J., & Yaryura–Tobias, J. (2004). *Overcoming compulsive hoarding.* Oakland, CA: New Harbinger.

Steketee, G., & Frost, R. (2013). *Compulsive hoarding and acquiring: Therapist guide* (2nd ed.). New York: Oxford University Press.

Steketee, G., & Frost, R. (2013). *Compulsive hoarding and acquiring: Client workbook* (2nd ed.). New York: Oxford University Press.

Tolin, D., Frost, R. O., & Steketee, G. (2014). *Buried in treasures: Help for compulsive hoarding* (2nd ed.). New York: Oxford.

Tompkins, M. A., & Hartl, T. L. (2009). *Digging Out: Helping Your Loved One Manage Clutter, Hoarding, and Compulsive Acquiring.* Oakland, CA: New Harbinger Publications, Inc.

Articles on Assessment of Hoarding

Frost, R. O., Hristova, V., Steketee, G., & Tolin, D. F. (2013). Activities of daily living in hoarding disorder. *Journal of Obsessive Compulsive and Related Disorders. 2*, 85–90.

Frost, R. O., Steketee, G., & Grisham, J. (2004). Measurement of compulsive hoarding: Saving Inventory–Revised. *Behaviour Research and Therapy, 42*, 1163–1182.

Frost, R. O., Steketee, G., Tolin, D. F., & Renaud, S. (2008). Development and validation of the Clutter Image Rating. *Journal of Psychopathology and Behavioral Assessment, 30*, 180–192.

Rasmussen, J. L., Steketee, G., Frost, R. O., & Tolin, D. F. (under review). Assessing squalor in compulsive hoarding: The Home Environment Index.

Steketee, G., Frost, R. O., & Kyrios, M. (2003). Beliefs about possessions among compulsive hoarders. *Cognitive Therapy & Research, 27*, 463–479.

Tolin, D. F., Frost, R., & Steketee, G. (2010). A brief interview for assessing compulsive hoarding: The Hoarding Rating Scale–Interview. *Psychiatry Research, 178*, 147–152.

Articles on Treatment of Hoarding

Ayers, C. R., Wetherell, J. L., Golshan, S., & Saxena, S. (2011). Cognitive-behavioral therapy for geriatric compulsive hoarding. *Behaviour Research and Therapy, 49*, 689–694.

Frost, R., & Hartl, T. (1996). A cognitive-behavioral model of compulsive hoarding. *Behaviour Research and Therapy, 34*, 341–350.

Frost, R. O., Pekorava-Kochergina, A., Maxner, S. (2011). The effectiveness of a biblio-based support group for hoarding disorder. *Behaviour Research and Therapy, 49*, 628–634.

Frost, R. O., Ruby, D., & Shuer, L. (2012). The Buried in Treasures Workshop: Wait list control trial of facilitated self-help for hoarding disorder. *Behaviour Research and Therapy, 50*, 661–667.

Gilliam, C. M., Norberg, M. M., Villavicencio, A., Morrison, S., Hannan, S. E., & Tolin, D. F. (2011). Group cognitive-behavioral therapy for hoarding disorder: an open trial. *Behaviour Research and Therapy, 49*(11), 802–807.

Hartl, T. L., & Frost, R. O. (1999). Cognitive-behavioral treatment of compulsive hoarding: a multiple baseline experimental case study. *Behaviour Research and Therapy, 37*, 451–461.

Muroff, J., Steketee, G., Rasmussen, J., Gibson, A., Bratiotis, C., & Sorrentino, C. (2009). Group cognitive and behavioral treatment for compulsive hoarding: A preliminary trial. *Depression and Anxiety, 26*(7), 634–640.

Muroff, J., Steketee, G., Bratiotis, C., & Ross, A. (2012). Group cognitive and behavioral therapy and bibliotherapy for hoarding: A pilot trial. *Depression and Anxiety, 29*(7), 597–604.

Saxena, S., Maidment, K. M., Vapnik, T., Golden, G., Rishwain, T., Rosen, R., ... & Bystritsky, A. (2002). Obsessive-compulsive hoarding: Symptom severity and response to multimodal treatment. *Journal of Clinical Psychiatry, 63*, 21–27.

Steketee, G., Frost, R. O., Tolin, D. F., Rasmussen, J., & Brown, T. A. (2010). Waitlist-controlled trial of cognitive behavior therapy for hoarding disorder. *Depression and Anxiety, 27*, 476–484.

Steketee, G., Frost, R. O., Wincze, J., Greene, K., & Douglass, H. (2000). Group and individual treatment of compulsive hoarding: A pilot study. *Behavioural and Cognitive Psychotherapy, 28*, 259–268.

Tolin, D. F., Frost, R. O., & Steketee, G. (2007). An open trial of cognitive-behavioral therapy for compulsive hoarding. *Behaviour Research and Therapy, 45*, 1461–1470.

Turner, K., Steketee, G., & Nauth, L. (2010). Treating elders with compulsive hoarding: A pilot program. *Cognitive and Behavioral Practice, 17*, 449–457.

Therapist Guides for Problems Related to Hoarding

Abramowitz, J. S. (2006). *Obsessive Compulsive Disorder*. Boston: Hogrefe & Huber Publishers.

Miller, W. R., & Rollnick, S. (2013). *Motivational interviewing: Helping people change* (3rd ed.). New York: Guilford.

Safren, S. A., Perlman, C. A., Sprich, S., & Otto, M. W. (2005). *Mastering your adult ADHD: A cognitive–Behavioral treatment program*. New York: Oxford University Press.

Wilhelm, S., & Steketee, G. (2006). *Treating OCD with cognitive therapy*. Oakland, CA: New Harbinger.

Self-Help Books on Organizing

Hemphill, B. (1992). *Taming the paper tiger: Organizing the paper in your life*. Washington, DC: The Kiplinger Washington Editors.

Kolberg, J., & Nadeau, K. (2002). *ADD—Friendly ways to organize your life*. New York: Routledge.

Smallin, D. (2002). *Organizing plain and simple: A ready reference guide with hundreds of solutions to your everyday clutter challenges*. North Adams, MA: Storey Publishing.

Waddill, K. (2001). *The organizing sourcebook: Nine strategies for simplifying your life*. New York: McGraw–Hill.

Report on Animal Hoarding

Patronek, G. J., Loar, L., & Nathanson, J. (Eds.) 2006. *Animal hoarding: structuring interdisciplinary responses to help people, animals and communities at risk*. Hoarding of Animals Research Consortium. Available at www.tufts.edu/vet/cfa/hoarding.

Web Resources

International Obsessive Compulsive Disorder Foundation: www.ocfoundation.org/hoarding

Hoarding Task Force List: http://www.ocfoundation.org/hoarding/task_forces.aspx

Association for Behavioral and Cognitive Therapies: www.abct.org/

Anxiety Disorders Association of America: www.adaa.org

National Association of Professional Organizers: www.napo.net

Institute for Challenging Disorganization: http://www.nsgcd.org/

International Hoarding Exchange: http://www.hoardingtaskforce.org/

Clutterers Anonymous: http://sites.google.com/site/clutterersanonymous/

Messies Anonymous: www.messies.com

Squalor Survivors Website: http://www.squalorsurvivors.com

Children of Hoarders Website: http://childrenofhoarders.com/wordpress/

Compulsive Hoarding Online Support Group: http://health.groups.yahoo.com/group/H-C/

The Hoarding of Animals Research Consortium: http://vet.tufts.edu/hoarding/

Boston University School of Social Work Hoarding Project: http://www.bu.edu/ssw/research/hoarding/

State-specific requirements and procedures:
https://www.childwelfare.gov/systemwide/laws_policies/state/
http://www.ncea.aoa.gov/Stop_Abuse/Get_Help/State/index.aspx

About the Authors

Jordana Muroff, PhD, is an assistant professor at Boston University School of Social Work in the Clinical Practice Department. She received her MSW and PhD in Social Work and Psychology from the University of Michigan. Her post-doctoral studies took place at the Center for Decision and Behavioral Medicine at the University of Michigan and at the Veterans Administration Ann Arbor Healthcare System. She participated in the National Institute of Mental Health Race and Mental Health pre-doctoral training program, focusing on reducing racial, ethnic, and gender disparities in mental health diagnosis, assessment, and interventions. Trained in cognitive behavioral therapy methods (CBT) with children and adults, Dr. Muroff is a licensed social worker with extensive clinical experience. She has published and presented widely on CBT for children and adults with anxiety disorders, especially obsessive-compulsive disorder (OCD) and hoarding, the use of technology in assessment and interventions, and the influence of race and ethnicity on clinical diagnostic decisions. She is the principal investigator on several studies examining group CBT treatment for hoarding. Her research and career interests are especially focused on the generation and dissemination of culturally responsive and empirically supported intervention methods (such as CBT), with the particular goal of reducing disparities and improving access among those seeking treatment for anxiety and related disorders. Her research has been funded by the International Obsessive Compulsive Disorder Foundation, the Massachusetts Department of Public Health, and the Substance Abuse and Mental Health Services Administration (SAMHSA). She teaches graduate-level courses in cognitive and behavioral treatment, assessment and intervention, and clinical research methods.

Patty Underwood, MSW, is a licensed independent clinical social worker in Massachusetts, and is a clinician at Riverside Community Care, a large community-based mental health agency. She is a part-time lecturer at Boston University School of Social Work (BUSSW), teaching courses in clinical practice. Ms. Underwood received her MSW and Group Work Certification from BUSSW. She provides direct clinical intervention for mental health problems and specializes in the treatment of individuals with hoarding disorder (HD). She has collaborated with Dr. Jordana Muroff since 2007 in developing and testing group treatment interventions for HD. She conducts workshops and trainings in cognitive and behavioral therapy for hoarding. Ms. Underwood has appeared on The Learning Channel's *Hoarding: Buried Alive* as a consulting clinician. She is trained in eye movement desensitization and reprocessing (EMDR), dialectical behavioral therapy (DBT), and cognitive behavioral therapy (CBT). Ms. Underwood is the current president of the Massachusetts Chapter of the International Association for Social Work with Groups (IASWG, Inc.) and has been a board member of the organization since 2007. She serves on the Dean's Advisory Board at the Boston University School of Social Work.

Gail Steketee, PhD, is dean of and professor at the Boston University School of Social Work. She received her MSS and PhD from the Bryn Mawr Graduate School of Social Work and Social Research. Her research has focused on understanding the causes and consequences of obsessive-compulsive (OC) spectrum conditions, especially hoarding disorder, and on developing and testing evidence-based treatments for these conditions. She has received several grants from NIMH and from the International OCD Foundation to examine family factors that influence treatment outcomes for anxiety disorders and to test cognitive and behavioral treatments for OCD, hoarding disorder, and body dysmorphic disorder. Her research on hoarding with collaborators Drs. Randy Frost and David Tolin has contributed significantly to the development of diagnostic criteria for hoarding disorder in the major revision of the *Diagnostic and Statistical Manual for Mental Disorders* (DSM-5, 2013). Dr. Steketee has published more than 200 articles and chapters and more than a dozen books on research findings and evidence-based treatments for OCD, hoarding, and related disorders. Her research has been funded by the National Institute of Mental Health and the International

OCD Foundation (IOCDF). Her best-selling book *Stuff: Compulsive Hoarding and the Meaning of Things*, co-authored with Dr. Frost, was a finalist for the Books for a Better Life Award. She is a Fellow in the American Academy of Social Work and Social Welfare and has received awards from the Association of Behavioral and Cognitive Therapies, the Society of Social Work Research, the International OCD Foundation, and the Aaron T. Beck Institute for Cognitive Studies. She serves on editorial boards and as ad hoc reviewer for multiple journals in social work, psychology, and psychiatry. She also serves on scientific advisory boards of U.S. and Canadian OCD foundations and on a Commission for the Council of Social Work Education. She has appeared in a variety of media venues regarding her work on hoarding.

Index